AMERICAN UNIVERSITY
NATIONAL SECURITY LAW BRIEF

American University Washington College of Law
Washington, D.C.

AMERICAN UNIVERSITY
NATIONAL SECURITY LAW BRIEF

Volume IX • Number 1 • Spring 2019

American University Washington College of Law
Washington, D.C.

NATIONAL SECURITY LAW BRIEF

American University National Security Law Brief, Volume 9, Number 1 (Spring 2019)

ISBN-13: 978-1090871367
ISBN-10: 1090871368

Founded in April 2009, the *American University National Security Law Brief* is the nation's first student-run law school publication to focus on the rapidly evolving field of national security law. The publication is published twice a year, with a complementary online component, and is edited and published by students at American University Washington College of Law.

The views and opinions expressed in the articles are solely those of the respective authors and do not necessarily represent those of the authors' employers, the publication, the editorial board, American University, or Washington College of Law.

The Brief welcomes manuscript submissions on relevant topics in national security law and policy.

For more information about the publication, submissions, or permissions, please visit the brief's website.

Website: nationalsecuritylawbrief.com
Twitter: @AUNatlSecLaw
Facebook: @AUNatlSecLaw
LinkedIn: linkedin.com/company/AUNatlSecLaw

Bluebook abbreviation: AM. U. NAT'L SEC. L. BRIEF

American University National Security Law Brief
Washington College of Law
American University
4300 Nebraska Avenue NW
Washington, DC 20016

Cover and design by Kevin D. Reyes (consulting editor) (kevindreyes.com)
Printed by Kindle Direct Publishing, an Amazon Company

AMERICAN UNIVERSITY

NATIONAL SECURITY LAW BRIEF

Volume IX • Number 1 • Spring 2019

Contents

EDITORIAL NOTE

Dear Reader,

This issue of the ninth volume of the *American University National Security Law Brief* marks a significant milestone for this publication. The *Brief* was founded ten years ago, in April 2009, and has since become one of the leading publications in the field of national security law. Hopefully, dear Reader, you will find this volume no less thought-provoking than the best of what we have published over the course of the last decade.

The legal issues presented in this volume are, in many respects, as original as they are profound. First, ask yourself, do you feel safe? I presume that you are aware the United States government collects foreign intelligence information around the globe as it attempts to assure your continued safety. However, there are times when the Government is faced with difficult decisions between balancing the collective national security with your individual privacy interests, as there are also times when sharing of vital intelligence between the United States and her allies can be, likewise, difficult.

The author of our lead article, Brian Mund, addresses these issues and proposes a first-of-its-kind, practical framework for you to consider when evaluating intelligence sharing. He presents his framework based on the following principles of international law: 1) legality; 2) safeguarding against abuse; 3) proportionality; 4) transparency and oversight; 5) notification and remedies; 6) complementarity; 7) good faith; and 8) an exigency exception. You will find that his proposed framework provides a heretofore unheard of level of transparency while still ensuring both the safety of nations and the privacy of their citizens.

In January 2018, Congress extended Section 702 of the Foreign Intelligence Surveillance Act for another six years, thereby preserving one of the intelligence community's most vital tools. But was it a good deal? Did the reauthorization give enough power and independence to the intelligence community to help ensure security or have things gone too far, only to infringe on individuals' right to privacy? John Schifalacqua examines this balance, whether Congress successfully cut the Gordian knot, and the avenues that potential plaintiffs have to challenge Section 702 in its newest form.

Our third author, Stephen Jackson, considers what the United States can and should do with American citizens and permanent aliens who joined the Islamic State or swore allegiance to it. Can the United States prosecute these individuals as traitors? Jackson will walk you through the history of treason and then consider what it means to be a traitor in the Age of Terrorism. In short, should the Department of Justice wish to pursue it, there is an additional charge they could bring in some of the cases sure to follow shortly after the eventual fall of the Caliphate.

This issue concludes with an article written by Clark Campbell, that presents what I think many of you will agree is an interesting, but rarely considered, constitutional conundrum: can a warlike Congress force a President to make war? This profound article considers the various means through which Congress could try to compel the President to act, and, in turn, what actions the President may have to take; but, Campbell ultimately, concludes that Congress has no effective means to force the President into war.

Dear Reader, I do hope that you find these four articles to be as fascinating as I do, and I thank you for taking the time, yet again, to read our publication. One successful decade down, and, hopefully, many more to come!

Very respectfully,

Prescott A. Heighton
Editor in Chief

Legalizing Intelligence Sharing: A Consensus Approach

Brian Mund*

Abstract

Governments face a decision between balancing collective national security interests with individual privacy rights and strike that balance to different degrees. Only recently has public attention turned to the lack of transparency surrounding cross-border international intelligence sharing agreements. Foreign intelligence cooperation is necessary for effective security, but differing intelligence governance standards create tension between clashing privacy regimes. This Article proposes a pragmatic pathway forward in the form of a palatable intelligence-sharing framework that respects state sovereignty and security needs, while simultaneously establishing revolutionary privacy protections. This first-of-its-kind framework identifies and builds upon principles of international law to construct this practical framework. These principles are: 1) principle of legality; 2) principle of safeguarding against abuse; 3) principle of proportionality; 4) principle of transparency and oversight; 5) principle of notification and remedies; 6) principle of complementarity; 7) principle of good faith; and 8) an exigency exception.

* **Brian Mund** is a 2018 graduate of Yale Law School, where he received his Juris Doctor, and a 2013 graduate of the University of Pennsylvania, from which he received a Bachelor of Arts degree. He is grateful to Professor Michael Reisman and Asaf Lubin as well as the 2018 Salzburg Cutler Global Seminar participants for their feedback on previous drafts of this Article. All errors are the author's alone.

TABLE OF CONTENTS

INTRODUCTION

> *Suppose that Jane Doe shows up at our border with a valid visa, but after that visa was issued . . . her home country learns that she is associated with a terrorist organization but doesn't tell us.*[1]

On April 25, 2018, United States Solicitor General, Noel Francisco, defended President Donald Trump's third travel ban — which targets nationals from Iran, Libya, Yemen, Somalia, North Korea, and Venezuela — before the Supreme Court on the basis of inadequate information sharing.[2] Setting aside the merits of this particular order, the case shines a light onto the commonplace reality of cross-border information sharing. This snippet above reflects the larger reality that in today's world, cross-border information sharing plays a vital role in ensuring national security for many states. In other words, governments keep their nations safe through exchanges of intelligence data.[3]

---

[1] Transcript of Oral Argument at 8, Trump v. Hawaii, 138 S. Ct. 2392 (2018) (No. 17–965).

[2] Adam Liptak, *Supreme Court Allows Trump Travel Ban To Take Effect*, N.Y. TIMES (Dec. 4, 2017), https://www.nytimes.com/2017/12/04/us/politics/trump-travel-ban-supreme-court.html. Chad has since been removed from the list countries. *See also Trump* 138 S. Ct. at 2405 (2018) ("Invoking his authority under 8 U. S. C. §§1182(f) and 1185(a), the President determined that certain entry restrictions were necessary to "prevent the entry of those foreign nationals about whom the United States Government lacks sufficient information").

[3] What is data? Merriam-Webster provides the comprehensive definition that data is "information in digital form that can be transmitted or processed." While data is a plural noun, this Article follows the popular singular constructive use. *See Data*, MERRIAM-WEBSTER, https://www.merriam-webster.com/dictionary/data (last visited Mar. 8, 2019). Privacy interests arise in data that contains personally identifiable information (PII), defined as "[a]ny representation of information that permits the identity of an individual to whom the information applies to be reasonably inferred by either direct or indirect means." *See, e.g., Guidance on the Protection of Personal Identifiable Information*, U.S. DEP'T LABOR, https://www.dol.gov/general/ppii (last visited Mar. 7, 2019). While this definition of PII is fairly inclusive, Paul Schwartz and Daniel Solove identify that "[a]t the same time, there is no uniform definition of PII in information privacy law." Paul M. Schwartz & Daniel J. Solove, *The PII Problem: Privacy And A New Concept Of Personally Identifiable Information*, 86 N.Y.U. L. REV. 1814, 1814 (2011).

Currently, countries share intelligence information through bilateral agreements.[4] Many of these agreements are secret and do not purport to be binding under international law.[5] In recent years, multinational intelligence exchange has continued to grow.[6] However, the public has only limited information regarding the extent and details of cooperative intelligence-sharing operations other than the fact that such cooperation exists.[7] For example, the Five Eyes Signal Intelligence Alliance, made up of the United States, the United Kingdom, Australia, Canada, and New Zealand operates according to the United Kingdom-United States Communication Intelligence (UKUSA) Agreement, but the last publically available version is from 1955.[8] Taken together, these signs indicate that improvements in international intelligence exchange since 9/11 have wrought "a qualitative change" in the nature of intelligence cooperation.[9]

---

[4] HANS BORN ET AL., MAKING INTERNATIONAL INTELLIGENCE COOPERATION ACCOUNTABLE 62 (2015).

[5] *Id.*

[6] *Id.* at 64; *see also* Didier Bigo et al., *National Security and Secret Evidence in Legislation and Before the Courts: Exploring the Challenges, in* EUR. PARL.: C.L., JUSTICE & HOME AFF. 8 (2014) (describing "a growing transnational exchange of intelligence"); Szabó & Vissy v. Hungary, App. No. 37138/14, Eur. Ct. H.R., Judgment, ¶ 78 (2016), http://hudoc.echr.coe.int/eng?i=001-160020 (noting that governments' more and more widespread practice of transferring and sharing amongst themselves intelligence retrieved by virtue of secret surveillance."); S.C. Res. 1373 (Sept. 28, 2001) (calling all United Nations member states to "[e]xchange information in accordance with international and domestic law and cooperate on administrative and judicial matters to prevent the commission of terrorist acts.")

[7] Craig Forcese, The Collateral Casualties of Collaboration: The Consequence for Civil and Human Rights of Transnational Intelligence Sharing 6–11 (Mar. 5, 2009) (unpublished manuscript), https://papers.ssrn.com/sol3/papers.cfm?abstract_id=1354022 (explaining the difficulty to piece together the full scope and extent of intelligence arrangements because these agreements are so closely guarded).

[8] *See* Scarlet Kim et al., *The "Backdoor Search Loophole" Isn't Our Only Problem: The Dangers of Global Information Sharing,* JUST SEC. (Nov. 28, 2017), https://www.justsecurity.org/47282/backdoor-search-loophole-isnt-problem-dangers-global-information-sharing/; *see also* U.K.-U.S. Communications Intelligence Agreement, U.S.-U.K., May 10, 1955, https://www.nsa.gov/news-features/declassified-documents/ukusa/assets/files/new_ukusa_agree_10may55.pdf.

[9] Richard J. Aldrich, *Global Intelligence Co-operation versus Accountability: New Facets to an Old Problem,* 24 INTELLIGENCE & NAT'L SEC. 26, 30, 54 (2009).

Intelligence sharing has also fallen under increased scrutiny by the privacy rights advocacy community. In September 2017, Privacy International spearheaded a campaign along with the Center for Democracy & Technology, the Electronic Frontier Foundation, the Electronic Privacy Information Center, and the Open Technology Institute to "seek increased transparency for intelligence sharing arrangements" from over forty governments.[10] Specifically, the Privacy International coalition has pressed for transparency on intelligence sharing, and has also identified intelligence cooperation among "the Nine-Eyes (the Five Eyes plus Denmark, France, the Netherlands and Norway), the 14-Eyes (the Nine-Eyes plus Belgium, Germany, Italy, Spain and Sweden), and the 43-Eyes (the 14-Eyes plus the 2010 members of the International Security Assistance Forces to Afghanistan)."[11] Other identified multilateral intelligence sharing arrangements include EUROPOL between the EU member states, the Africa-Frontex Intelligence Community between European and African states, intelligence cooperation between eleven countries in the Great Lakes Region, the Shanghai Cooperation Organization between China, Russia, Kazakhstan, Kyrgyzstan, Tajikistan, and Uzbekistan,

---

[10] Letter from Gus Hosein et al., Exec. Director, Privacy Int'l, to Elizabeth B. Collins, Board Member, Privacy & Civ. Liberties Board, Re: Oversight of intelligence sharing between your government and foreign governments (Sep. 13, 2017), https://www.documentcloud.org/documents/4000688-US-Open-Letter-on-Intelligence-Sharing-and.html; *see also* PRIVACY INT'L, EVIDENCE ON THE DATA PROTECTION BILL AND PROPOSED AMENDMENTS FOR THE HOUSE OF COMMONS PUBLIC BILL COMMITTEE 6 (2018) (explaining that "[t]he Bill provides for almost unfettered powers for cross-border transfers of personal data by intelligence agencies without appropriate levels of protection.") https://publications.parliament.uk/pa/cm201719/cmpublic/dataprotection/memo/dpb07.pdf.

[11] *Privacy International Launches International Campaign For Greater Transparency Around Secretive Intelligence Sharing Activities Between Governments*, PRIVACY INT'L (Oct. 23, 2017), https://www.privacyinternational.org/press-release/51/privacy-international-launches -international-campaign-greater-transparency-around [hereinafter Privacy International]; *see also* Scarlet Kim et al., *Newly Disclosed Documents on the Five Eyes Alliance and What They Tell Us about Intelligence-Sharing Agreements*, LAWFARE (Apr. 23, 2018), https://www.lawfareblog.com/newly-disclosed-documents-five-eyes-alliance-and-what-they-tell-us-about-intelligence-sharing (describing pressure for US disclosure of secret intelligence agreements).

and an anti-Islamic State intelligence sharing coalition of Russia, Iraq, Iran, and Syria.[12]

This Article responds to the demand for greater intelligence sharing accountability by offering a detailed and thorough governmental intelligence cooperation framework. This type of pragmatic, compromising approach is sorely missing from a literature filled with idealistic yet wholly impractical measures. With intelligence sharing propelled under the public spotlight with renewed vigor in late 2017, the time is ripe for such an intervention. This Article offers a pragmatic pathway forward for governments and activists in the form of a palatable proposal that respects state sovereignty and security needs while simultaneously establishing revolutionary privacy protections.

The Article further emphasizes the distinct tension that arises from government intelligence sharing of personal information. This tension primarily arises when government intelligence agencies transfer information related to national security threats: specifically, cross-border intelligence transfers to combat serious crime and national security threats.[13] Government intelligence transfers occur most frequently among allied countries,[14] but as

---

[12] *See Human Rights Implications of Intelligence Sharing*, PRIVACY INT'L (Sept. 2017), https://www.privacyinternational.org/sites/default/files/2017-11/PI-Briefing-to-National-Intelligence-Oversight_0.pdf; Stephane Lefebvre, *The Difficulties and Dilemmas of International Intelligence* Cooperation, 16 INT'L J. INTELLIGENCE & COUNTERINTELLIGENCE 527, 529–534 (2003).

[13] Privacy-security tradeoff considerations are also engaged during inter-governmental law enforcement data sharing and involve information transfers to one another for the exchange of evidence and information in criminal and related matters. These transfers usually occur through the formalized process outlined within a Mutual Legal Assistance Treaty (MLAT). *See generally 2012 International Narcotics Control Strategy Report*, U.S. DEP'T OF STATE (Mar. 7, 2012) https://www.state.gov/j/inl/rls/nrcrpt/2012/vol2/184110.htm (detailing United States' use of MLATs). A considerable literature has been emerging over the appropriate process for MLAT reform. *See infra* note 186. While MLAT reform poses an important step to strengthen the international data sharing regime, law enforcement sharing, and intelligence sharing are most appropriately addressed separately for reasons addressed *infra*, notes 211–286.

[14] *See, e.g.*, Data Protection Bill, 20 Mar. 2018, Parl Deb HL (2018) col. 161 (UK), https://hansard.parliament.uk/Commons/2018-03-20/debates/c72d5ec6-a472-4c53-be4c-8c80f291bd2f/DataProtectionBill(Lords)(FifthSitting) (quoting Victoria Atkins in saying that "[i]n the vast majority of cases, intelligence sharing takes place with

the *Trump v. Hawaii* oral argument transcript suggests, not exclusively.[15] These transfers directly engage profound questions with respect to the proper relationship between actions taken in the name of national security and ensuring appropriate privacy protections for the dissemination of private information. Intelligence sharing between foreign intelligence agencies provides tangible national security benefits. However, such benefits must be balanced against the costs to privacy and open expression.

The world of intelligence sharing is understandably opaque. Hans Born, Ian Leigh, and Aidan Wills provide a useful taxonomy for conceptualizing international intelligence cooperation, and this paper adopts their thoughtful framework.[16] Born *et al.* identifies five types of international intelligence cooperation: 1) information sharing, 2) covert operational cooperation, 3) hosting facilities and equipment, 4) training and capacity building, and 5) providing software and equipment.[17] This paper focuses on the first type: information sharing. Information sharing includes strategic information, operational information, and tactical information. Strategic information includes policy analyses related to foreign policy developments or larger security trends.[18] Operational information generally involves threat assessments of groups' or actors' current capabilities, and unlike policy-oriented strategic analyses, tends to be directed at security personnel. Finally, tactical information relates to the specifics relevant for current operations — the specific details necessary for answering the "who, what, where, when, and how."[19]

Shared intelligence information splits into two further subcategories: "raw intelligence" or an analyzed "end product."[20] Raw intelligence has not been altered from its initial collection form, whereas the "end product" has

---

countries with which the intelligence services have long-standing and well-established relationships.").

[15] *See generally* Transcript of Oral Argument, Trump v. Hawaii, 138 S. Ct. 2392 (2018) (No. 17–965).

[16] BORN ET AL., *supra* note 4.

[17] *Id.*

[18] *Id.*

[19] *Id.*

[20] *Id.*

already received initial treatment by intelligence operatives. The sensitivity of the collection source will impact the likelihood of raw data sharing, as will the relationship between the two agencies. Lastly, the process of information sharing can manifest in two distinct forms. Most often, information sharing is "reactive," and results from *ad hoc* requests from a foreign partner for any information on a given subject.[21] However, close allies may also share information on an "automated basis."[22] These arrangements may rely on joint databases or other shared receptacles of gathered intelligence information.

I.   EXISTENCE OF PRIVACY-SECURITY TRADEOFF

Throughout the world, people care deeply about their privacy. Common-law courts have long recognized the importance of privacy from governmental intrusion. This long-standing common law principle announces, "the house of every one is to him as his castle and fortress, as well for his defense against injury and violence as for his repose."[23] As expounded by American courts, the privacy right allows one "to retreat into his own home and there be free from unreasonable governmental intrusion."[24] For European countries, Article 8 of the European Convention on Human Rights grants "[e]veryone . . . the right to respect for his private and family life, his home and his correspondence."[25] Many other countries also protect the privacy of its citizens. For example, Articles 23–25 of the Russian Constitution grant

---

[21] *Id.*

[22] *Id.*

[23] Pavesich v. New England Life Ins. Co., 50 S.E. 68, 71 (1905).

[24] Kyllo v. United States, 533 U.S. 27, 31 (2001) (quoting Silverman v. United States, 365 U.S. 505, 511 (1961)

[25] *See* Convention for the Protection of Human Rights and Fundamental Freedoms, Art. 8, Nov. 4, 1950, 213 U.N.T.S. 222 [hereinafter "European Convention on Human Rights"]. European Courts have also explicitly held that that private life "includes personal identity, such as a person's name, and that the protection of personal data is of fundamental importance to a person's enjoyment of his right to respect for private life." Case C-92/09, Volker und Markus Schecke GbR v. Land Hessen, 2010 E.C.R. I-11063, http://curia.europa.eu/juris/document/document.jsf?text=&docid=80291&pageIndex=0&doclang=en&mode=lst&dir=&occ=first&part=1&cid=1680697.

substantial privacy rights, including the protection against "the collection, keeping, use and dissemination of information about the private life of a person."[26] Article 40 of the Constitution of the People's Republic of China notes that "freedom and privacy of correspondence of citizens of the People's Republic of China are protected by law."[27] In August 2017, the Indian Supreme Court overturned its precedent and unanimously declared, "The right to privacy is protected as an intrinsic part of the right to life and personal liberty under Article 21 and as a part of the freedoms guaranteed by Part III of the Constitution."[28] Notwithstanding this background of general respect for privacy rights, government security practices threaten to intrude upon citizens' rights.

However, the very purpose of privacy rights continues to be a source of debate among various countries. The debate over the contours and purpose of privacy rights does not map along a simple East-West or North-South divide; for example, scholars have recognized "two western cultures of privacy"[29] with fundamentally different approaches to privacy and surveillance.[30] Recent scholarship has also recognized that China's unique cultural and historical foundation of privacy have generated a wholly

---

[26] RUSSIAN CONST., art. 23–25, http://www.constitution.ru/en/10003000-03.htm.

[27] CHINESE CONST., March 14, 2004, art. 40, http://www.hkhrm.org.hk/english/law/const03.html.

[28] Justice K. S. Puttaswamy (Retd.) and Anr. v. Union Of India & Ors., (2017) Writ Petition (Civ.), No. 494 of 2012, http://supremecourtofindia.nic.in/supremecourt/2012/35071/35071_2012_Judgement_24-Aug-2017.pdf.

[29] See generally James Whitman, The Two Western Culture of Privacy: Dignity Versus Liberty, 113 YALE L. J. 1151 (2004).

[30] See David Cole & Federico Fabbrini, Bridging the Transatlantic Divide? The United States, the European Union, and the Protection of Privacy Across Borders, 14 INT'L J. CONST. L. 220, 237 (2016). For an informative survey of 13 countries' surveillance and data privacy laws, see generally Peter Swire & DeBrae Kennedy-Mayo, How Both The Eu And The U.S. Are "Stricter" Than Each Other For The Privacy Of Government Requests For Information, 66 EMORY L. J. 617 (2017) http://law.emory.edu/elj/content/volume-66/issue-3/articles/both-eu-us-stricter-privacy-requests-information.html;   Ira   S. Rubinstein et al., Systematic Government Access to Personal Data: A Comparative Analysis, 4 INT'L DATA PRIVACY L. 96 (2014), https://doi.org/10.1093/idpl/ipu004.

different conception of privacy.[31] These fundamentally different views of privacy have prevented the formation of any internationally accepted right to privacy or data protection.[32] Even among the subset of countries that recognize such rights, deep disagreement persists over the appropriate scope or content of those rights, and the appropriate role of courts in reviewing security practices.[33]

If the expansion of privacy rights were purely a positive-sum-game, then few would oppose the implementation of greater individual privacy protections. However, as alluded to above, privacy protections come at a cost to security interests, and vice versa.[34] Government security interests encourage information-gathering tactics that impose limitations on citizens' interests in their privacy and family life, as well as their "right to be let alone."[35] Furthermore, the fear of government surveillance may chill

---

[31] *See generally* Tiffany Li et al., *Saving Face: Unfolding the Screen of Chinese Privacy Law*, J. L. INFO. & SCI. (forthcoming), https://ssrn.com/abstract=2826087.

[32] *See, e.g.,* Bert-Jaap Koops & Morag Goodwin, Cyberspace, the Cloud, and Cross-Border Criminal Investigation. The Limits and Possibilities of International Law 1, 47 (Tilburg L. Sch., Research Paper No. 5/2016), https://papers.ssrn.com/sol3/papers.cfm?abstract_id=2698263 (stating, in relevant part, that "there is no universally shared content for the right to privacy or data protection at the international level."); Data Protection Bill, 10 October 2017, Parl Deb HL (2017) col. 785 (UK), https://hansard.parliament.uk/Lords/2017-10-10/debates/A0271CAB-90BC-49BD-B284-664918EE70CA/DataProtectionBill(HL) (quoting the Earl of Lytton in saying, "[a]s regards international cross-jurisdictional data— I am thinking of beyond the EU—I wonder how successfully the proposed arrangements will carry forward in the longer term, bearing in mind that the world market contains numerous players who for their own purposes and advantage might not be that keen to match the standards we claim to set for ourselves.").

[33] *Id.*

[34] As former President Barack Obama put it, "You can't have 100% security and also then have 100% privacy and zero inconvenience, . . . we're going to have to make some choices as a society." Peter Nicholas & Siobhan Gorman, *Obama Defends Surveillance*, WALL ST. J. (June 8, 2013), https://www.wsj.com/articles/SB10001424127887324299104578531742264893564.

[35] Samuel D. Warren & Louis D. Brandeis, *The Right to Privacy*, 4 HARV. L. R. 193, 193 (1890). *See also* Charter of Fundamental Rights of the European Union, art. 8, Oct. 10, 2012 O.J. (C 326) 02, http://fra.europa.eu/en/charterpedia/article/8-protection-personal-data (stating, in relevant part, that "[e]veryone has the right to the protection of personal data concerning him or her."). Such an approach views one's personal

individual freedoms of speech, assembly, and association.[36] On the other hand, privacy protective measures that reduce government access to information-gathering methods could hamstring efforts to identify and thwart dangerous threats to the societies' collective security interests.[37] Accordingly, the government mandate to ensure the safety of its citizenry requires the government to undertake some behaviors that intrude into the sphere of personal privacy.[38]

---

information as commensurate with ownership over one's identity and sense of self. Allowing governments to share that information can be deeply injurious to one's sense of identity. *See, e.g.,* Julie E. Cohen, *What Privacy Is For,* 126 HARV. L. REV. 1904, 1911 (2013), https://harvardlawreview.org/wp-content/uploads/pdfs/vol126_cohen.pdf (stating, in relevant part, that "[s]ubjectivity is a function of the interplay between emergent selfhood and social shaping; privacy, which inheres in the interstices of social shaping, is what permits that interplay to occur.").

[36] There are several famous examples from United States' jurisprudence. *See, e.g.,* United States v. U.S. Dist. Court for E. Dist. of Mich., S. Div., 407 U.S. 297, 314 (1972) ("The price of lawful public dissent must not be a dread of subjection to an unchecked surveillance power. Nor must the fear of unauthorized official eavesdropping deter vigorous citizen dissent and discussion of Government action in private conversation. For private dissent, no less than open public discourse, is essential to our free society."); *see also* United States v. Jones, 565 U.S. 400, 416, 132 S. Ct. 945, 956, 181 L. Ed. 2d 911 (2012) (Sotomayor, J., concurring) ("[a]wareness that the Government may be watching chills associational and expressive freedoms."). Researchers have sought to show that the fear of government surveillance does in fact change citizen behavior. *See* Brynne O'Neal, *What Americans Actually Do When the Government Is Watching,* HUFFINGTON POST (Jul. 20, 2015), https://www.huffingtonpost.com/brynne-oneal/what-americans-actually-do-when-the-government-is-watching_b_7833408.html; *see also* BORN ET AL., *supra* note 4, at 45.

[37] [Irish] Data Prot. Comm'r, v. Facebook Ireland Ltd. & Maximillian Schrems [2016 No. 4809 P.], 40 (H. Ct.) (Ir.), http://www.europe-v-facebook.org/sh2/HCJ.pdf ("A degree of surveillance for the purposes of national security, counterterrorism and combating serious crime is vital for the safeguarding of the freedoms of all citizens of the union. This necessarily involves interference with the right to privacy, including data privacy.").

[38] As former FBI Agent Asha Rangappa explains, "[a]s any law enforcement official will tell you, criminals and spies don't show up on the doorstep of law enforcement with all of their evidence and motives neatly tied up in a bow. Cases begin with leads, tips, or new information obtained in the course of other cases. . . . However, anytime the FBI receives a credible piece of information that could indicate a potential violation of the law or a threat to national security, it has a legal duty determine whether a basis for further investigation exists." Asha Rangappa, *Don't Fall for the Hype: How the FBI's*

The privacy-security tradeoff is not a new phenomenon. In the prelude to the American independence, colonial Americans well understood the "difficult tradeoff between safety and freedom."[39] As Alexander Hamilton argued:

> The violent destruction of life and property incident to war; the continual effort and alarm attendant on a state of continual danger, will compel nations the most attached to liberty, to resort for repose and security to institutions which have a tendency to destroy their civil and political rights. To be more safe, they, at length, become willing to run the risk of being less free.[40]

The challenge that Hamilton faced was the same difficulty that government decision makers continue to struggle with today: where to strike the appropriate tradeoffs between privacy and security.[41] As the British government recently declared, "There are circumstances where the processing of data is vital for our economy, our democracy and to protect us against illegality."[42] Today, the question facing states involves grappling with:

> how [do] we get the balance right between protecting the freedoms and civil liberties that underpin our functioning liberal democracy

---

Use of Section 702 Surveillance Data Really Works, JUST SEC. (Nov 29, 2017), https://www.justsecurity.org/47428/dont-fall-hype-702-fbi-works. Inevitably, some of these suspicions will not translate into actual threats to national security or even legal infractions. This necessary reality of overreach means that bulk data searches must be "adequately authorised and limited by domestic law." BORN ET AL., *supra* note 4, at 70. Presently, such protection "seems to be the exception rather than the norm". *Id.*

[39] Hamdi v. Rumsfeld, 542 U.S. 507, (2004) (Scalia, J., dissenting); see also Medina v. California, 505 U.S. 437, 443 (1992) (providing, in relevant part, that "[t]he Bill of Rights speaks in explicit terms to many aspects of criminal procedure, and the expansion of those constitutional guarantees under the open-ended rubric of the Due Process Clause invites undue interference with both considered legislative judgments and the careful balance that the Constitution strikes between liberty and order.").

[40] *Id.* (citing THE FEDERALIST No. 8, p. 33).

[41] *See* Eugene Volokh, *Liberty, Safety, and Benjamin Franklin*, WASH. POST (Nov. 11, 2014), https://www.washingtonpost.com/news/volokh-conspiracy/wp/2014/11/11/liberty-safety-and-benjamin-franklin (emphasizing that the "real challenge is in deciding which tradeoffs are wise and which are foolish.").

[42] Dep't Digital, Culture, Media & Sport, *Data Laws To Be Made Fit For Digital Age*, UK GOV. (Sep. 14, 2017), https://www.gov.uk/government/news/data-laws-to-be-made-fit-for-digital-age.

> while protecting that democracy from the various threats to our safety and well-being. The sophisticated use of new technologies by terrorist groups and organised crime means that we have to make a sober assessment of exactly what powers our police and security services need to combat the terrorist attack and disrupt the drug or people trafficker or the money launderer. The fact that those threats are often overlapping and interconnected makes granting powers and achieving appropriate checks and balances ever more difficult.[43]

When Hamilton considered this question, the debate concerned a wholly domestic issue. The Continental Congress had to engage in introspection and begin carving a tradeoff consonant with American values. The national nature of this decision meant that different sovereign countries could strike different tradeoffs without friction. However, the privacy-security tradeoff for modern, international intelligence sharing changes that paradigm.

States' national privacy-security balance generates difficult decisions when considering information-sharing arrangements with other governments. While the privacy concerns are considerable, state security interests mandate cooperative data sharing as a crucial component of state practice. Before exploring solutions to conflicting surveillance regimes, the sections below expand upon the privacy-security tension in cross-border intelligence sharing.

II.   PRIVACY-SECURITY TRADEOFF FOR INTELLIGENCE SHARING

A. Intelligence Sharing Raises Privacy Concerns

As outlined above, domestic privacy protections play an important role in limiting government intrusion into the private lives of its citizens.[44]

---

[43] Data Protection Bill, 10 October 2017, Parl Deb HL (2017) col. 785 (UK), https://hansard.parliament.uk/lords/2017-10-10/debates/22188EC1-6BAB-4F06-BE64-5831ABAF78E2/DataProtectionBill(HL).

[44] *See, e.g.,* Myres S. McDougal et al., *The Intelligence Function and World Public Order,* 46 TEMP. L.Q. 365, 397 (1973) ("Much intelligence inevitably touches upon the private lives and pursuits of individuals and its dissemination is bound to have at least some adverse effects.").

Unchecked intrusion threatens to chill the important freedoms of speech, assembly, and association.[45] If these fears arise from one's own government surveillance, *a fortiori*, they are exponentially amplified by data sharing with foreign governments.[46] Every citizen enjoys national citizenship[47] and retains the peace of mind that their national government owes some obligations and fealty to protect the interests of their own nationals.[48] No such commitment exists for foreign government actors, and citizens have no reason to expect foreign governments to consider foreign citizens' interests when accessing personal data.[49] To the contrary, if a government receives private information that allows it to further its own national interests at the foreign citizen's expense, that government would assuredly do so. Thus, the government's data sharing practices with foreign governments jeopardize its citizens' private sense of security, a feeling further enhanced by foreign governments' freedom to further circulate the private information.[50]

Of course, one should not discount the possibility that not only will *fear* create chilling effects but that the private information might actually be used to stifle the above-mentioned rights. Regimes may utilize shared information

---

[45] *See supra* notes 23–36.

[46] *See, e.g.,* Privacy Int'l, *supra* note 11 ("States may share intelligence with States known for violating international law, ... Such sharing can place individuals in those States at particular risk.").

[47] *See, e.g.,* United Nations Convention on the Reduction of Statelessness art. 1, Aug. 30, 1961, 989 U.N.T.S. 175.

[48] *See, e.g.,* Myres S. McDougal et al., *Nationality and Human Rights*, 83 YALE L. J. 900, 960 (1974) (stating that "on the transnational level[,] nationality is the right to have protection in rights").

[49] *See, e.g.,* Robin Simcox, *Europe, Stop Trying to Make 'Intelligence Sharing' Happen*, FOREIGN POL'Y (Apr. 14, 2016), http://foreignpolicy.com/2016/04/14/europe-stop-trying-to-mak-brussels-paris-bombings ("Brits may have become used to the CCTV cameras and Automatic Number Plate Recognition technology that allows their own government to monitor their travel—but they would be considerably more dubious about letting the Germans and the French do the same.").

[50] *See generally* Jennifer Daskal, *Law Enforcement Access to Data Across Borders: The Evolving Security and Rights Issues*, 8 J. NAT'L SEC. L. & POL'Y 473 (2016), http://jnslp.com/wp-content/uploads/2016/11/Law_Enforcement_Access_to_Data_Across_Borders_2.pdf (detailing ways through which collection of private information can stifle rights and freedoms).

to monitor political dissidents or regime opponents living as part of a foreign diaspora community.[51] Such privacy and even safety concerns may pose a barrier to data sharing agreements with countries bearing shaky human rights records.[52] Even when shared information would not lead to concrete harm, countries may also hesitate to share information to partners with poor privacy safeguards due to the belief that the mere access to the private information constitutes severe dignitary harm.

Similar considerations also weigh in favor of caution before utilizing shared data received from an intelligence partner. If the intelligence partner does not honor the same degree of privacy as the home state, the home state may fear complicity in privacy or human rights violations.[53] The "Originator Rule" allows the original collector of information to govern the subsequent downstream flow of the information.[54] If an intelligence agency receives information from a foreign counterpart, the information originator may choose to not include the sources or procedures by which the agency acquired this information. As such, the recipient agency may unknowingly utilize private information that was unlawfully gathered under foreign laws.

Agencies can also take advantage of disparate protective regimes through the deliberate use of a "revolving door" tactic. The "revolving door" describes a mechanism through which government intelligence agencies rely on foreign

---

[51] BORN ET AL., *supra* note 4, at 45. By the same token, however, sharing information about domestic dissidents might have a significantly *smaller* chilling effect. American political dissidents might fear retaliatory action by the United States yet would probably be far less concerned about repercussions from a removed country like China. *See* Stephen J. Schulhofer, *An International Right to Privacy? Be Careful What You Wish For*, 14 INT'L J. CONST. L. 238 (2016), https://doi.org/10.1093/icon/mow013; Ashley Deeks, *An International Legal Framework for Surveillance*, VA. J. INT'L L. 291, 346 (2015) https://ssrn.com/abstract=2490700; Asaf Lubin, *'We Only Spy on Foreigners': The Myth of a Universal Right to Privacy and the Practice of Foreign Mass Surveillance*, 18 CHI. J. INT'L L. 502, 534 (2018) https://ssrn.com/abstract=3008428 ("Chinese, French, and Russian intelligence agents do not have the time or inclination to harass random Americans, nor the capability as long as Americans remain in the United States.").

[52] Lefebvre, *supra* note 12, at 535.

[53] AIDAN WILLS, UNDERSTANDING INTELLIGENCE OVERSIGHT 25 (2010), http://www.dcaf.ch/sites/default/files/publications/documents/IntelligenceOversight_en.pdf.

[54] Lubin, *supra* note 51.

collection to collect information that they could not have legally collected under their domestic legal frameworks.[55] This is not merely an abstract concern. Part 0 describes the United States' lack of privacy protection for non-U.S. citizens located abroad. Insofar as foreign intelligence partners such as the Five Eyes coalition have access to United States intelligence databases, U.S. overseas collection practices may directly facilitate a legal quagmire for those foreign agencies.[56] While the bulk collection may have been legal under United States law, these partners might not have legal authorization to collect such information. The revolving door is not a one-way street: the Wall Street Journal has also reported that Europeans have also collected intelligence information for American intelligence agencies.[57] As David Cole and Federico Fabrinni note, "Reports of cooperation and mass intelligence sharing between the NSA and the General Communication Headquarters (GCHQ), the United Kingdom's surveillance agency, make these concerns even more immediate."[58] Thus, intelligence sharing agreements should account for the legitimate privacy interests implicated in inter-governmental data transfers.

B. *Effective Security Requires Intelligence Sharing*

Policing and counterterrorism efforts necessarily depend on cross-border data sharing.[59] The modern era has ushered in an age of advanced communications technologies and increasingly sophisticated threats that do not confine themselves to national borders. In the globalized 21st century, effective national security practices require not only data access among national law

---

[55] *Id.*

[56] *See* Kim et al., *supra* note 8.

[57] Adam Entous & Siobhan Gorman, *Europeans Shared Spy Data With U.S.*, WALL ST. J. (Oct. 29, 2013), https://www.wsj.com/articles/us-says-france-spain-aided-nsa-spying-1383065709.

[58] Cole & Fabbrini, *supra* note 30, at 222.

[59] Andrew Keane Woods, *Against Data Exceptionalism*, 68 STAN. L. REV. 729, 742 (2016) (stating, in relevant part, that "Governments seek lawful access to Internet data for a host of reasons, including counterterrorism operations, immigration control, and many other administrative matters.").

enforcement and intelligence agencies but also cooperative data sharing with international intelligence partners.[60]

In today's global economy, the idea of data fails to comport with traditional borders, and security threats have adopted a transnational nature.[61] As Professor Jennifer Daskal points out, "The ease and speed with which data travels across borders, the seemingly arbitrary paths it takes, and the physical disconnect between where data is stored and where it is accessed critically test these foundational premises [of territoriality]."[62] In a world of non-territorial data, blocking foreign security data streams can have significantly adverse consequences. As President Obama observed, "[E]merging threats from terrorist groups and the proliferation of weapons of mass destruction place new and in some ways more complicated demands on our intelligence agencies. Globalization and the Internet made these threats more acute, as technology erased borders and empowered individuals to project great violence . . . ."[63] One Irish Court recently recognized that limitations on legal

---

[60] *Id.* at 745 ("This is striking: a police officer now must cross an international border in order to do her job, whereas twenty or even ten years ago, the same officer might have been able to investigate a routine crime like kidnapping without leaving her country. Just as crime has become increasingly global, evidence gathering has followed suit."). This trend has long been in the works. *See* McDougal et al., *supra* note 44, at 424 (noting that increasing global interrelation has "rendered intelligence gathering a global operation requiring more institutional and ad hoc cooperation across political boundaries.").

[61] *But see* Woods, *supra* note 59, at 763 ("At a deep conceptual level, data is not as novel as the data exceptionalists suggest. None of the features that are thought to make data novel are in fact novel-whether the features are considered individually or as a whole-and in fact, data is an easier case than some other assets because data has a physical location wherever it is stored").

[62] Jennifer Daskal, *The Un-Territoriality of Data*, 125 YALE L. J. 326 (2015).

[63] Ashley Deeks, *Confronting and Adapting: Intelligence Agencies and International Law*, 102 VA. L. REV. 599, 622 (2016) https://papers.ssrn.com/sol3/papers.cfm? abstract_id=2768339 (citing *Remarks by the President on Review of Signals Intelligence*, WHITE HOUSE OFFICE PRESS SEC'Y (Jan. 17, 2014), https://obamawhitehouse.archives.gov/the-press-office/2014/01/17/remarks-president-review-signals-intelligence).

security sharing "has potentially extremely significant implications for the safety and security of residents within the European Union."[64]

This reflects a larger truth that as transnational integration has developed, so too has state susceptibility to intervention or interruption by individuals located around the world. As criminal activity takes an increasingly international flavor,[65] domestic information alone proves insufficient to provide safety in the twenty-first century. This position does not merely reflect theoretical rhetoric arising from the desire to shape the modern global citizen. Rather, this position has been cemented by empirical experience: it is widely accepted among the global intelligence community that international data sharing incidents have contributed to saving many lives.[66] To highlight one well-cited example, Canada's refusal to accept Indian intelligence information regarding a threat of homegrown Canadian Sikh extremist nationalists resulted in the destruction of Air India Flight 182 and cost 329 lives.[67]

In addition to preventing the loss of life, intelligence-sharing agreements provide a number of important benefits. Intelligence sharing with foreign governments helps provide a more complete picture of often-cryptic circumstances that allow "military commanders, law enforcement officials,

---

[64] [Irish] Data Prot. Comm'r, v. Facebook Ireland Ltd. & Maximillian Schrems [2016 No. 4809 P.], 3 (H. Ct.) (Ir.), http://www.europe-v-facebook.org/sh2/HCJ.pdf.

[65] For example, "between October 2014 and September 2015, the UK Financial Intelligence Unit (UKFIU) received 1,566 requests from international partners for financial intelligence. Of these, at least 800 came from EU Member States. In the same period, the UKFIU proactively disseminated 571 pieces of financial intelligence to international financial intelligence units, 200 of which went to Europol." *The Exchange and Protection of Personal Data: A Future Partnership Paper*, HM GOV'T (2017), https://www.gov.uk/government/uploads/system/uploads/attachment_data/file/6398 53/The_exchange_and_protection_of_personal_data.pdf; *see also* Woods, *supra* note 59, at 744–745 (2016) (presenting U.K. Government Requests for Internet Data from Major U.S. Service Providers in 2014).

[66] *See, e.g.*, BORN ET AL., *supra* note 4, at 33 ("[I]nternational intelligence cooperation can help to safeguard the right to life, and it can prevent serious threats to public safety. It is widely accepted that information sharing has contributed to the prevention of numerous terrorist attacks over the past decade, saving many lives.")

[67] *See id.* at 41 (citing COMMISSION OF INQUIRY INTO THE INVESTIGATION OF THE BOMBING OF AIR INDIA FLIGHT 182, 422–31 (2010)).

and policymakers to improve the quality of their decision making."[68] Additionally, data sharing provides for significant cost-savings and enables operational efficiencies. Data sharing delivers benefits in the division of labor, reducing the burden of duplicative investigative efforts, and leveraging specialized areas of expertise.[69] Take the example of human intelligence.[70] As the self-proclaimed Islamic State loses the last of its territory and resources, many fear that it will increasingly turn its focus to conducting international terrorism.[71] As such, governments who fear that they are potential targets will seek to place clandestine operatives within the organization or recruit informants. Such measures are extremely costly, and the duplication of effort may itself compromise the efficacy of individual missions. Moreover, certain governments will have comparative advantages—in this scenario, Middle Eastern governments will likely have more native language speakers and citizens with plausible ties to the region or conflict. At first glance, the ISIS case might seem distinguishable from the privacy concerns explored in this Article. However, even in this extreme scenario of the Islamic State, the Islamic State's international ambitions involve cross-border communications and association with and surveillance of individuals located around the world. When intelligence agencies can engage in information sharing, they benefit from the collective efficiencies.

---

[68] *Id.* at 34.

[69] *Id.* at 36 ("Close allies can work to avoid duplication of information collection efforts . . .. It may be easier for a service to work with a foreign partner whose intelligence officials and/or agents share these [specialized] characteristics"); Janine McGruddy, *Multilateral Intelligence Collaboration and International Oversight*, 6 J. STRATEGIC SEC. 214, 215 (2013) http://scholarcommons.usf.edu/cgi/viewcontent.cgi?article=1317&context=jss ("No one country can effectively cover all the areas of interest that their intelligence collection requirements demand.")

[70] Human Intelligence (HUMINT) is defined by the Central Intelligence Agency as "any information that can be gathered from human sources." *INTelligence: Human Intelligence*, CENT. INTELLIGENCE AGENCY (last updated Apr. 30, 2013), https://www.cia.gov/news-information/featured-story-archive/2010-featured-story-archive/intelligence-human-intelligence.html.

[71] *See, e.g.*, Daniel Byman, *Beyond Iraq and Syria: ISIS' Ability to Conduct Attacks Abroad*, LAWFARE (Jun. 15, 2017, 11:14 AM), https://www.lawfareblog.com/beyond-iraq-and-syria-isis-ability-conduct-attacks-abroad ("This loss of territory and resources, however, increases the Islamic State's desire to conduct international terrorism.").

Intelligence sharing practices also lead to security improvements by effectuating peer review.[72] The nature of intelligence-sharing work can often insulate such practices from substantive agency review by other areas of the government.   Through coordination with foreign government agencies, intelligence sharing establishes an avenue for an outside party to provide the intelligence agency with professional feedback. In doing so, intelligence-sharing agreements play an invaluable role in providing an objective and critical review of practices that lay "largely shielded" from external review.[73] While peer review provides a helpful informal model for intelligence feedback, it should not serve as the only source of oversight—an issue that receives extensive attention *infra*.

Finally, intelligence-sharing agreements permit governments to control the external information flow to other governments.   Through such arrangements, governments can tailor the amount of information that they share with partners and can withhold sensitive material or titrate the circumstances in which they distribute such information. Cooperation can limit the degree to which foreign governments expend the resources to surveil non-citizens, thereby decreasing the risk of incidental foreign espionage threatening national security. These positive externalities of lessened foreign government espionage have encouraged even privacy advocates to push for data sharing regimes motivated by the belief that agreements will bolster citizens' protections against foreign government surveillance.[74]

---

[72] *See* Deeks *supra* note 63, at 640.

[73] BORN ET AL., *supra* note 4, at 36 ("Exchanging information and intelligence analyses with foreign partners can provide services with alternative perspectives on key issues and help them to challenge their own assumptions . . . the professional criticism that foreign partners can provide may be invaluable. Accordingly, services with close relationships will sometimes solicit comments on their strategic analyses.")

[74] *See* Cole & Fabbrini, *supra* note 30, at 236–37.

III.   COUNTRIES STRIKE DIFFERENT PRIVACY-SECURITY BALANCES FOR NATIONAL INTELLIGENCE REGIMES

While popular imagery may paint a privacy-loving Europe and a security-obsessed United States, the reality is that when it comes to government surveillance, experts have recognized that "[s]afeguards under American law, for all their shortcomings, are far more robust than those now found or likely to emerge elsewhere," including in Europe.[75] European Union member states themselves hold widely varying views on the appropriate tradeoff balance on "such fundamental issues as the required level of suspicion, the role of suspect-specific judicial approval ex-ante, and the degree to which transparency and oversight."[76]

Taken holistically, EU law provides substantially more protection against government surveillance in three ways. First, it does not accept the third-party doctrine found in American jurisprudence, which robs individuals of a reasonable expectation of privacy—in other words, a privacy interest—in information that has been revealed to a third party.[77] The third-party doctrine has led American courts to reject a privacy interest in information given to a third party "even if the information is revealed on the assumption that it will be used only for a limited purpose."[78] The EU also imposes greater privacy

---

[75] Schulhofer, *supra* note 51, at 245. *See, e.g.*, Entous & Gorman, *supra* note 57, (statement of Rep. Mike Rogers) ("[The U.S. is] the only intelligence service in the world that is forced to go to a court before they even collect on foreign intelligence operations, which is shocking to me.").

[76] Schulhofer, *supra* note 51, at 245 ("There is wide variation, even among Western democracies, on such fundamental issues as the required level of suspicion, the role of suspect-specific judicial approval *ex ante*, and the degree to which transparency and oversight are relaxed in the national security context.").

[77] *Id.*

[78] United States v. Miller, 425 U.S. 435, 443 (1976). However, the United States jurisprudence on the third-party doctrine may be shifting for online information. *See, e.g.*, Carpenter v. United States, 138 S. Ct. 2206 (2018) (limiting the scope of third-party doctrine by requiring a warrant for cell phone geo-location data lasting longer than a week); *see also* Brian Mund, *Social Media Searches and the Reasonable Expectation of Privacy*,

restrictions on the private sector, including limitations on the retention and use of data and has recognized a right to be forgotten.[79] The EU is also subject to the European Court of Human Rights (ECtHR), where the Court has built a considerable foundation for privacy protection, including a right against secret monitoring of postal and telephonic communications,[80] real-time communications interceptions,[81] and bulk data collection.[82] However, the ECtHR maintained wide discretion to state actors by granting a "margin of appreciation" in the national security and surveillance context.[83]

That is not to say that the United States is insensitive to privacy concerns; the central understanding of American privacy arises from the notion of freedom from state surveillance.[84] In three other ways, American law provides more privacy protections than the EU for government intelligence. First, while American law requires FISA authorization, EU law does not require judicial oversight.[85] Second, EU law does not require individualized suspicion for intelligence searches, which allows for greater bulk collection flexibility than is allowed in the U.S.[86] Third, EU law lacks "the detailed specificity of the US

---

19 YALE J. L. & TECH. 238, 256-57 (2017) http://yjolt.org/sites/default/files/mund19yjolt238_0.pdf (arguing that the U.S. Supreme Court has indicated a willingness to reconsider the third party doctrine for digital information).

[79] Schulhofer *supra* note 51, at 249.

[80] Klass v. Germany, App. No. 5029/71, Eur. Ct. H.R. (ser. A), Judgment (1978), http://hudoc.echr.coe.int/eng?i=001-57510.

[81] Malone v. United Kingdom, App. No. 8691/79, (1984) Eur. H.R. Rep. 14 (telephone interception); Copland v. United Kingdom, App. No. 62617/00, Eur. Ct. H.R., Judgment (2007), http://hudoc.echr.coe.int/eng?i=001-79996 (email interception).

[82] Rotaru v. Romania, App. No. 28341/95, Eur. Ct. H.R., Judgment (2000), http://hudoc.echr.coe.int/eng?i=001-58586; Marper v. United Kingdom, Apps. No. 30562/04 & 30566/04, Eur. Ct. H.R., Judgment (2008), http://hudoc.echr.coe.int/eng?i=001-90051.

[83] Cole & Fabbrini, *supra* note 30, at 227.

[84] James Q. Whitman, *The Two Western Cultures of Privacy: Dignity Versus Liberty*, 113 YALE L. J. 1151, 1211–13 (2004), https://www.yalelawjournal.org/pdf/246_ftn7jo8w.pdf ("Suspicion of the state has always stood at the foundation of American privacy thinking.").

[85] Schulhofer, *supra* note 51, at 249.

[86] *Id* at 249–50.

Foreign Intelligence Surveillance Act (FISA)," which has left national security practices largely unregulated.[87]

However, the U.S. Fourth Amendment's protection against "unreasonable searches and seizures"[88] is not absolute, and the United States has shifted towards a greater security emphasis in the aftermath of the September 11 attacks. Most notably, the USA PATRIOT Act[89] has realigned the balance between the government and American citizens over the scope of reasonable privacy intrusions for national security purposes.[90] The PATRIOT Act included provisions that added a broad new definition of domestic terrorism under 18 U.S.C. § 2331[91] and allowed for delayed notice for certain searches and interceptions,[92] thereby facilitating extended covert operations.[93] Furthermore, the United States has extended Fourth Amendment procedural protections for domestic national security gathering[94] and has prevented the bulk data collection of all American telephone metadata records.[95] The United States offers much less protection to non-U.S. persons located abroad and has

---

[87] *Id.* at 250.

[88] U.S. CONST. Amend. IV.

[89] Pub. L. No. 107-56, § 1, 115 Stat. 272, 272–75.

[90] Patricia Mell, *Big Brother at the Door: Balancing National Security with Privacy under the USA Patriot Act*, 80 DENV. U. L. REV. 375, 379 (2002) ("The PATRIOT Act attacks the balance between the government and the individual by a systematic circumvention of established doctrine and procedures guarding against unreasonable governmental intrusion").

[91] *See* 18 U.S.C. § 2331; Patriot Act, H.R. 3162, 107th Cong. § 802 (2001).

[92] 18 U.S.C. § 3103(a).

[93] *USA Freedom Act: What's In, What's Out*, WASH. POST (Jun. 2, 2015), https://www.washingtonpost.com/graphics/politics/usa-freedom-act (stating that the USA Freedom Act reauthorized the PATRIOT Act while modifying some of the government's bulk data collection powers). *See generally* USA FREEDOM Act of 2015, Pub. L. No. 114-23, 129 Stat. 267 (2015), https://www.congress.gov/bill/114th-congress/house-bill/2048?q={%22search%22%3A[%22\%22hr2048\%22%22]}.

[94] United States v. U.S. Dist. Court for E. Dist. of Mich., S. Div., 407 U.S. 297, 321 (1972) (holding government's national security concerns "do not justify departure in this case from the customary Fourth Amendment requirement of judicial approval prior to initiation of a search or surveillance.").

[95] *See* Am. Civil Liberties Union v. Clapper, 785 F.3d 787, 796 (2d Cir. 2015) (interpreting §215 of the PATRIOT Act, 50 U.S.C. § 1861, to not authorize bulk data collection of American telephone records).

authorized extensive foreign collection data collection, even if the data also captures communications concerning persons located within the United States.[96]

The United States and Europe also differ in their approach to judicial review.[97] The European Union tilts heavily towards judicial engagement to protect individual privacy rights.[98] The contrast between the United States and European Union approach on the scope of judicial reviewability shines through a conclusion by the United States Foreign Intelligence Surveillance Court of Review (FISCR). Rather than allow substantive privacy interests to narrow legitimate national security methods, the FISCR judges instead recognized that "where the government has instituted several layers of

---

[96] United States v. Mohamud, 2014 WL 2866749, at *15 (D. Or. June 24, 2014), *aff'd*, 843 F.3d 420, 440 (9th Cir. 2016) ("The § 702 acquisition targeting a non-U.S. person overseas is constitutionally permissible, so, under the general rule, the incidental collection of defendant's communications with the extraterritorial target would be lawful."). *See also* Redacted, 2011 WL 10945618, at *27 (FISA Ct. Oct. 3, 2011) (providing, in relevant part, that "incidental collections occurring as a result of constitutionally permissible acquisitions do not render those acquisitions unlawful."). President Obama's Presidential Policy Directive 28 added additional safeguards for non-U.S. citizens located abroad and required that "signals intelligence activities must take into account that all persons should be treated with dignity and respect[.]" *See also Presidential Policy Directive No. 28, Signals Intelligence Activities* § 1 (Jan. 17, 2014) [hereinafter PPD-28], https://obamawhitehouse.archives.gov/the-press-office/2014/01/17/presidential-policy-directive-signals-intelligence-activities.

[97] This difference has been characterized as a "ballot-box democracy" in the U.S. versus a "fundamental rights" model of judicial review in Europe. *See* Francesca Bignami & Giorgio Resta, *Human Rights Extraterritoriality: The Right to Privacy and National Security Surveillance* at 19, *in* EYAL BENVENISTI & GEORG NOLTE, THE RIGHT TO PRIVACY AND NATIONAL SECURITY SURVEILLANCE IN COMMUNITY INTERESTS ACROSS INTERNATIONAL LAW (forthcoming), https://scholarship.law.gwu.edu/cgi/viewcontent.cgi?referer=https://scholar.google.com/&httpsredir=1&article=2562&context=faculty_publications.

[98] *See, e.g.*, Joined Cases C-293/12 and C-594/12, Digital Rights Ireland & Others v Minister for Communications, Marine & Natural Resources and Others, E.C.J., Judgment (Grand Chamber Apr. 8, 2014), https://eur-lex.europa.eu/legal-content/EN/TXT/PDF/?uri=CELEX:62012CJ0293&from=EN (holding that "EU legislature's discretion is reduced" because of the fundamental right to respect for private life, the government's stated legitimate interest in national security notwithstanding.).

serviceable safeguards to protect individuals against unwarranted harms and to minimize incidental intrusions, its efforts to protect national security should not be frustrated by the courts."[99]

Neither the United States nor the European Union represents the full range in which states establish their privacy-security tradeoff. For example, Japan has traditionally sat at the extreme "privacy" end of the privacy-security spectrum.[100] The Japanese government's ability to engage in surveillance and interception practices has been highly curtailed, including for national security purposes.[101] Japan has a wiretap law, but "Japanese culture strongly opposes government interceptions, and the authority is rarely used."[102] Until June 2017, Japan did not have a statutory basis for authorizing communications interceptions for counter-terrorism purposes.[103] However, Japan's robust privacy anti-interception laws do not translate to a complete lack of authorization for counter-terror activity. In 2016, the Japanese Supreme Court granted $880,000 to Muslim plaintiffs for privacy violations related to a leak of police files that revealed blanket surveillance of religious Muslims in Japan.[104] Nevertheless, Japan's Supreme Court affirmed a lower

---

[99] *In re* Directives Pursuant to Section 105B of Foreign Intelligence Surveillance Act, 551 F.3d 1004, 1016 (FISA Ct. Rev. 2008).

[100] *See* Rubinstein et al., *supra* note 30, at 104 ("At the opposite extreme, Japan and Brazil are notable for the severe limits they impose on interceptions undertaken for foreign intelligence security purposes.").

[101] *Id.*

[102] *Id.* at 109 ("Japanese society strongly disfavours the use of wiretaps and the number of communications intercepts is miniscule."). *See also* Toshimaru Ogura, *Toward Global Communication Rights: Movements Against Wiretapping and Monitoring in Japan*, TRANSNATIONAL INSTITUTE (2018), https://www.tni.org/en/archives/act/2691 (last visited Oct. 11, 2018).

[103] Andy Sharp, *Abe Passes Controversial Bill Boosting Japan Surveillance Powers*, BLOOMBERG (Jun. 14, 2017 10:06 PM), https://www.bloomberg.com/news/articles/2017-06-15/abe-passes-controversial-bill-boosting-japan-surveillance-powers; Rubinstein et al., *supra* note 30, at 109 ("Japanese law lacks any statutory basis for authorizing wiretaps for counter-terrorism purposes.").

[104] Ian Monroe, *Top Court Green-Lights Surveillance of Japan's Muslims*, AL JAZEERA (Jun. 29, 2016), http://www.aljazeera.com/news/2016/06/top-court-green-lights-surveillance-japan-muslims-160629040956466.html.

court ruling permitting intelligence profiling and surveillance as "necessary and inevitable" to guard against the threat of international terrorism.[105]

At the other end of the spectrum, China and India heavily subordinate privacy interests to possible security needs in a way that neither the United States, the European Union, nor Japan would find appropriate. Both China and India are distinguished by their "almost total" lack of privacy protection from government monitoring and oversight. In India, the Indian Intelligence Bureau (IB) faces little public accountability.[106] In fact, the IB, which has existed since 1887, might not even have any legislative basis in modern Indian law.[107] The Indian government has also bolstered its surveillance capabilities through establishing a Central Monitoring System that enables government interception of emails, chats, voice calls and text messages without the assistance of third party service providers.[108] In addition, the Indian government has over 1.18 billion citizens[109] in its Aadhaar identification system based on biometric and demographic information and has disabled encryption between telephones and network stations, which facilitates government interception of communications transmissions.[110] The

---

[105] *Id.*

[106] Pranesh Prakash, *How Surveillance Works in India*, N.Y. TIMES (Jul. 10 2013, 2:29 AM), https://india.blogs.nytimes.com/2013/07/10/how-surveillance-works-in-india (stating that "[n]o intelligence agency in India has been created under an act of Parliament with clearly established roles and limitations on powers, and hence there is no public accountability whatsoever.").

[107] *See Subramanium to Katju: The Dangerous Elevation of the IB Report*, FIRST POST (Jul. 24, 2014), http://www.firstpost.com/india/subramanium-to-katju-the-dangerous-elevation-of-the-ib-report-1631981.html (noting that the IB is "agency established under an administrative order without any constitutional or statutory identity"). *See also Explain Intelligence Bureau's Legality, HC Tells Centre*, TIMES INDIA (Mar. 26, 2012), https://timesofindia.indiatimes.com/india/Explain-Intelligence-Bureaus-legality-HC-tells-Centre/articleshow/12408605.cms.

[108] Rubinstein et al., *supra* note 30, at 98; Leo Mirani, *Think US snooping is bad? Try Italy, India or . . . Canada*, QUARTZ (Jun. 10, 2013), https://qz.com/92648/think-us-snooping-is-bad-try-italy-india-or-canada.

[109] Unique Identification Authority of India, *Welcome to AADHAAR Dashboard*, GOV'T INDIA, https://uidai.gov.in/aadhaar_dashboard (last visited Feb. 28, 2019).

[110] *See generally* Stephanie K. Pell & Christopher Soghoian, *Your Secret Stingray's No Secret Anymore: The Vanishing Government Monopoly over Cell Phone Surveillance and Its*

government has wide discretion in utilizing this information for national security and other "public interest" purposes.[111] While a 1996 Supreme Court decision recognized that wiretapping constitutes an invasion of privacy,[112] the Indian government retains relatively wide discretion in collecting and utilizing information for national security and other "public interest" purposes.[113] Finally, India's laws grant procedural review by a committee of the law enforcement official's colleagues but critics have questioned its procedural credibility.[114]

China grants broad security powers to its security forces. As China scholar James Fry notes, "there are only a few legal limitations on the authorities when it comes to Internet surveillance, with the vast majority of laws providing the authorities many express powers over content censorship."[115] The Chinese Ministry of Public Security has undertaken the ambitious "Police Cloud" project, which, similarly to the Indian Aadhaar, collects a vast amount of information tied to citizens' unique national identification number.[116] China has also installed over 20 million cameras in

---

Impact on National Security and Consumer Privacy, 28 HARV. J. L. & TECH. 1 (2014), https://ssrn.com/abstract=2437678.

[111] Rhyea Malik & Subhajit Basu, *India's Dodgy Mass Surveillance Project Should Concern Us All*, WIRED (Aug. 25, 2017), http://www.wired.co.uk/article/india-aadhaar-biometrics-privacy; Prashant Reddy, *Data Protection: Can India Overcome the Spy-Security State and Big Tech To Enact a Strong Law?*, SCROLL (Aug. 22, 2017), https://scroll.in/article/846946/data-protection-can-india-overcome-the-spy-security-state-and-big-tech-to-enact-a-strong-law. *See also Data Protection Laws of the World: India*, DLA PIPER (Jan. 24, 2017), https://www.dlapiperdataprotection.com/index.html?t=law&c=IN (stating that "[t]here is no specific legislation on privacy and data protection in India.").

[112] *See* Prakash, *supra* note 106; Bhairav Acharya, *Mastering the Art of Keeping Indians Under Surveillance*, WIRE (May 30, 2015), https://thewire.in/2756/mastering-the-art-of-keeping-indians-under-surveillance.

[113] *See supra* note 109.

[114] *See* Acharya, *supra* note 112.

[115] James D. Fry, *Privacy, Predictability And Internet Surveillance In The U.S. And China: Better The Devil You Know?*, 37 U. PA. J. INT'L L. 419, 478 (2016), http://scholarship.law.upenn.edu/cgi/viewcontent.cgi?article=1910&context=jil.

[116] *China: Police 'Big Data' Systems Violate Privacy, Target Dissent*, HUMAN RIGHTS WATCH (Nov. 19, 2017), https://www.hrw.org/news/2017/11/19/china-police-big-data-systems-violate-privacy-target-dissent.

the past few years as means of more closely monitoring its population.[117] With its extensive infrastructure, China has also introduced real-time facial recognition tracking[118] as well as voice recognition forensics for unidentified targets in phone conversations.[119] Chinese policies have also generated less expectation of privacy among the Chinese public. In one recent study, only 50 percent of Chinese consumers acknowledged the need for caution in sharing personal information online, and reflected a "more cavalier approach" towards data privacy among Chinese citizens.[120] In contrast, the average acknowledgment of data privacy caution in ten other countries exceeded 75 percent.[121] The Washington Post reports that spying in China is so pervasive that government officials often spy upon one another—leading to a practice of hugging at the beginning of meetings in order to pat down their counterparts for hidden microphones.[122]

China's trajectory appears to continue empowering widespread national security surveillance activity. China's Anti-Terrorism Law (ATL) requires telecommunication and Internet providers within Chinese jurisdiction to

---

[117] Frank Langfitt, *In China, Beware: A Camera May Be Watching You*, NAT'L PUB. RADIO (Jan. 29, 2013), https://www.npr.org/2013/01/29/170469038/in-china-beware-a-camera-may-be-watching-you.

[118] Ms. Smith, *Skynet in China: Real-life 'Person of Interest' spying in real time*, CSO ONLINE (Sep. 28, 2017), https://www.csoonline.com/article/3228444/security/skynet-in-china-real-life-person-of-interest-spying-in-real-time.html.

[119] *See China: Voice Biometric Collection Threatens Privacy*, HUMAN RIGHTS WATCH (Oct. 22, 2017), https://www.hrw.org/news/2017/10/22/china-voice-biometric-collection-threatens-privacy.

[120] *See* George G. Chen & Tiffany G. Wong, *Waiting for China's Data Protection Law*, DIPLOMAT (Aug. 12, 2017), https://thediplomat.com/2017/08/waiting-for-chinas-data-protection-law. *See also* Peter Fuhrman, *Government Cyber-Surveillance is the Norm in China—And Its Popular*, WASH. POST (Jan. 29, 2016), https://www.washingtonpost.com/opinions/cyber-surveillance-is-a-way-of-life-in-china/2016/01/29/e4e856dc-c476-11e5-a4aa-f25866ba0dc6_story.html (stating that "none [of my Chinese friends] expressed the slightest quibble about their government knowing where they travel or when they receive international calls.").

[121] *See* Chen & Wong, *supra* note 120.

[122] Max Fisher, *Chinese Government Officials Are Constantly Wiretapping And Spying On One Another*, WASH. POST (Feb. 13, 2013), https://www.washingtonpost.com/news/worldviews/wp/2013/02/19/chinese-government-officials-are-constantly-wiretapping-and-spying-on-one-another.

grant data access and decryption support to government authorities under the ambit of national security.[123] Given the government's sweeping authority to take "all necessary" steps to guard China's sovereignty,[124] the ATL effectively grants access to any and all locally stored data that the Chinese government might want.[125] Finally, an updated Intelligence Law promotes a similar purpose, broadly allowing Chinese security officials to "make inquiries of any individuals as part of their intelligence-gathering, and to examine their reference materials and files [and] commandeer the communications equipment, transportation, buildings, and other facilities of individuals as well as organizations and government organs."[126]

In short, countries ranging from Japan, the European Union, the United States, India and China all display a wide array of preferences and values regarding their internal balance between privacy and national security interests. In the age of transnational data, these balances necessarily bleed

---

[123] Courtney M. Bowman et al., *A Primer on China's New Cybersecurity Law: Privacy, Cross-Border Transfer Requirements, and Data Localization*, PROSKAUER (May 9, 2017), https://privacylaw.proskauer.com/2017/05/articles/international/a-primer-on-chinas-new-cybersecurity-law-privacy-cross-border-transfer-requirements-and-data-localization (stating that decryption assistance has not included a requirement to surrender decryption keys); Alyssa Abkowitz & Eva Dou, *Apple to Build China Data Center to Meet New Cybersecurity Law*, WALL ST. J. (Jul. 12, 2017), https://www.wsj.com/articles/apple-to-build-china-data-center-to-meet-new-cybersecurity-law-1499861507; Dante D'Orazio, *China Passes Controversial Anti-Terrorism Law To Access Encrypted User Accounts*, VERGE (Dec. 27, 2015), https://www.theverge.com/2015/12/27/10670346/china-passes-law-to-access-encrypted-communications (stating that "[t]he new law does not require that companies operating in China hand over encryption keys.").

[124] This *carte blanche* is conferred pursuant to China's National Security Law. *See* Bowman et al., supra note 123.

[125] *See* D'Orazio *supra* note 123 ("President Obama raised his concerns over draft regulations with China's President Xi Jinping, saying that the rules amounted to a dangerous backdoor to internet services.").

[126] Murray Scot Tanner, *Beijing's New National Intelligence Law: From Defense to Offense*, LAWFARE (Jul. 20, 2017), https://www.lawfareblog.com/beijings-new-national-intelligence-law-defense-offense; *China Activists Fear Increased Surveillance With New Security Law*, REUTERS (May 25, 2017), https://www.reuters.com/article/us-china-security-int/china-activists-fear-increased-surveillance-with-new-security-law-idUSKBN18M09U.

beyond state borders and create difficult questions for intelligence sharing between various agencies. The next section explores some of the barriers to intelligence sharing that have arisen in the face of this tradeoff.

IV.   BARRIERS TO CROSS-BORDER INTELLIGENCE REGIME

The privacy-security value disparity has led to pressure on intelligence sharing regimes. Most notably, the European Union has engaged in unilateral pressure to push states to modify their intelligence sharing practices and adopt greater privacy rights protections. The European Union has most actively imported privacy requirements onto other countries' intelligence gathering practices. Taking action in the name of international human rights, European Courts have led the effort to institute intelligence-sharing safeguards consistent with its interpretation of European human rights obligations. Europe's extraterritorial privacy governance has not been limited to national security practices, but has rather been part of a larger effort to govern global privacy law.[127] As legal scholars Jack Goldsmith and Tim Wu recognize, "For many purposes, the European Union is today the effective sovereign of global privacy law."[128] While European Courts have seized control of the EU's

---

[127] Canada has undertaken similar efforts more recently, but its actions have not had the same effect. For example, the Canadian Supreme Court also ordered Google to erase search results worldwide associated with a regarding an accusation of misappropriating confidential information and trade secrets. *See* Google Inc. v. Equustek Solutions Inc., 2017 SCC 34, ¶3, https://scc-csc.lexum.com/scc-csc/scc-csc/en/16701/1/document.do; *see also* Jacob Gershman, *Judge Rules Canada Can't Make Google Delete Search Results in U.S.,* WALL ST. J. (Nov. 3, 2017), https://www.wsj.com/articles/judge-rules-canada-cant-make-google-delete-search-results-in-u-s-1509745395. A U.S court rejected the attempt to apply the Canadian ruling to U.S. jurisdiction. Google LLC v. Equustek Sols. Inc., 2017 WL 5000834, at *4 (N.D. Cal. Nov. 2, 2017) ("By forcing intermediaries to remove links to third-party material, the Canadian order . . . threatens free speech on the global internet."). As one analyst explains, this decision suggests that countries will not succeed in extraterritorial enforcement in the United States. Gershman, *supra.*

[128] *See* Jack Goldsmith & Tim Wu, *Who Controls the Internet?: Illusions of a Borderless World,* 126 HARV. L. REV. 1966, (2006). *See also* Paul M. Schwartz, *The EU-U.S. Privacy*

privacy exportation, many of the European Union member states would like to strike a different balance—especially in the intelligence sphere.[129]

In recent years, the Court of Justice of the European Union (CJEU) has increasingly expanded its authority to review Member States' national security activity. In particular, the CJEU has actively policed data sharing practices for national security purposes, thereby influencing the security tradeoff for both the EU member states and also EU national security partners. The primary barrier of cross-border influence lies in CJEU's commitment to enforcing "an adequate level of protection"[130] for data transfers beyond the

---

Collision: A Turn to Institutions and Procedures, 126 HARV. L. REV. 1966, 1966 (2013) ("The EU has played a major role in international decisions involving information privacy, a role that has been bolstered by the authority of EU member states to block data transfers to third party nations, including the United States."); Graham Greenleaf, *The Influence of European Data Privacy Standards Outside Europe: Implications for Globalisation of Convention 108*, 2 INT'L DATA PRIVACY L. 68, 77 (2012) (stating, in relevant part, that "something reasonably described as 'European standard' data privacy laws are becoming the norm in most parts of the world.").

[129] Privacy watchdog Privacy International has reported inconsistencies between EU member state practice and CJEU decisions. For example, as of July 2017, *zero* EU member states had adjusted their data retention practices or surveillance laws into compliance consistent with the 2016 CJEU *Watson* decision. *See National Data Retention Laws Since the CJEU's Tele-2/Watson Judgment*, PRIVACY INT'L (Sept. 2017), https://privacyinternational.org/sites/default/files/Data%20Retention_2017.pdf.
Analysts have also noted that the UK's departure from the European Union was motivated at least in part by its antipathy towards the CJEU. *See, e.g.*, Elizabeth Piper, *Britain Outlines Plans To Break Free of European Court*, BUS. INSIDER (Aug. 22, 2017), http://www.businessinsider.com/r-britain-outlines-plans-to-break-free-of-european-court-after-brexit-2017-8 ("The European court, or ECJ, is hated by many pro-Brexit lawmakers in May's governing Conservative Party, who say it has slowly sucked power from British courts and parliament."). While the UK currently remains a European Union member state, it has reiterated its position on the CJEU's limited jurisdiction during the introduction of its recent data protection bill. According to the UK government, "National security is outside the scope of EU law. Consequently, the processing of personal data for national security purposes is not within scope of the GDPR or the Law Enforcement Directive ("LED")." Home Office, *Data Protection Bill: Factsheet—National Security Data Processing*, DEP'T DIGITAL, CULTURE, MEDIA & SPORT, https://www.gov.uk/government/uploads/system/uploads/attachment_data/file/6448 29/2017-09-13_Factsheet04_national_security__1_.pdf.
[130] Proposal for a Regulation of the European Parliament and of the Council on the Protection of Individuals with Regard to the Processing of Personal Data and on the

EU, even when it blends into the sphere of national security. In *Schrems v. Data Protection Commissioner* (Case C-362/14), the CJEU invalidated the transatlantic Safe Harbor agreement allowing for personal data sharing between European Union member states and the United States.[131] The CJEU overruled the Irish Data Protection Commissioner and found that in light of the Snowden revelations, the United States did not provide "adequate" protection to the personal data of E.U. citizens under the Safe Harbor framework.[132] In rejecting the 15-year old agreement that governed the data transfers for over 4,500 companies,[133] the CJEU pronounced that its preferred tradeoff balance must govern both the European Union, and the United States. The CJEU held:

> The right to respect for private life, guaranteed by Article 7 of the Charter and by the core values common to the traditions of the Member States, would be rendered meaningless if the State authorities were authorised to access electronic communications on a casual and generalised basis without any objective justification based on considerations of national security or the prevention of crime that are specific to the individual concerned and without those practices being accompanied by appropriate and verifiable safeguards.[134]

The CJEU asserted its ability to review the validity of national security interests as essential to accomplishing its mission to protect other human rights that fell within its jurisdiction. However, as expanded upon *infra*, the CJEU operates off an implicit assumption that human rights operate

---

Free Movement of Such Data, art. 45 (Jan. 25, 2012), http://eur-lex.europa.eu/legalcontent/EN/TXT/PDF/?uri=CELEX:52012PC0011&from=EN [http://perma.cc/4ZY8-82A4.

[131] Robert Levine, *Behind the European Privacy Ruling That's Confounding Silicon Valley*, N.Y. Times (Oct. 9, 2015), http://www.nytimes.com/2015/10/11/business/international/behind-the-european-privacy-ruling-thats-confounding-silicon-valley.html.

[132] Case C-362/14, Schrems v. Data Prot. Comm'r, 2005 E.C.R. I-627, http://curia.europa.eu/jcms/upload/docs/application/pdf/2015-10/cp150117en.pdf.

[133] Natalia Drozdiak & Sam Schechner, *EU Court Says Data-Transfer Pact With U.S. Violates Privacy*, Wall Street J., (Oct. 6, 2015 1:42 P.M.), https://www.wsj.com/articles/eu-court-strikes-down-trans-atlantic-safe-harbor-data-transfer-pact-1444121361.

[134] Case C-362/14, Schrems v. Data Prot. Comm'r, 2015 E.C.R. I-31–32.

unilaterally in the privacy security tradeoff.[135] It also assumes the CJEU's right to give precedence to the CJEU's preferred balance point vis-à-vis other sovereign states. This assumption seemingly contradicts the CJEU's explicit finding that

> In a democratic society, a balance must be struck between these competing concerns, interests and values. Not every State will strike the same balance. One will place a greater emphasis on the right to privacy and one will place a greater emphasis on the requirements of national security. *It is important to state that it is not the function of this court to assess, still less resolve, the relative merits of these positions.*[136]

In light of the CJEU's stated position on the limited roles of the courts, the Court's decision was quite remarkable. Nevertheless, CJEU's resolution of "the relative merits of these [privacy tradeoff] positions" has created tensions with the privacy-security balances employed in other states' intelligence practices.

In addition to direct judicial review of national security data sharing arrangements, the European Union has also conditioned cross-border data sharing on its review of, among other factors, a non-EU country's national security practices.[137] Thus far, Andorra, Argentina, the Faroe Islands, Guernsey, Israel, the Isle of Man, Japan, Jersey, New Zealand, Switzerland and Uruguay have received adequacy decisions,[138] and both Canada and the

---

[135] *See* discussion *infra* Part IV.

[136] Case 2016 No. 4809 P., Data Prot. Comm'r v. Facebook Ireland Limited & Maximillian Schrems, §47 (Oct. 3, 2017), http://www.europe-v-facebook.org/sh2/HCJ.pdf (emphasis added).

[137] *See* Resolution of 6 April 2017 on the adequacy of the protection afforded by the EU-U.S. Privacy Shield, EUR. PARL. DOC. 2016/3018 ¶ 20 (RSP), http://www.europarl.europa.eu/sides/getDoc.do?pubRef=-//EP//NONSGML+TA+P8-TA-2017-0131+0+DOC+PDF+V0//EN. Interview with Iain Bourne, Group Manager – Parliamentary and Government Affairs Department, United Kingdom Information Commissioner's Office (Aug. 1, 2017) (notes on file with author).

[138] European Union Comm.: 3rd Report of Session 2017–19, *Brexit: The EU Data Protection Package*, HOUSE OF LORDS §67 (2017) https://publications.parliament.uk/pa/ld201719/ldselect/ldeucom/7/7.pdf; *see also Adequacy of the Protection of Personal Data in non-EU Countries*, EUROPEAN COMM., https://ec.europa.eu/info/strategy/justice-and-fundamental-rights/data-protection/data-transfers-outside-eu/adequacy-protection-personal-data-non-eu-countries_en; HM GOV'T , *supra* note 65, at ¶ 37.

United States have received "partial" adequacy decisions.[139] By leveraging the stick of forbidding corporate-to-corporate cross-border information sharing, the CJEU has been able to exercise a powerful *de facto* influence on U.S. intelligence practices, and a significant barrier to intelligence sharing to the extent that the U.S. refuses to amend its practices.[140] As one European legal scholar described this success, "It is no exaggeration to state that in future, transnational privacy law will not be written in Brussels, but in Luxembourg."[141] For example, in order to achieve the new US-EU Privacy Shield agreement, the United States has assigned a State Department official to serve as an Ombudsperson charged with the role of serving as the point of contact for foreign governments to raise concerns regarding US signals intelligence activities.[142] The Ombudsperson also collaborates with independent oversight bodies in the US government like the Inspectors

---

[139] Canada has a partial adequacy with respect to only commercial organizations subject to the PIPED Act, and the United States has an adequacy decision for organizations certified under the Privacy Shield only. *Id.*

[140] Alexander Garrelfs, *GDPR Top Ten: #3 Extraterritorial Applicability Of The GDPR*, DELOITTE, Apr. 3, 2017, https://www2.deloitte.com/nl/nl/pages/risk/articles/gdpr-top-ten-3-extraterritorial-applicability-of-the-gdpr.html. Even if one were to contest that the regulations only apply to those operating in EU jurisdiction negate the extraterritorial reach, the de facto extraterritorial imposition still applies. *See, e.g.,* Gregory Shaffer, *Globalization and Social Protection: The Impact of EU and International Rules in the Ratcheting Up of U.S. Privacy Standards*, 25 YALE J. INT'L L. 1, 78 (2000) ("Most importantly, once U.S. businesses adopt internal data privacy policies to avoid EU transfer restrictions, they subject themselves to potential FTC enforcement proceedings for failure to comply with proclaimed policies. In any case, it will be pragmatically difficult for businesses to employ two sets of data privacy practices, one for EU residents (providing for greater privacy protection) and one for U.S. residents (providing for less."). Thomas Wischmeyer, *Faraway, So Close!' – A Constitutional Perspective on Transatlantic Data Flow Regulation, in* OBAMA'S COURT: RECENT CHANGES IN U.S. CONSTITUTIONAL LAW IN TRANSATLANTIC PERSPECTIVE (Anna-Bettina Kaiser, Niels Petersen & Johannes Saurer eds.) 14 (2017), https://ssrn.com/abstract=2877548 ("Moreover, the CJEU's strict scrutiny standard from Schrems coupled with the extraterritorial scope of EU privacy law established in Google Spain amount to a de-facto implementation of EU law on non-EU actors, in particular private actors based in the U.S.").

[141] Wischmeyer, *supra* note 140.

[142] *EU - U.S. Privacy Shield Ombudsperson*, U.S. DEP'T STATE, https://www.state.gov/e/privacyshield/ombud.

General to ensure that appropriate safeguards and procedures are in place.[143] This Privacy Shield, a creature of compromise,[144] is now under attack as privacy activists hope to use litigation to further heighten U.S. intelligence safeguards.[145] As illustrated through the Privacy Shield example, European judicial oversight poses the challenge of holding foreign government intelligence agencies to a privacy-security tradeoff different than the one that they have traditionally chosen.[146]

However, the United States is not entirely blameless in this regard. The CJEU *Schrems* decision responded to the United States' jurisprudence on the Fourth Amendment's inapplicability to non-U.S. citizens located outside of United States territory.[147] The United States Supreme Court has ruled that the Fourth Amendment does not "restrain the actions of the Federal Government against aliens outside of the United States territory."[148] In other words, when

---

[143] *Id.*

[144] *See, e.g.*, Paul M. Schwartz, *The EU-U.S. Privacy Collision: A Turn to Institutions and Procedures*, 126 HARV. L. REV. 1966, 1967 (2013) (arguing that privacy "policymaking has not been led exclusively by the EU, but has been a collaborative effort marked by accommodation and compromise."); Maria Tzanou, *The War against Terror and Transatlantic Information Sharing: Spillovers of Privacy or Spillovers of Security*, 31 UTRECHT J. INT'L & EUR. L. 87 (2015) (arguing that EU-US privacy agreement might not actually have the privacy forcing effect on the United States that many analysts suggest).

[145] *Second Legal Challenge Launched Against "Privacy Shield"*, ELECTRONIC PRIVACY INFO. CENTER, Nov. 3, 2016, https://epic.org/2016/11/second-legal-challenge-launche.html.

[146] However, these changes in privacy-security balance may have thus far been mostly cosmetic. Maria Tzanou's assessment of EU data sharing agreements with the U.S. suggest that in practice, the United States has drawn the EU towards the security end of the privacy-security tradeoff without conceding any security powers. Tzanou, *supra* note 144, at 95 ("While potential 'spillovers of privacy' are not visible yet, 'spillovers of security' looking in the opposite direction, are certainly here.").

[147] *See generally* Wischmeyer, *supra* note 140, at 4.

[148] United States v. Verdugo-Urquidez, 494 U.S. 259, 266 (1990). One must however note the irony that the justification for the decision rested in part on a need for international comity: "For better or for worse, we live in a world of nation-states in which our Government must be able to "functio[n] effectively in the company of sovereign nations." . . . Some who violate our laws may live outside our borders under a regime quite different from that which obtains in this country. Situations threatening to important American interests may arise half-way around the globe, situations which . . . [require cooperation] through diplomatic understanding, treaty, or legislation." *Id.*

it comes to foreign nationals located abroad, the United States' privacy-security tradeoff determines that for intelligence purposes, foreigners do not receive any privacy protection.   This lack of constitutional procedural protection has culminated in foreign opposition to United States' Upstream surveillance practices authorized under Section 702 of the FISA Amendment Act of 2008.[149] The Amendment eliminated the previous statutory warrant and probable cause requirements for the collection of electronic communication by non-United States persons located extraterritorially.[150]   The § 702 standard requires joint authorization by the Attorney General and the Director of the National Intelligence with a showing that the targets are "reasonably believed to be located outside the United States to acquire foreign intelligence information."[151] The Upstream collection physically taps the fiber-optic cables responsible for data traffic, and enables bulk communication interception.[152]

---

at 275. *See also* Wischmeyer , *supra* note 140, at 7 (discussing *Verdugo-Urquidez* effects); *see* discussion *supra* note 96 (detailing recent §702 jurisprudence).

[149] Daskal, *supra* note 62, at 346.

[150] *Id.* In contrast, the Act retains explicit due process safeguards for United States citizens. *See* Matt Olsen, *"Fixes" to Surveillance Law Could Severely Harm FBI National Security Investigations*, JUST SEC. (Nov. 27, 2017), https://www.justsecurity.org/47349/section-702-privacy-surveillance-law-severely-harm-fbi-national-security-investigations.   However, there are still concerns of incidental collection of U.S. persons' communications. *See* Elizabeth Goitein, *Closing Section 702's Front-Door Search Loophole: A Critical Protection for Americans*, JUST SEC. (Oct. 24, 2017), https://www.justsecurity.org/46239/closing-section-702s-front-door-search-loophole-critical-protection-americans.   Additionally, the Open Technology Institute has carefully documented the public record of FISA Section 702 compliance violations. Robyn Greene, *A History of FISA Section 702 Compliance Violations*, NEW AM.: OPEN TECH. INST. (Sep. 28, 2017), https://www.newamerica.org/oti/blog/history-fisa-section-702-compliance-violations/#. *But see* PRIVACY & C.L. OVERSIGHT BD., REPORT ON THE SURVEILLANCE PROGRAM OPERATED PURSUANT TO SECTION 702 OF THE FOREIGN INTELLIGENCE SURVEILLANCE ACT 2 (2014), https://www.pclob.gov/library/702-Report.pdf (providing, in relevant part, that "[o]peration of the Section 702 program has been subject to judicial oversight and extensive internal supervision, and the Board has found no evidence of intentional abuse.").

[151] Daskal, *supra* note 62, at 346.

[152] Scarlet Kim, *How Bulk Interception Works*, PRIVACY INT'L (Sep. 30, 2016), https://medium.com/privacy-international/how-bulk-interception-works-d645440ff6bd; *see also* Daskal, *supra* note 62, at 349 ("Whereas collection through the PRISM program is done with the assistance of the ISP or phone service providers with

2019]   LEGALIZING INTELLIGENCE SHARING

While in the past, Upstream collection included "to, from or about" information about a Section 702 Selector, beginning in May 2017, the Upstream collection only intercepted "to or from" communication data.[153] This interception capability takes advantage of the United States' domestic access control over Internet infrastructure,[154] and may set a precedential model for other states to engage in similar fiber-optics tapping practices.[155] Of note, despite the CJEU's condemnation of U.S. intelligence gathering practices, it is not clear that European governments provide greater safeguards against foreign government surveillance.[156] Other practices notwithstanding, the balance struck by U.S. government surveillance plays an outsized role given the effective control that U.S. companies exert over vast swaths of the Internet.[157] When the United States intelligence agencies need information,

---

whom the target interacts, "upstream" collection is done with the assistance of the Internet and telecommunications companies that control the fiber-optic cables over which a target's communications travel."); Ashley Gorski & Patrick Toomey, *Unprecedented and Unlawful: The NSA's 'Upstream' Surveillance*, AM. C.L. UNION (Sep. 23, 2016), https://www.aclu.org/blog/national-security/privacy-and-surveillance/unprecedented-and-unlawful-nsas-upstream (describing Upstream and accompanying concerns).

[153] *NSA Stops Certain Section 702 "Upstream" Activities*, NAT'L SEC. AGENCY: CENTRAL SEC. SERV., Apr. 28, 2017, https://www.nsa.gov/news-features/press-room/statements/2017-04-28-702-statement.shtml.

[154] *See* Kim, *supra* note 152 ("The geographic location of the US features a high concentration of cables emanating from its east and west coasts."); Ian Brown, *The Feasibility Of Transatlantic Privacy-Protective Standards For Surveillance*, 23 INT'L J. L. & INFO. TECH. 23, 29 (2014), https://academic.oup.com/ijlit/article/23/1/23/2907405 ("USA is reluctant to accept limitations on its abilities to monitor data and communications relating to non-US persons that physically transit US territory—which NSA Director Keith Alexander has called a huge 'home-field advantage'.").

[155] *See* Daskal, *supra* note 50, at 474 ("The approach taken by the United States is likely to become a model for others, thus providing the United States a unique opportunity to set the standards.").

[156] *See* Schulhofer, *supra* note 51, at 250; *see also* Deeks, *supra* note 51, at 332 (detailing bulk collection practices in the United Kingdom, Germany, Sweden, and France).

[157] Daskal, *supra* note 50, at 474 ("While the problem of cross-border access to data is inherently international, the United States has an outsized role to play, given a combination of the U.S.-based provider dominance of the market"); Rubinstein et al., *supra* note 30, at 118 (stating, in relevant part, that "[t]he USA is perceived as having unique advantages in [transborder surveillance].").

they can (with the appropriate domestic safeguards) utilize the information in question. As viewed by non-Americans, U.S. hegemony over Internet services allows for intrusions by the United States government, irrespective of domestic national privacy protections.[158] While the United States has stated that it is undeterred by the possible consequences of its unchecked § 702 collection,[159] in practice, the US has taken steps to regulate its collection of foreign intelligence to account for privacy interests of those located abroad.[160]

---

[158] *See, e.g.*, Brief for Appellate at 8, In the Matter of A Warrant To Search A Certain E-Mail Account Controlled & Maintained By Microsoft Corporation. Microsoft Corp. v. United States (2014) (No. 14-2985-cv.), 2014 WL 7277561, at *8 ("European citizens are highly sensitive to the differences between European and U.S. standards on data protection. Such concerns are frequently raised in relation to the regulation of cross-border data flows and the mass-processing of data by U.S. technology companies. The successful execution of the warrant at issue in this case would extend the scope of this anxiety to a sizeable majority of the data held in the world's datacenters outside the U.S. (most of which are controlled by U.S. corporations) and would thus undermine the protections of the EU data protection regime, even for data belonging to an EU citizen and stored in an EU country."). *See also* Farhad Manjoo, *Why The World Is Drawing Battle Lines Against American Tech Giants*, N.Y. TIMES (Jun. 1, 2016), https://www.nytimes.com/2016/06/02/technology/why-the-world-is-drawing-battle-lines-against-american-tech-giants.html; *Internet Firms Face A Global Techlash*, ECONOMIST (Aug. 10, 2017), https://www.economist.com/news/international/21726072-though-big-tech-firms-are-thriving-they-are-facing-more-scrutiny-ever-internet-firms ("Some governments are unsettled by the growing role in their national lives of firms whose values are distinctively American, in particular in their commitment to free speech ahead of privacy.").

[159] Ahmed Ghappour, *Searching Places Unknown: Law Enforcement Jurisdiction on the Dark Web*, 69 STAN. L. REV. 1075, 1130 (2017), https://review.law.stanford.edu/wp-content/uploads/sites/3/2017/04/69-Stan-L-Rev-1075.pdf ("[T]he [U.S. Department of Justice] has made it clear that it intends to use hacking techniques for all crimes, regardless of the potential cross-border implications."). In late 2017 and early 2018, § 702 underwent a heated reauthorization debate in the USA Liberty Act. *See, e.g.,* Olsen, *supra* note 150 (defending "national security imperative" for full reauthorization). In January 2018, Congress reauthorized FISA Section 702 for another six years. Ted Barrett & Ashley Killough, *Senate Passed FISA Section 702 Reauthorization*, CNN (Jan. 18, 2018), https://www.cnn.com/2018/01/18/politics/fisa-reauthorization-senate-vote.

[160] President Obama's Presidential Policy Directive 28 added additional safeguards for non-U.S. citizens located abroad and required that "signals intelligence activities must take into account that all persons should be treated with dignity and respect[.]" *See* PPD-28, *supra* note 96. *But see* Eric Manpearl, *The Privacy Rights of Non-U.S. Persons*

In short, the European Courts have taken steps to govern the intelligence sharing practices of not only the European Union Member States, but also their intelligence partners. This jurisprudence catches other states in a bind; states have their historical privacy-security tradeoff on one hand, and a legitimate need to engage in intelligence sharing with EU member states as well. Moreover, the United States' lack of extraterritorial privacy protection has further aggravated these barriers to intelligence sharing. The United States' legal stance, that the privacy-security considerations grant *no* privacy protections to foreigners located abroad, has generated understandable discomfort among partnering countries. In particular, foreign onlookers fear that the dissonance between domestic and foreign surveillance protections can facilitate a "revolving door" method by which their own intelligence services may partner with the United States to circumvent national limitations on domestic surveillance.[161]

The EU Court's approach to intelligence governance leads the EU to strike a particular privacy-security tradeoff for cross-border intelligence sharing. Privacy rights do not dissolve in the face of security; as the famous quote attributed to Benjamin Franklin goes, "Those who would give up essential Liberty, to purchase a little temporary Safety, deserve neither Liberty nor Safety."[162] However, the human rights interests weigh on both sides of the scale—too much privacy jeopardizes the human right to life and security. The European Courts have approached intelligence sharing with a privacy idealism that has infused their jurisprudence, but has met practical resistance by security apparatuses, including within EU member states.[163] Unless

---

in Signals Intelligence, 29 FL. J. INT'L L. 303 (2017) https://heinonline.org/HOL/P?h=hein.journals/fjil29&i=323 (arguing that "the United States should rescind PPD-28's expansion of privacy protections to non-U.S. persons because of its cost to U.S. intelligence capabilities, which are critical to protecting U.S. national security interests, the American people, and the U.S. Homeland.").

[161] *See, e.g.*, Kim et al., *supra* note 8.

[162] Benjamin Franklin, *Pennsylvania Assembly: Reply to the Governor, in* VOTES AND PROCEEDINGS OF THE HOUSE OF REPRESENTATIVES, 1755-1756 (1756), http://franklinpapers.org/franklin/framedVolumes.jsp?vol=6&page=238a.

[163] *See, e.g.*, Lorna Woods, *Transferring Personal Data Outside the EU: Clarification from the ECJ?*, EU L. ANALYSIS (Aug. 4, 2017), http://eulawanalysis.blogspot.com/2017/08/transferring-personal-data-outside-eu.html; *New Privacy International report shows that*

European law enforcement and intelligence partners comport with the requisite privacy data collection and data sharing standards, Europe may not be able to lawfully access or utilize the proffered foreign intelligence. As such, this standard has the potential to undermine Europe's effectiveness in receiving foreign information. It also undermines the national security of European partners who may no longer have the ability to share European intelligence.[164] Below, this Article tackles the challenge of designing criteria by which states may share intelligence with agencies that may strike a different privacy balance yet still ensuring the legitimate safeguarding of privacy interests.

V. ADOPTING CRITERIA FOR GOVERNMENT INTELLIGENCE SHARING

A. *International Law Governing Intelligence Sharing*

As Professor Ashley Deeks recognizes, when it comes to international law and the intelligence landscape, "few guideposts exist on how to proceed."[165] Professor Michael Reisman and James Baker have suggested that "the legality of any proactive covert operation should be tested by whether it promotes the basic policy objectives of the Charter, for example, self-determination; whether it adds to or detracts from minimum world order; whether it is consistent with contingencies authorizing the overt use of force; and whether covert coercion was implemented only after plausibly less coercive measures

---

21 European countries are unlawfully retaining personal data, PRIVACY INT'L (Oct. 23, 2017), https://www.privacyinternational.org/press-release/52/new-privacy-international-report-shows-21-european-countries-are-unlawfully; Schulhofer, *supra* note 51, at 253 (noting that the European Council of Ministers have spent years resisting "efforts to put EU privacy-protective legislation on a firmer footing.").

[164] Assuming that leaving the threat to national security unchecked is not a viable option, then the absence of foreign intelligence sharing will likely lead to increased surveillance of foreigners by European governments.

[165] Deeks, *supra* note 63, at 667. *See also* BORN ET AL., *supra* note 4, at 70 (stating that "relatively few countries have legislation on strategic surveillance and the jurisprudence of international courts is sparse.").

were tried."[166] Reisman and Baker's operational approach, while practically oriented, has received criticism for granting almost "unfettered discretion" to the state analyzing the issue.[167]

Some legal scholars have sought to find an international human right to privacy in the International Covenant on Civil and Political Rights (ICCPR), an international treaty with 169 parties.[168] Article 2(1) of the ICCPR requires: "Each State Party to the present Covenant undertakes to respect and to ensure to all individuals within its territory and subject to its jurisdiction the rights recognized in the present Covenant, without distinction of any kind, such as race, colour, sex, language, religion, political or other opinion, national or social origin, property, birth or other status."[169] However, the United States has consistently taken the position that the ICCPR does not apply extraterritorially,[170] and state practice demonstrates "few, if any" extraterritorial privacy protections against intelligence surveillance.[171] As Asaf Lubin notes: "Despite this prevalent state practice, U.N. experts, human rights treaty bodies, and privacy NGOs have been adamant about protecting the myth of a singular and universal right to privacy. By doing so, they seem to 'abet the deception, avoiding the truth like someone pulling blankets over his head to avoid the cold reality of dawn.'"[172] Other scholars have identified

---

[166] W. MICHAEL REISMAN & JAMES E. BAKER, REGULATING COVERT ACTION: PRACTICES, CONTEXTS, AND POLICIES OF COVERT COERCION ABROAD IN INTERNATIONAL AND AMERICAN LAW 26–27 (1992).

[167] Deeks, *supra* note 63, at 668.

[168] International Covenant on Civil and Political Rights, Dec. 19, 1966, 999 U.N.T.S. 171 [hereinafter ICCPR], https://treaties.un.org/doc/Treaties/1976/03/19760323%2006-17%20AM/Ch_IV_04.pdf.

[169] *Id.* at art. 2, ¶ 1.

[170] *See, e.g.*, U.N. Hum. Rts. Comm., 53d Sess., 1405th mtg., ¶ 20, U.N. Doc. CCPR/C/SR.1405 (Mar. 31, 1995) (statement of Conrad Harper, Legal Advisor, U.S. Dep't of State) ("The Covenant was not regarded as having extraterritorial application. . . . During the negotiating history, the words 'within its territory' had been debated and were added by vote, with the clear understanding that such wording would limit the obligations to within a Party's territory.").

[171] Lubin, *supra* note 51, at 551.

[172] *Id.* at 515 (citing W. Michael Reisman, *Myth System and Operational Code*, 3 YALE STUD. WORLD PUB. ORD. 229, 237 (1977)). To take a few recent examples, *see, e.g.*, ANA VANESSA MIRANDA ANTUNES DA SILVA, ENHANCING SURVEILLANCE THROUGH THE

that even if one accepts that the ICCPR has extraterritorial effect, Article 17 of the ICCPR does not create an absolute limitation on intrusion, but rather only forbids "arbitrary or unlawful interference."[173] As a result, despite the ardent advocacy, most scholars agree that as a practical matter, United States opposition and state practice do not provide a viable implementation of universal privacy rights on the basis of the ICCPR.[174]

PATRIOT ACT AND THE FOREIGN INTELLIGENCE SURVEILLANCE AMENDMENT ACT, AND THEIR IMPACT ON CIVIL LIBERTIES: CAN HUMAN SECURITY BE COMPROMISED BY SECURITIZATION? 138 (2014), https://repositorium.sdum.uminho.pt/bitstream/1822/ 33875/1/Ana%20Vanessa%20Miranda%20Antunes%20da%20Silva.pdf ("[T]here is an increasing perception, not only but particularly in the EU, that the international human rights law applies extraterritorially and should be respected in order to abide by these international obligations."); Bignami & Resta, *supra* note 97, at 1 ("[Privacy] is a fundamental right enjoyed by all members of the human community and deserving of respect by all states whenever they act on their territory or enjoy "effective control" over persons."); Eliza Watt, *The Right To Privacy And The Future Of Mass Surveillance*, 21 INT'L J. HUM. RTS. 773, 776 (2017) ("Article 17 ICCPR and Article 8 ECHR apply extraterritorially, which means that states must respect the right to privacy whenever individuals are within their territory as well as their jurisdiction."). The U.N. General Assembly also adopted consensus resolution, G.A. Res. 68/167, ¶ 3 (Dec. 18, 2013), which "[a]ffirms that the same rights that people have offline must also be protected online, including the right to privacy." However, the U.S., which joined the resolution, issued an explanation reiterating that the ICCPR does not apply extraterritorially. U.S. Envoy at U.N., Explanation of Position on Draft Resolution L.26/Rev. 1 The Right to Privacy in the Digital Age (Nov. 25, 2014) (cited in Deeks, *supra* note 51, at 334).

[173] ICCPR, *supra* note 168, at art. 17. *See also* Bignami & Resta, *supra* note 97, at 6 ("The wording of Article 17 of the ICCPR makes clear that privacy is only protected against "unlawful" and "arbitrary" interferences."); Peter Margulies, *The NSA in Global Perspective: Surveillance, Human Rights, and International Counterterrorism*, 82 FORDHAM L. REV. 2137, 2138 (2014), http://ir.lawnet.fordham.edu/cgi/viewcontent.cgi? article=4980&context=flr ("This Article takes a middle ground that acknowledges that the United States has an extraterritorial duty under Article 2(1) to "respect" ICCPR rights including privacy, but then construes Article 17's prohibition on arbitrary interference narrowly to permit NSA surveillance abroad, given the legal constraints already in place governing the NSA's efforts."); Deeks, *supra* note 51, at 307 ("The Commentary to the ICCPR does indicate, however, that when states were negotiating Article 17, they understood the prohibition on "unlawful" or "arbitrary" interference to refer to acts that conflicted with the state's domestic legal system (which tends to run with the state's territory).").

[174] *See* Schulhofer, *supra* note 51, at 254 ("For these reasons, privacy advocates are right not to place all hopes on the broad jurisprudence of international human rights.")

International law governing state sovereignty might also seem to prevent foreign intelligence collection and its subsequent sharing. As Bert-Jaaps Koop and Morag Goodwin contend,

> In the strict—and still dominant—interpretation of international law, any evidence-gathering activity in a foreign state, including the making of a mere phone call, can be considered a breach of state sovereignty. Accessing data that is, or later turns out to be, stored on a server located in the territory of another state, without the prior consent of that state, constitutes a breach of the territorial integrity of that state and thus a wrongful act.[175]

In other words, according to Koop and Goodwin, non-consensual intelligence gathering violates the international legal principle of state territorial integrity. The authors point to Article 19 of the Cybercrime Convention, which provides that extended computer network searches should not cross national borders in the absence of two circumstances outlined in Article 32: a) lawful and voluntary consent from foreign actors, or b) if the targeted information is publicly available.[176] If states violated international law in collecting shared intelligence, then one might consider international law to forbid any subsequent use of the information.

Koops and Goodwin's point notwithstanding, further case law developed by the rights-protective European Court of Human Rights may have cabined the effect of international law limitations for cross-border computer searches. In *Weber and Saravia v. Germany*, the Plaintiffs charged Germany's Federal Intelligence Service (*Bundesnachrichtendienst*) with the interception of telecommunications and the subsequent use of personal data.[177] The Court took important notice of the fact that while the data may have been relayed from foreign countries, the devices used to monitor the wireless

---

[175] Koops & Goodwin, *supra* note 32, at 9.

[176] *Id.* at 53 (citing Convention on Cybercrime, Nov. 23, 2001, C.E.T.S. 185). A similar provision is included in article 40 of the League of Arab States' Arab Convention on Combating Information Technology Offences (available at https://cms.unov.org/DocumentRepositoryIndexer/GetDocInOriginalFormat.drsx?DocID=3dbe778b-7b3a-4af0-95ce-a8bbd1ecd6dd).

[177] Weber & Saravia v. Germany, App No 54934/00, 2006-XI [2006] Eur. Ct. H.R. 1173, Admissibility (2006), http://hudoc.echr.coe.int/webservices/content/pdf/001-76586.

communications were situated in sovereign German territory.[178] In doing so, the Court held that this German interception did not constitute conduct "which interfered with the territorial sovereignty of foreign States as protected in public international law."[179] Under parallel reasoning, a state would not interfere with the territorial sovereignty of any foreign state as long as that state accessed the wireless Internet data from a computer located in its own country. Additionally, in contrast to criminal evidence collection, foreign intelligence gathering constitutes acts of espionage. When it comes to espionage,

> one can identify scores of sources in international law to establish the existence of the *Jus Ad Explorationem* (the Right to Spy). So much so, in fact, that "to claim that espionage is not a priori permissible as a sovereign prerogative is simply inconceivable in our public world order" and certainly in discontent with both vast bodies law and practice.[180]

As such, state sovereignty does not provide a barrier to intelligence gathering under international law. Therefore, the subsequent intelligence sharing does not constitute 'fruit of the poisonous tree.'

Finally, at least one court—the European Court of Human Rights—has tied the international law principles governing surveillance and intelligence gathering to intelligence sharing. In *Liberty v UK*, the ECtHR held that the privacy safeguards on intelligence data must detail the "procedure to be followed for selecting for examination, *sharing*, storing and destroying intercepted material."[181] In the absence of conflicting jurisprudence, the ECtHR case law makes a plausible contention that any international law

---

[178] *Id*. at ¶ 86 ("The Court observes that the impugned provisions of the amended G 10 Act authorise the monitoring of international wireless telecommunications, that is, telecommunications which are not effected via fixed telephone lines but, for example, via satellite or radio relay links, and the use of data thus obtained. Signals emitted from foreign countries are monitored by interception sites situated on German soil and the data collected are used in Germany.").

[179] *Id*.

[180] Asaf Lubin, *The Dragon-Kings Restraint: Proposing a Compromise for the EEZ Surveillance Conundrum*, 57 WASHBURN L. J. 17, 56 (2018).

[181] Liberty v. United Kingdom, App. No. 58243/00, Eur. Ct. H.R., Judgment (July 1, 2008), § 69, http://hudoc.echr.coe.int/eng?i=001-87207 (emphasis added).

governing intelligence collection mandates some privacy consideration in intra-governmental intelligence sharing.

B. Scholarship on Intelligence Governance Frameworks

The legal field has proliferated substantial writing on international intelligence bodies and covert operations, but far less attention has been paid to intelligence sharing.   Some of the classic literature recognizes the importance of data sharing but does not address the challenges arising from various privacy regimes. For example, work by Professors Myres McDougal, Harold Lasswell and Michael Reisman note the importance of intelligence sharing across governments: "The model of Interpol may be simulated by 'Interspy,' a service that draws upon the sources available to all organizations willing and able to work together to expose threats to world public order."[182] While McDougal *et al* recognize the importance of intelligence sharing,[183] they do not address the differences in privacy-security balances.[184] Over the past few decades, with what Professor Margo Schlanger has recognized a rise of "intelligence legalism," legal scholarship has taken a renewed interest between law and the intelligence community.[185]   Much of the effort has focused on MLAT reform, which grapples with the more circumscribed problem of obstruction in law enforcement data sharing requests.[186] Other

---

[182] McDougal et al., *supra* note 44, at 447.

[183] *Id.* at 422 ("As global interdependence increases, this imbalance will ultimately prove to be detrimental to planning on the part of even the most developed communities, and will give greater impetus to the sharing of processing technology.").

[184] *Id.*

[185] Margo Schlanger, *Intelligence Legalism and the National Security Agency's Civil Liberties Gap*, 6 HARV. NAT'L SEC. J. 112, 113 (2015).

[186] *See* Jennifer Daskal & Andrew Keane Woods, *Cross-Border Data Requests: A Proposed Framework*, LAWFARE (Nov. 24, 2015, 8:00 AM), https://www.lawfareblog.com/cross-border-data-requests-proposed-framework; *see also* Daskal, *supra* note 50; Daskal, *supra* note 62, at 393 ("these concerns highlight the need for new cross-border mechanisms that facilitate law enforcement access to data, yet also respect the sovereign interest in setting privacy protections and controlling law enforcement operations within one's jurisdiction."); ANDREW K. WOODS, DATA BEYOND BORDERS: MUTUAL LEGAL ASSISTANCE IN THE INTERNET AGE (2015), https://globalnetworkinitiative.org/wp-content/uploads/2016/12/GNI-MLAT-Report.pdf; MICHAEL CHERTOFF & PAUL ROSENZWEIG, A PRIMER ON GLOBALLY

proposals tackle "government data collection" with a broad scope and do not clarify whether they intend their proposals to address the MLAT process or also include government intelligence sharing.[187]

Inter-governmental data-sharing regimes have been woefully under-theorized by the legal literature.[188] Nearly all the work focuses on domestic privacy governance over the home regime and does not seriously engage with the question of harmonizing the different privacy-security tradeoffs for intelligence sharing between allied governments. Instead, the goal is to regulate the surveillance practices of each country, so a uniform sharing

---

HARMONIZING INTERNET JURISDICTION AND REGULATIONS (Global Comm'n on Internet Gov., Paper No. 10 2015), https://www.cigionline.org/sites/default/files/gcig_paper _no10_0.pdf; Peter Swire & Justin Hemmings, *Stakeholders in Reform of the Global System for Mutual Legal Assistance, in* BULK COLLECTION: SYSTEMATIC GOVERNMENT ACCESS TO PRIVATE-SECTOR DATA (Fred H. Cate & James X. Dempsey eds., 2017), http://dx.doi.org/10.2139/ssrn.2696163; Jonah Force Hill, *Problematic Alternatives: MLAT Reform for the Digital Age*, HARV. NAT'L SEC. J. ONLINE (Jan. 28, 2015), http://harvardnsj.org/2015/01/problematic-alternatives-mlat-reform-for-the-digital-age; Gail Kent, Sharing Investigation Specific Data with Law Enforcement—An International Approach (Feb. 14, 2014) (Stanford Pub. L. working paper), http://ssrn.com/abstract=2472413. For a useful overview of the current status of UK-UK MLAT negotiations as well as some of the remaining concerns, see Tiffany Lin & Mailyn Fidler, *Cross-Border Data Access Reform: A Primer on the Proposed U.S.-U.K. Agreement* (Berkman Klein Center Research Pub. No. 2017-7, 2017), https://ssrn.com/abstract=3035563.

[187] *See, e.g.*, Microsoft Corporate Blog, *Time For An International Convention On Government Access To Data*, MICROSOFT (Jan. 20, 2014), https://blogs.microsoft.com/on-the-issues/2014/01/20/time-for-an-international-convention-on-government-access-to-data (writing generally about "government access to data"). However, given Microsoft's well-documented challenges navigating conflicts over compelled data disclosures, see United States v. Microsoft Corp., SCOTUSBLOG, http://www.scotusblog.com/case-files/cases/united-states-v-microsoft-corp, one may reasonably assume that the Microsoft's principle concern centers on government access to data stored by private companies, not exchanged with foreign intelligence agencies.

[188] Rubinstein et al., *supra* note 30, at 105 ("Although most of the countries appear to consider multinational access and sharing essential to national security and law enforcement activities, these arrangements received relatively little attention in the papers that were commissioned. Overall, it seems, there has been relatively little discussion of the complex legal and political issues associated with asserting jurisdiction over data stored in other countries or relating to citizens of other countries.").

standard is often assumed. Professor Peter Margulies' article presents an exception to this rule; while Margulies does not consider intelligence sharing, he envisions complementarity providing procedural pluralism to legitimate differing state surveillance practices under international law.[189] More typical is the stance epitomized by Edward Snowden supporters, who have clamored for the introduction of a "Snowden Treaty," which calls to outlaw mass surveillance and create whistleblower protections.[190]

Some scholars and human rights groups have sought to forge limiting principles conjured from international human rights law. Rubinstein *et al* have sought to design a privacy framework directly based on the principles governing surveillance (for law enforcement and intelligence gathering) extrapolated from the European Court of Human Rights jurisprudence,[191] and suggest fourteen principles from the ECtHR.[192] However, the Rubinstein analysis does not directly consider intelligence sharing with foreign governments. Similarly, privacy activist group Necessary & Proportionate has outlined thirteen principles that they believe provide the international human rights law standards for government communications surveillance.[193] While at first blush, one of the principles, safeguards for international cooperation, seems to cover the subject of this inquiry—intelligence sharing, it entirely elides the issue. The principle discusses international cooperation within the context of MLATs. MLATs are used only for criminal

---

[189] Margulies, *supra* note 173, at 2157 ("A state could choose from a number of procedural options that would accomplish these goals, without being locked into specific measures that might not fit with that state's history or traditions. Procedural pluralism would also minimize conflicts with other international rules, such as the law of armed conflict and Security Council resolutions mandating counterterrorism efforts.").

[190] *What is the Snowden Treaty,* SNOWDEN TREATY, http://www.snowdentreaty.org; *The Snowden Treaty: A new International Treaty on the Right to Privacy, Protection Against Improper Surveillance and Protection of Whistleblowers,* SNOWDEN TREATY, http://media.wix.com/ugd/fb845b_89e20fe385844f348fbc79a6ede39a4d.pdf.

[191] Rubinstein et al., *supra* note 30, at 111.

[192] *Id.*

[193] *Necessary and Proportionate: International Principles On The Application Of Human Rights To Communications Surveillance,* NECESSARY & PROPORTIONATE COALITION (May 2014), https://necessaryandproportionate.org/principles.

investigations, and do not cover intelligence sharing.[194] It is possible that Necessary & Proportionate have implicitly adopted the position that intelligence sharing should fall within the MLAT framework, although this delivers a strained reading given MLATs' traditional scope. Finally, President Obama's Presidential Policy Directive 28 establishing voluntary minimum protections for foreigners during government intelligence activities has introduced another helpful framework, as the protections outlined in PPD-28 benefited from the insight of the real security needs that government intelligence seeks to address.[195] However, the PPD-28 framework is incomplete, both in its lack of legal discussion and lack of detail.

The few works that do directly consider inter-governmental intelligence sharing almost unfailingly adopt a tunnel vision towards only the "privacy" elements of the privacy-security tradeoff.[196] Take, for example, Eliza Watt's effort supporting the proposed Intelligence Codex for the Council of Europe.[197] David Cole and Federico Fabbrini argue for a comprehensive transatlantic privacy between the EU and US that would close the protection gap endemic in the lack of extraterritorial privacy protection under each jurisdiction.[198] Ian Brown *et al* undertakes the project to outline "privacy-conscious intelligence reform," and proposes a series of standards, but do not actually consider

---

[194] Greg Nojeim, *MLAT Reform: A Straw Man Proposal*, CTR. FOR DEMOCRACY & TECH. (Sep. 3, 2015), https://cdt.org/insight/mlat-reform-a-straw-man-proposal.

[195] PPD-28, *supra* note 96 (committing to 1) proportionality, 2) use, dissemination, and retention limitations 3) data security and accuracy protections 4) oversight procedures.).

[196] *See* Schulhofer, *supra* note 51, at 253 ("[T]he international law scholarship, even on its own terms, is often incomplete, because much of it is framed in terms applicable only to ordinary law enforcement, without taking on board the extra flexibility and secrecy that is arguably "necessary in a democratic society" in the case of surveillance for national security purposes.").

[197] Watt, *supra* note 172, at 784 ("There can be no doubt that a binding treaty, such as the proposed Codex, is necessary."). The Council of Europe suggested four principles to govern intra-European intelligence cooperation: 1) prohibition on mutual political and economic espionage; 2) foreign intelligence activity must receive *ex ante* approval from the target state; 3) prohibition on tracking, analyzing, or storing data without individualized suspicion from a friendly state, and 4) prohibition on compelled disclosures from telecommunication and internet companies without a court order. *Id.*

[198] Cole & Fabbrini, *supra* note 30, at 223.

intelligence-sharing.[199]   Privacy International's recent call for greater transparency over government intelligence sharing reflects the renewed interest in bringing law into the shadowy sphere of government intelligence, but the privacy advocacy group does not suggest a framework for intelligence governance beyond public transparency.[200]

Professor Stephen Schulhofer rejects "the developing consensus" that a comprehensive multilateral agreement to abide by surveillance principles or minimum standards would help regulate expansive state surveillance activity.[201] Instead, Schulhofer argues that a "privacy-conscious international framework" would allow "the fox to design th[e] henhouse," and his "ultimate concern [] for privacy and democracy worldwide" leads him to reject an agreement that would almost inevitably lead to an arrangement at less than maximal privacy.[202] Instead, Schulhofer promotes bilateral commitment in which each party grants whichever safeguards it observes when engaging in surveillance over its own citizens.[203]

Schulhofer is right. A multinational arrangement would necessarily result in less privacy safeguards than required for national security activity in the maximally protective states. But from here we differ. Unlike Schulhofer, I reject the premise that privacy rights are the only rights at play here and

---

[199] Ian Brown et al., Towards Multilateral Standards for Surveillance Reform (Jan. 5, 2015) (Oxford Internet Institute Discussion Paper), https://ssrn.com/abstract=2551164 (outlining standards of 1) legitimate national security purposes for surveillance, 2) establishment of extraterritorial privacy standards, 3) tailored limitations on data collection beyond a broad "relevant to national security interest," 4) minimization standards, 5) methods of oversight, 6) protection against unauthorized access.). Their closest standard is "onward transmission/purpose limitation," but this limitation refers to alternative non-intelligence uses, not sharing with another intelligence agency. See id. at 5–6. The paper also provides an excellent recap of some of the existing intelligence reform proposals. Id. at 20–24.

[200] Privacy International Launches International Campaign For Greater Transparency Around Secretive Intelligence Sharing Activities Between Governments, PRIVACY INT'L (Oct. 23, 2017), https://www.privacyinternational.org/press-release/51/privacy-international-launches-international-campaign-greater-transparency-around.

[201] See Schulhofer, supra note 51, at 242.

[202] Id.

[203] Id. at 261.

contend that security considerations also implicate human rights in a way that justifies tailored departures for intelligence-sharing purposes. Security officials are not the "fox in the henhouse," but rather serious stakeholders in a privacy-security duet balancing competing human rights.

Ashley Deeks and Peter Margulies are possibly the only scholars who have employed a true balance-oriented approach in designing an intelligence-sharing framework.[204] However, both works only treat intelligence sharing as an incidental measure to a state's domestic intelligence program. Deeks recognizes that "[there is no] disagreement that the right to privacy is a qualified right, subject to lawful and non-arbitrary interference by a state."[205] Instead, she suggests six "procedural norms" that would create meaningful privacy protections without harming national security.[206] Deeks touches briefly on intelligence sharing by recognizing that a preference for domestic surveillance would help address the "revolving door" concern, and notes that such a principle "could increase the need for ongoing coordination among allies' intelligence agencies."[207] Similarly, Margulies offers a list of procedural protections.[208] Like Deeks, Margulies recognizes that harmonizing standards "could also remove any barriers to cooperation between the United States and foreign states."[209] This Article goes further in providing a cooperation

---

[204] Margulies, *supra* note 173, at 2157; Deeks, *supra* note 51, at 346.

[205] Deeks, *supra* note 51, at 305. This is not to say that other frameworks do not recognize that the privacy right is not absolute. To the contrary, they uniformly allow for privacy intrusions in some circumstances. However, what distinguishes Deeks' scholarship from the other works is an explicit recognition that the *goal* of the framework should not be to achieve the maximum privacy protections possible.

[206] Deeks, *supra* note 51, at 351–63 (the six procedural norms are 1) notice to public of applicable rules, 2) limits on the reasons for data collection and use, 3) requirement for periodic reviews, 4) limits on data retention, 5) preference for domestic surveillance, and 6) neutral oversight body).

[207] *Id*. at 366.

[208] Margulies, *supra* note 173, at 2157. Margulies' procedural protections include 1) notice about grounds for surveillance, 2) oversight of surveillance programs, 3) deterrence of arbitrary official conduct, including targeting of political opponents or disfavored ethnic, racial, or religious groups, and includes procedural flexibility for state implementation. *Id*.

[209] *Id*. at 2165.

framework tailored to a thorough and detailed exploration of inter-governmental intelligence sharing.

C. Proposed Framework

As noted *supra* in Part 0, widespread disagreement persists over the relevant international law governing intelligence sharing. This framework utilizes commonly cited principles of international law as a helpful starting point. Drawing on prior literature, I condense the fourteen international law principles of government surveillance identified by Necessary & Proportionate[210] into 5 primary categories: 1) principle of legality 2) principle of safeguarding against abuse 3) principle of proportionality 4) principle of transparency and oversight 5) principle of notification and remedies. In order to tailor this framework to the challenges of intelligence sharing, I include three additional considerations: 6) the principle of complementarity 7) the principle of good faith and 8) the exigency exception. Using this framework, I outline a way forward for governing intelligence sharing while respecting legitimate differences in countries' privacy-security balance.

In devising a framework for governmental intelligence sharing, one approach would be to adopt a highest common denominator and to use the same standards to govern intelligence sharing as are used for law enforcement sharing and other police activities. Some privacy rights advocates, including Privacy International, have opted for this approach.[211] Such individuals can point to American law, which grants the same Fourth Amendment privacy protection to American citizens, regardless of whether the surveillance arises in the context of petty crime or dire threats to national security.[212] As the U.S. Supreme Court famously held in the *Keith* case, a government's national security concerns "do not justify departure in this case from the customary Fourth Amendment requirement of judicial approval prior to initiation of a

---

[210] *See* Rubinstein et al., *supra* note 30, at 104 (condensing the fourteen necessary and proportionate principles into thirteen categories).

[211] *See* Brown, *supra* note 154, at 23–25 (conflating intelligence and law enforcement privacy standards).

[212] *See infra* note 218.

search or surveillance." [213] However, as Professor Schulhofer notes, for many democratic countries, "such fundamental issues as the required level of suspicion, the role of suspect-specific judicial approval ex ante, and the degree to which transparency and oversight are relaxed in the national security context."[214]

There are good reasons for differentiating intelligence and law enforcement data collection. For example, intelligence purposes may fundamentally differ from those of law enforcement: "Intelligence often searches for new information, whereas law enforcement often looks for additional information."[215] This purposive difference reasonably leads to one to expect different evidentiary standards—"probable cause" often poses a prohibitively challenging standard when searching for new information. Therefore, this paper rejects the notion that the same criminal law enforcement information sharing standards should also apply to intelligence sharing.

"In the field of monitoring bilateral and multilateral intelligence sharing arrangements, there has been particular inadequacy of oversight."[216] Thus far, the European Court of Human Rights (ECtHR) has developed the most comprehensive case law on surveillance. However, as the Court's name suggests, the ECtHR "takes the community interest in the right to privacy and the corresponding state duty to respect that community obligation very seriously."[217] As such, it comes as little surprise that privacy advocates

---

[213] *See* United States v. U.S. Dist. Court for E. Dist. of Mich., S. Div., 407 U.S. 297, 321 (1972) (holding government's national security concerns "do not justify departure in this case from the customary Fourth Amendment requirement of judicial approval prior to initiation of a search or surveillance.").

[214] Schulhofer, *supra* note 51, at 245 ("There is wide variation, even among Western democracies, on such fundamental issues as the required level of suspicion, the role of suspect-specific judicial approval *ex ante*, and the degree to which transparency and oversight are relaxed in the national security context.").

[215] Mailyn Fidler, *MLAT Reform: Some Thoughts From Civil Society*, LAWFARE (Sep. 11, 2015), https://www.lawfareblog.com/mlat-reform-some-thoughts-civil-society.

[216] Lubin, *supra* note 51, at 548.

[217] Bignami & Resta, *supra* note 97, at 2. Because the European Court of Human Rights (ECtHR) views privacy as a human right, its jurisprudence has found that "all persons are covered and are guaranteed the same treatment by the state." *Id.* As noted in Part VII.A, this interpretation is contested as a matter of international law.

campaign for the ECtHR as the privacy floor. The CJEU decision in *Kadi v. Commission* has provided ammunition for the "privacy floor" approach by establishing that "EU concepts on fundamental rights prevail, whenever this is necessary, over international law."[218]

Nevertheless, the ECtHR has developed its jurisprudence while leaving some room for discretion, and despite its privacy-protective orientation, many of the ECtHR privacy decisions have recognized the need for flexibility in the intelligence space.[219] For example, while the ECtHR has recognized "rather strict standards" governing the interception of communication, the Court has expressly recognized that those standards do not necessarily apply in other intelligence gathering contexts.[220] Furthermore, the European Court has taken the reasonable approach of recognizing the existence of tradeoffs, and has not perpetuated the mistaken notion that surveillance constitutes a per se violation of human rights.[221] Even Privacy International acknowledges that intelligence activities necessarily cannot operate with complete transparency over the scope and nature of government intelligence-sharing agreements.[222] While the ECtHR provides one possible approach, its institutional mission-

---

[218] Hielke Hijmans, *The European Union As Guardian of Internet Privacy: The Story of Art 16 TFEU*, 31 L. GOVERNANCE & TECH. SERIES 1, 473 (2016) https://link.springer.com/content/pdf/10.1007/978-3-319-34090-6.pdf.

[219] Respondent's Open Response, Privacy Int'l v. United Kingdom, Case No. IPT/13/92/CH, (Investigatory Powers Trib. 2014) (U.K.) and Liberty v. United Kingdom, Case No. IPT/13/77/H (Investigatory Powers Trib. 2014) (U.K.) [hereinafter UK IPT Response], https://www.liberty-human-rights.org.uk/sites/default/files/The%20Intelligence%20Services%20open%20response%20to%20Liberty%E2%80%99s%20and%20Privacy%20International%E2%80%99s%20claims%2015th%20November%202013.pdf.

[220] *Id.* (citing Uzun v. Germany (2011) 53 EHRR 24, at §66). *See also* McE v. Prison Service of Northern Ireland [2009] 1 AC 908, per Lord Carswell at § 85.

[221] Rubinstein et al., *supra* note 30, at 119.

[222] *Human Rights Implications of Intelligence Sharing*, PRIVACY INT'L 9 (2017), https://www.privacyinternational.org/sites/default/files/2017-12/PI%20Briefing%20to%20National%20Intelligence%20Oversight%20Bodies_12_Sept.pdf ("Privacy International specifically urges national intelligence oversight bodies, to the extent permitted under their mandates, to: make publicly available as much information as possible as to the nature and scope of intelligence sharing arrangements to which their governments are party, as well as the rules governing such arrangements[.]").

orientation leads to an uncompromising approach that does not accommodate the privacy-security balance adopted by most countries. In contrast, the framework below secures meaningful privacy protections while still preserving maximal respect for sovereign discretion.

i.   Principle of Legality

A basic requirement for the rule of law is that rules must be based in law, with a degree of foreseeability and accessibility. This principle of legality is generally uncontroversial and considered a core principle of international law.[223] Intelligence-sharing arrangements should have these provisions to the extent reasonably practicable. It is true that political considerations may weigh in favor of preventing the public disclosure of intelligence cooperation with some countries,[224] but the principles by which governments conduct themselves in the intelligence-sharing process would not adversely affect their capacity to conduct their jobs. At the same time, such principles would also provide a circulated standard against which intelligence agencies, their counterparts, and oversight bodies could hold agency action accountable.

Both the United States and the EU agree that the ICCPR requires some respect for privacy rights of those under a country's domestic jurisdiction. Specifically, that states have an obligation to refrain from "arbitrary or unlawful interference" into the private lives of those under the state's domestic jurisdiction.[225] This principle of legality is expressed in the first clause of Article 8(2) of the European Convention on Human Rights, stating

---

[223] Beth Van Schaack, *The Principle of Legality in International Criminal Law*, 103 Am. Soc. of Int'l L. 101, 101 (2009) ("The principle of *nullum crimen sine lege* is a fundamental principle of criminal law. It has particular resonance at the international level given the relative lack of clarity surrounding certain international legal norms.").

[224] *See generally* Ashley Deeks, *A (Qualified) Defense of Secret Agreements*, 49 Ariz. St. L.J. 713 (2017) http://arizonastatelawjournal.org/wp-content/uploads/2017/09/Deeks_Pub.pdf.

[225] Deeks, *supra* note 51, at 305 ("The United States, for example, believes that states may engage in surveillance that is in accordance with transparent laws and that furthers a legitimate aim. Human rights groups favor a higher standard drawn from ECtHR case law: The interference must be necessary in the circumstances of the case and proportional to the end sought, and the surveillance must be conducted under specific and clearly defined laws.").

that "[t]here shall be no interference by a public authority with the exercise of this right except such as is *in accordance with the law.*"[226] In other words, the exercised powers have some basis in domestic law and meet a foreseeability requirement.[227] Accordingly, secret rules without any basis in domestic legislation cannot be in accordance with the law for the purposes of restricting rights.[228] This 'accordance with the law' requirement poses a low standard; even broad delegations of power, such as those in the Chinese National Security Law,[229] have a basis in domestic law.[230] This delegation may be analogized to the broad "intelligible principle" requirement in American administrative law and is unlikely to carry significant substantive impact beyond public accessibility to the relevant law.[231]

However, the law must also enable a degree of foreseeability. This has led international privacy scholars to argue that privacy rights require that "[a]ny limitations to the right to privacy 'must be provided for by law, and the law must be sufficiently accessible, clear, and precise so that an individual may look to the law and ascertain who is authorized to conduct data surveillance and under what circumstances.'"[232] As interpreted by the ECtHR, the essential test for foreseeability asks whether the laws sufficiently indicate the scope of discretion and the manner of exercise "to give the individual adequate protection against arbitrary interference."[233] However, the ECtHR highlights

---

[226] European Convention on Human Rights, *supra* note 25 (emphasis added).

[227] Brown et al., *supra* note 199.

[228] *Id.*

[229] *See supra* notes 124, 125.

[230] *But see* Szabó & Vissy v. Hungary, App. No. 37138/14, Eur. Ct. H.R., Judgment, ¶ 78 (2016), http://hudoc.echr.coe.int/eng?i=001-160020.

[231] *See* J.W. Hampton, Jr., & Co. v. United States, 276 U. S. 394, 409 ("If Congress shall lay down by legislative act an intelligible principle to which the person or body authorized to fix such rates is directed to conform, such legislative action is not a forbidden delegation of legislative power.").

[232] Lubin, *supra* note 51, at 542.

[233] Malone v United Kingdom, App. No. 8691/79, (1984) 7 Eur. H.R. Rep 14, §86. *See also* Weber & Saravia v. Germany, App No 54934/00, 2006-XI [2006] Eur. Ct. H.R. 1173, Admissibility, §§ 78–79 (2006), http://hudoc.echr.coe.int/webservices/content/pdf/001-76586 (the laws must be sufficiently detailed to give "an adequate indication" to the times and circumstances under which the government may engage in surveillance activities).

that the foreseeability requirement should not be taken to preclude effective surveillance: "the requirement of foreseeability cannot mean that an individual should be enabled to foresee when the authorities are likely to intercept his communications so that he can adapt his conduct accordingly."[234] The UN High Commissioner for Human Rights (UNHCHR) has echoed the generally-accepted the legality requirement, interpreting surveillance carried out on the basis of a law to require (a) public accessibility and (b) sufficient precision for reasonable foreseeability of the consequences of certain conduct.[235]

In the intelligence-sharing context, applying the legality principle makes sense. States should have laws governing intelligence sharing. The U.N. Special Rapporteur on Counter-Terrorism and Human Rights has noted

> The absence of laws to regulate information-sharing agreements between States has left the way open for intelligence agencies to enter into classified bilateral and multilateral arrangements that are beyond the supervision of any independent authority. Information concerning an individual's communications may be shared with foreign intelligence agencies without the protection of any publicly accessible legal framework and without adequate (or any) safeguards . . .. Such practices make the operation of the surveillance regime unforeseeable for those affected by it.[236]

While security concerns may weigh in favor of limiting the disclosure of specific information sharing arrangements, laws delineating the general circumstances and procedures under which a government engages in intelligence sharing would allow "sufficient adequate protection against arbitrary interference" and offset concerns of unbridled government power to

---

[234] Malone v United Kingdom, App. No. 8691/79, (1984) 7 Eur. H.R. Rep 14, § 67. *See also* OFFICE OF THE SPECIAL RAPPORTEUR FOR FREEDOM OF EXPRESSION OF THE INTER-AMERICAN COMMISSION ON HUMAN RIGHTS, FREEDOM OF EXPRESSION AND THE INTERNET 75 (2013) ("The State must be transparent with respect to the laws regulating communications surveillance and the criteria used for their application. The principle of 'maximum disclosure' is applicable to this issue.").

[235] *See* Bignami & Resta, *supra* note 97. The UNHCHR elements also include (c) provisions ensuring legitimate aims and (d) effective safeguards against abuse, but (c) and (d) simply suggest a divergent taxonomy, as both concern safeguards against abuse addressed below.

[236] Lubin, *supra* note 51, at 548–49.

exchange private information without due consideration of individual privacy interests. Adopting public intelligence sharing standards would achieve this goal and provide the legally grounded governance standards expected in the international community.

Getting states to recognize the legality principle should prove relatively uncontroversial, and states' acceptance would not likely face ideological resistance. The difficulty arises at the implementation stage over which safeguards adequately ensure that the government does not engage in arbitrary or unlawful interference. For example, the United States believes that this limitation is satisfied as long as its surveillance is consistent with transparent laws and furthers a legitimate aim, whereas the ECtHR adds additional principles of necessity and proportionality.[237] The next section seeks to untangle the morass over what should count as sufficient safeguards against abuse.

ii.   Principle of Safeguards against Abuse

The appropriate intelligence-sharing framework should delineate procedural requirements that safeguard against abuse. In order to fulfill the legality principle, countries sharing information should both have publically issued safeguarding procedures governing their intelligence practices. In *Weber and Saravia v. Germany*, the ECtHR helpfully identified six procedural safeguards to govern European communications interception:

> [1] the nature of the offences which may give rise to an interception order;
>
> [2] a definition of the categories of people liable to have their telephones tapped;
>
> [3] a limit on the duration of telephone tapping;

---

[237] Deeks, *supra* note 51, at 305–06 ("The United States, for example, believes that states may engage in surveillance that is in accordance with transparent laws and that furthers a legitimate aim. Human rights groups favor a higher standard drawn from . . . [ECtHR] case law: The interference must be necessary in the circumstances of the case and proportional to the end sought, and the surveillance must be conducted under specific and clearly defined laws.").

[4] the procedure to be followed for examining, using and storing the data obtained;

[5] the precautions to be taken when communicating the data to other parties;

[6] and the circumstances in which recordings may or must be erased or the tapes destroyed[238]

For the purpose of intelligence sharing, Categories [1], [3], [4] and [5] are most important.

First, states should publically disclose the nature of the offenses and purposes that warrant intelligence sharing. Intelligence sharing should remain limited to exchanges of intelligence information for national security purposes and should not operate as a loophole for the transfer of other types of information. In order for the information to be shared through intelligence channels, the collected information should have been collected for security purposes. For example, the United States has committed to exclusively collecting signals intelligence for foreign intelligence or counterintelligence purposes to support national and departmental missions.[239] Intelligence sharing agreements should provide similar commitments to exclusive national security utilization among both the collecting and transferring parties. This is particularly important in light of concerns that signals intelligence may be utilized for the "purpose of suppressing or burdening criticism or dissent, or for disadvantaging persons based on their ethnicity, race, gender, sexual orientation, or religion."[240] While states will differ on the extent to which these protected categories may factor into national security practices, establishing clear purposes for intelligence exchange facilitates effective oversight and provides clear normative guidelines for the state's intelligence apparatus. While Category [2] would help provide foreseeability to know the specific categories of individuals liable to have their information

---

[238] Lubin, *supra* note 51 (citing Weber & Saravia v. Germany, App No 54934/00, 2006-XI [2006] Eur. Ct. H.R. 1173, Admissibility, ¶ 95 (2006), http://hudoc.echr.coe.int/webservices/content/ pdf/001-76586,).

[239] *See* PPD-28, *supra* note 96.

[240] *See id.*

shared, a definition of the purposes for which states may exchange intelligence information provides greater utility in parsing foreseeable exchanges.

Category [3] and [6] highlight the procedures governing temporal limitations on information sharing. While the sharing of analyzed information does not contain a temporal aspect, joint intelligence ventures collecting raw information could persist for an undisclosed amount of time. As a result, intelligence-sharing laws should incorporate procedures for determining the appropriate duration of raw intelligence sharing operations. All transferred information could be subject to a sunset clause requiring the erasure of shared intelligence information after six months absent explicit reauthorization.[241]

Category [4] concerns important procedures related to accessing, retaining, and storing transferred information. The procedures should address technological procedures related to the safe storage of intelligence information in a secure server, record keeping procedures, and logs to account for the use or forensic inspection of the information use. Moreover, while analyzed information should be appropriately tailored to the scope of the request, both raw intelligence and analyzed intelligence will usually contain personal information, and the transfer of such information should not result in a total abdication of access controls. Therefore, states should clarify the scope of their access controls and related procedures. For example, the German surveillance authorization act examined in *Weber* provided "detailed rules on storing and destroying any data obtained using these search terms, and the authorities storing the data had to verify every six months whether the data were still necessary to achieve the purpose for which they had been obtained or transmitted to them."[242]

Access controls are especially important given the variation in the conceptualization of privacy harms. On the one hand, European Courts have found that "that the storage of private information amounts to or is akin to

---

[241] *See, e.g.*, Gesetz zur Beschränkung des Brief-, Post- und Fernmeldegeheimnisses [Artikel 10-Gesetz] [G 10] [Act to Restrict the Privacy of Correspondence, Mail, and Telecommunications] [Article 10 Act], June 26, 2001, BGBl. I at 1254, 2298, as amended, http://www.gesetze-im-internet.de/bundesrecht/g10_2001/gesamt.pdf (requiring authorities storing the data had to verify every six months whether the data were still necessary to achieve the purpose for which it had been gathered).

[242] Rubinstein et al., *supra* note 30, at 113.

secret surveillance."[243]   Under this conception, the mere collection of information constitutes a privacy harm. However, many states take a different approach to data access and argue that "[u]ntil the data are accessed by humans and used as a means of investigating or identifying particular people . . . , no concrete intrusion has occurred."[244] As Deeks reports, "states seem committed to the idea that they require access to as much data as possible to accurately locate terrorist plots and connections among suspected terrorists, among other threats." [245]   Both offer legitimate approaches to balancing

---

[243] Matthew White, *Protection by Judicial Oversight, or an Oversight in Protection?*, 2 J. INFO. RTS., POL'Y, & PRACTICE 1, 33 ("The ECtHR has previously noted that e-mail and internet usage fall within the ambit of Article 8334 and on numerous occasions has held that the storage of private information amounts to or is akin to secret surveillance."). *See also* Lubin, *supra* note 51, at 515 ("As was explained by Commissioner Pillay, an interference with the right to privacy already occurs at the point of interception.").

[244] Christopher Slobogin, *Policing, Databases and Surveillance: Five Regulatory Categories*, 28 (Nat'l Const. Ctr. White Paper Series, 2017), https://papers.ssrn.com/sol3/papers.cfm?abstract_id=2551164 ("It is further assumed by the intelligence community that the infringement of the data subjects' rights takes place only at the point at which their data is retrieved from the "haystack on the basis of a search term, keyword, or other selector."). Deeks points to some United States courts that have taken this approach. Deeks, *supra* note 51, at 357 ("This is consistent, for instance, with the approach some U.S. courts have taken to the Fourth Amendment; for them, a search (and therefore an infringement on privacy) occurs when information is exposed to possible human observation, rather than when it is copied or processed by a computer."). *But see* Daskal, *supra* note 62, at 354 (cataloging the "rich and thick literature" contending that simple data collection inflicts severe privacy harm); Neil M. Richards, *The Dangers of Surveillance,* HARV. L. REV. 1934, 1936 (2013), https://ssrn.com/abstract=2239412 (arguing that surveillance "menaces intellectual privacy and increases the risk of blackmail, coercion, and discrimination" and should comprise a harm sufficient for constitutional standing).

[245] Deeks, *supra* note 51, at 357. Such logic proceeds as follows: The retention of information is critical because one cannot know when it will come in handy. One can analogize to the use of Box, Dropbox or an external hard drive. You never know which document is going to crash, so you back up all documents. Similarly, with intelligence collection—there is a vast degree of available information, and intelligence officials don't know what will come in handy later down the line. While one might push back to suggest that, using the back-up example, there is no need to save every piece of information. Instead, one prioritizes different documents to different degrees. For example, losing a shopping list would carry far less severe consequences than the loss of a 70-page research paper. However, such an argument misunderstands the nature

privacy and security.[246] Brown et al disagree, arguing that the latter approach "cannot be reconciled with international human rights law."[247] However, Brown and his colleagues ground their claim of international human rights law on *European* human rights law; thereby conflating the privacy-security tradeoff for one regime with that of the entire international community.[248]

Nevertheless, the differing points of restriction should encourage states to consider access control safeguards. States that impose a higher barrier to data

---

of data retention. The problem with discordant pieces of information is that, prior to an incident in question, one does not know which information will prove most necessary. As such, the more appropriate analogy would be to ask which sources would prove most valuable at the very onset of a research project. Without knowing the direction of the project, it can be nearly impossible to know which information to prioritize in advance.

[246] The collection process and storage of information, in addition to the distribution of information under the control of private companies versus government entities are important questions beyond the scope of this discussion.

[247] Brown et al., *supra* note 199.

[248] To be sure, Brown et al. is correct as a matter of European law. The Court in Szabó & Vissy v. Hungary, App. No. 37138/14, Eur. Ct. H.R., Judgment, ¶ 78 (2016), http://hudoc.echr.coe.int/eng?i=001-160020, recognized that mass surveillance could undermine citizen freedom if all privacy barriers were eliminated.

Indeed, it would defy the purpose of government efforts to keep terrorism at bay, if the terrorist threat was paradoxically substituted for by a perceived threat of unfettered executive power intruding into citizens' private spheres by virtue of uncontrolled yet far-reaching surveillance techniques and prerogatives.

However, such a portrayal rests on the notion that there must in fact be an intrusion—that information is actually accessed. It is also true that the Report of the Special Rapporteur on the Promotion and Protection of Human Rights and Fundamental Freedoms While Countering Terrorism, argued that despite "[t]he prevention and suppression of terrorism [being] a public interest imperative of the highest importance," bulk collection programs "pose a direct and ongoing challenge to an established norm of international law." Ben Emmerson (Special Rapporteur on the promotion and protection of human rights and fundamental freedoms while countering terrorism), *Promotion and protection of human rights and fundamental freedoms while countering terrorism*, U.N. Doc. A/69/397 (Sep. 23, 2014). However, United Nations officials' pontifications on international law do not determine the state of international law.

collection tend to employ fewer safeguards at the data access phase.[249]   In contrast, states that do not consider privacy interests at the collection state will likely employ measures that restrict access to more limited criteria of conditions and circumstances.[250] Thus, access procedures for transferred data should include measures to condition access to exchanged information, even if state surveillance practices do not contain any access requirements.[251] Conditioning access on state-specific safeguards—further expanded in Part 0—plays a critical role in protecting the legitimate privacy interests in disparate privacy-security regimes.

Finally, Category [5] concerns third party transfers. As such, it necessarily incorporates all of the suggested procedures and principles outlined in this framework for cross-border intelligence sharing. However, it also concerns onward transfers from the receiving agency. The onward transfers may be internal; many countries have seen a decline in the "wall" separating national security and other law enforcement uses.[252] Intelligence transfers should be limited to national security purposes, and measures should be undertaken to maintain a wall over transferred information. If the recipient country would also like to access shared intelligence for law enforcement purposes, it should pursue that information through the appropriate channels.   Intelligence sharing should not serve as a shortcut around MLAT agreements.

---

[249] For example, the United Kingdom, which imposes collection restrictions, does not distinguish between collection and access. DAVID ANDERSON, A QUESTION OF TRUST– REPORT OF THE INVESTIGATORY POWERS REVIEW, 292-94, 2015, https://terrorismlegislationreviewer.independent.gov.uk/wp-content/uploads/2015/ 06/IPR-Report-Web-Accessible1.pdf (illustrating that the United Kingdom does not distinguish between collection and access).

[250]See Rangappa, *supra* note 36 (discussing the United States bulk data collection pursuant to § 702 which contain access protections that ensure that "neither the metadata nor the content of that communication is immediately accessible to all agents.").

[251] See Deeks *supra* note 51, at 305 (explaining the United States permits surveillance as long as its surveillance is consistent with transparent laws and furthers a legitimate aim but does not require proportionality or necessity).

[252] Rubinstein et al., *supra* note 30, at 105 ("In many countries, this wall has been dismantled, with the result that intelligence agencies may now, at least as a matter of legal authority, pass information to law enforcement officials. . . .").

The receiving agency might also seek onward transfers of shared information to external parties. Governments receiving information should commit to ensuring that exchanged intelligence information is not shared with non-governmental parties. However, government intelligence agencies should have the flexibility to share such information with other government intelligence partners, in the event that the receiving party commits to the same transfer restrictions as binding the original recipient. Of course, governments have no obligation to share information with a third party, and political considerations effectively restrain third-party intelligence sharing against the originator's wishes. Integrating data access and data sharing procedures would help offset a major barrier to intelligence sharing: the difficulties that countries face in verifying how a foreign government will use information sent to it.[253]

In sum, safeguards against abuse should include 1) public limitations on the purposes of government intelligence sharing; 2) public limitations on the duration of sharing agreements and the implementation of sunset clauses; 3) public access, retention, and storage procedures for exchanged information; 4) and public commitment to third-party transfer procedures ensuring that exchanged intelligence information remains limited to government intelligence use.

iii. Principle of Transparency and Oversight

Intelligence sharing agreements should not operate in a vacuum of accountability. The UN General Assembly Resolution on the Right to Privacy in the Digital Age, which calls upon all states "[t]o establish or maintain existing independent, effective, adequately resourced and impartial judicial, administrative and/or parliamentary domestic oversight mechanisms capable of ensuring transparency, as appropriate, and accountability for State surveillance of communications, their interception and the collection of personal data . . ."[254] Furthermore, modern norms have led to a public

---

[253] BORN ET AL., *supra* note 4, at 38 ("[I]ntelligence services lose full control of information as soon as they transmit it to another body.").

[254] G.A. Res 69/166, at 4 (Dec. 18, 2014). *See* Emmerson, *supra* note 248 ("One of the core protections afforded by article 17 is that covert surveillance systems must be

expectancy of greater transparency over intelligence activities.[255] By establishing publically available governance measures for intelligence sharing agreements, states will take significant steps towards transparent practices. While the government cannot provide complete transparency to the public, it can provide more searching internal oversight procedures.

Intelligence sharing agreements would benefit from the designation of a specific independent official or officials responsible for overseeing intelligence sharing exchanges and subsequent access. Many countries already have independent oversight of surveillance and government access, with China as a notable exception.[256] Significantly, independent oversight does not implicate the government's chosen privacy-security tradeoff, but instead ensures that intelligence information is handled commensurate with that government's standards. For example, the United States has a Privacy and Civil Liberties Official who ensures the legitimate privacy interests of data handled by the intelligence community.[257] Such a role should operate similarly to Inspector Generals, embedded in United States executive agencies.

In order to effectively implement intelligence transfer access controls, each country must implement *ex ante* review. This oversight process already exists through Sweden's Defense Intelligence Inspection (SIUN) body, which monitors whether the procedural conditions have been complied with before transferring the information in question for use by Swedish intelligence.[258]

---

attended by adequate procedural safeguards to protect against abuse. These safeguards may take a variety of forms, but generally include independent prior authorization and/or subsequent independent review."). However, the Special Rapporteur goes too far in asserting the mass collection schemes are necessarily inconsistent with principles of individualized suspicion.

[255] Deeks, *supra* note 63, at 618 ("Overall, the public now expects greater transparency about intelligence activities and some governments have begun to provide it.").

[256] Rubinstein et al., *supra* note 30, at 104.

[257] PPD-28, *supra* note 96 (describing the principles of United States signals intelligence collection).

[258] European Commission for Democracy through Law (Venice Commission), *Update of the 2007 Report on the Democratic Oversight of the Security Services and Report on the Democratic Oversight of Signals Intelligence Agencies*, CDL-AD(2015)006, Study No. 719/2013, ¶¶131-133 (Apr. 7, 2015), http://www.venice.coe.int/webforms/documents/default.aspx?pdffile=CDL-AD(2015)006-e ("An example of a model which combines judicial authorization with expert follow-up comes from Sweden.").

Former Independent Reviewer of Terrorism Legislation David Anderson has proposed a series of possible *ex ante* criteria that the UK could implement for bulk data access.[259] This *ex ante* review requirement aligns with a CJEU emphasis on the importance of independent authorization.[260] When assessing government access to retained data, the CJEU has held that all access should "be subject to a prior review carried out either by a court or by an independent administrative body."[261] Prior review constitutes a best practice and should be implemented across all states. Oversight independence should be established through the criteria that 1) the overseer can only be removed for cause; 2) the overseer is not appointed by the executive branch; and 3) the overseer is not involved in the intelligence exchange mission.

Professor Richard Aldrich conceives the possibility of "Inspectors General with extended authority to operate in more than one country."[262] Given that countries will display a variety of different procedures and processes, a roving Inspector General should not be a requirement for sharing compliance. Nevertheless, a joint Inspector General would add particular value in joint raw data collection enterprises. These joint enterprises, such as the compilation of joint databases, poses greater privacy risks and would be well-served by another layer of protection. Furthermore, this close-knit form of "far reaching" cooperation is only likely to occur if the states maintain a "close,

---

[259] ANDERSON, *supra* note 249, at 292–94 (following the British model which does not distinguish between collection and access).

[260] *Ex ante* authorization is not a uniquely European requirement, and the U.S. has played a significant role in promulgating an *ex ante* review ethos. As Jennifer Daskal reports, "[t]he UK government supported a new judicial review mechanism for intercept orders in part because it knew that this would be a precondition entering into such an agreement under US law." Jennifer Daskal, *New Bill Would Moot Microsoft Ireland Case—And Much More!*, JUST SEC. (Feb. 6, 2018), https://www.justsecurity.org/51886/bill-moot-microsoft-ireland-case-more.

[261] Joined Cases C-203/15 & C-698/15, Tele2 Sverige AB v. Post-Och telestyrelsen, 2016 EUR-Lex 62015CJ0203 (Dec. 21 2016), https://eur-lex.europa.eu/legal-content/EN/TXT/PDF/?uri=CELEX:62015CJ0203&from=EN ("In order to ensure, in practice, that those conditions are fully respected, it is essential that access of the competent national authorities to retained data should, as a general rule, except in cases of validly established urgency, be subject to a prior review carried out either by a court or by an independent administrative body[.])".

[262] Aldrich, *supra* note 9, at 56.

trust-based relationship."[263]   Given the muted secrecy concerns, such a cooperative arrangement with an objective third-party Inspector General is conceivable for a subset of states with a high commitment to public transparency.[264]   Such bodies could operate along lines similar to the International Committee for the Red Cross (ICRC) in its designation and ability to inspect treatment of prisoners of war,[265] or the International Atomic Energy Agency (IAEA) mandate to inspect nuclear sites. Specifically, joint intelligence operations could include an arrangement to allow an objective party to inspect and provide reports on compliance of procedural privacy safeguards.[266]

Intelligence sharing agreements should also require states to include a measure of *ex post* review to ensure that the surveillance measures undertaken are done so according to the procedures in place. Particularly when security exigencies require urgent government action, *ex post* review provides prospective control over future behavior. As the ECtHR recognizes "a subsequent judicial review can offer sufficient protection if a review procedure at an earlier stage would jeopardise [sic] the purpose of an investigation or

---

[263] BORN ET AL., *supra* note 4, at 19.

[264] *See* Aldrich, *supra* note 9 (suggesting inspectors general with extended authority in more than one state).

[265] *See, e.g., Rule 124.   ICRC Access to Persons Deprived of Their Liberty*, INT'L COMM. RED CROSS, https://ihl-databases.icrc.org/customary-ihl/eng/docs/v1_rul_rule124 ("The right of the ICRC to visit detainees in international armed conflicts is provided for in the Third and Fourth Geneva Conventions.").

[266] Preexisting bilateral and multilateral exchanges between external oversight bodies might provide a foundational framework for building international acceptance. Examples of such bodies include "periodic meetings with national parliamentary oversight committees organized by the European Parliament's Committee on Civil Liberties, Justice and Home Affairs; the annual Southeast European Parliamentary Oversight Bodies' Conference; the biennial International Intelligence Review Agency Conference (IIRAC); and the (now defunct) Conference of the Parliamentary Committees for the Oversight of Intelligence and Security Services of the European Union Member States." BORN ET AL., *supra* note 4, at 156. An institutional entity could also provide other benefits, such as a rigorous training program that could provide best practices for privacy protection. Such a training program could help promote responsible handling of personal information and diminish the fears of privacy harm stemming from intelligence practices. *See* Kent, *supra* note 186, at 12 (recommending international standards of training for law enforcement data requests).

surveillance."[267] Domestic audits offer one effective form of *ex post* review. Such an inspection process should occur at regular intervals, with reviewable information based on the time of access or, in exceptional circumstances, as promptly as possible. In addition, an oversight body could scrutinize the procedural compliance through methods such as hearings, documentary analysis, interviews and sampling.[268] Scheduled inspections could be further supplemented by surprise visits. In Norway, a national model is already in place, where the Parliament's Intelligence Oversight Committee (EOS) has the power to conduct surprise inspection visits for shared data.[269]

Finally, each state should provide whistleblower protection in the event of abuse of intelligence sharing agreements. Given the sensitivity of intelligence operations, whistleblower protections do not need to extend to the release of information to the public.[270] However, each state should ensure that government employees or officials may report violations of protocols and procedures to the relevant oversight bodies without fear of retribution.

iv. Principle of Proportionality

States disagree about the need for a proportionality analysis in their own surveillance operations. The United States, for example, only requires surveillance to meet a legitimate national security purpose, but the European Union requires proportionality.[271] The ECtHR in *Weber and Saravia* established

---

[267] Sommer v. Germany, App. No. 73607/13, Eur. Ct. H.R., 15 (2016), http://hudoc.echr.coe.int/eng?i=001-173091. However, this model contests the ECtHR's' subsequent proclamation that "the effectiveness of a subsequent judicial review is inextricably linked to the question of subsequent notification about the surveillance measures. There is, in principle, little scope for recourse to the courts by an individual unless he or she is advised of the measures taken without his or her knowledge and thus able to challenge the legality of such measures retrospectively." *Id.*

[268] BORN ET AL., *supra* note 4, at 147-48 (discussing some principle methods of review for data sharing).

[269] *Id.* at 148.

[270] This more circumscribed view almost certainly departs from the whistleblower protection envisioned by the Snowden Treaty Advocates calling for "international protections for whistleblowers." *The Snowden Treaty, supra* note 195.

[271] *See* Deeks, *supra* note 51 (assessing the differences between the United States' and the ECtHR approach).

a European balancing test that weighs "all the circumstances of the case, such as the nature, scope and duration of the possible measures, the grounds required for ordering them, the authorities competent to authorise, carry out and supervise them, and the kind of remedy provided by the national law."[272] Countries will continue to differ in their decisions whether to insert proportionality considerations in their intelligence practices. Nonetheless, when it comes to sharing intelligence, proportionality considerations should not be wholly absent from either the sharing or accessing of foreign intelligence information.

First, states should condition their access of shared intelligence information on a proportionality assessment. In order to access foreign analyzed intelligence information, states should engage in a balancing analysis weighing the degree of privacy intrusion, demonstrated by the nature of the data sought and the amount of data sought,[273] against the specific purpose for which the information is being accessed. It is important to note that the privacy intrusion calculation should focus on the *content and volume* of the information shared, and not the means by which that content was collected. While some might prefer that all foreign intelligence include the means by which such intelligence was collected, foreign states will not realistically divulge such information in most circumstances. Moreover, attempting to apply procedural collection processes across countries fails to account for the fact that another agency could have gathered the same information through a different process. For example, one intelligence agency might have obtained telephone records through a targeted bulk data collection, and another agency might have obtained the same telephone records with a warrant—or would have been able to do so if the relevant telephone company were located under its jurisdiction.

Nevertheless, states' domestic legislatures should retain significant leeway in applying access controls for accessing foreign-sourced analyzed information. These legislatures could prescribe the weight given to different factors in a proportionality assessment. For example, the United States might

---

[272] Weber & Saravia v. Germany, App No 54934/00, 2006-XI [2006] Eur. Ct. H.R. 1173, Admissibility, 24 (2006), http://hudoc.echr.coe.int/webservices/content/pdf/001-76586.

[273] Slobogin, *supra* note 244.

decide that U.S. intelligence services might only access foreign intelligence reports that target non-U.S. citizens. Alternatively, the U.S. might require the anonymization of U.S. citizen's personal information unless granted permission to reinsert redacted information by the FISA court. Any such access controls should be implemented by the receiving state. Through such a process, domestic legislation could control the parameters and risk of incidental use of domestically unattainable information. As explained in Part 0, this process should be further bolstered by internal oversight to ensure that intelligence agencies do not abuse foreign intelligence sharing to circumvent their own collection limitations. Due to widely differing privacy-security tradeoffs, the access standards would likely exhibit wide variation. This framework does not recommend substantive access standards beyond the exigency exception in Part 0, but instead urges substantial flexibility in allowing sovereign states to determine the content of its access controls.

States could create more robust access barriers that include collection methods for the transfer of raw intelligence. Since raw intelligence has not been altered from its initial collection form, its mode of collection is far more easily discernable. If sharing raw intelligence, states should be willing to either disclose the intelligence collection method or stipulate that the collection method would not have violated the intelligence collection laws of the partner state. Joint overseers, as suggested by Aldrich,[274] could facilitate the more rigorous implementation of state-specific access controls.

States should also avoid transferring requested information without the partner state sharing a purpose or justification. Due to access control variations in state intelligence practice, states should adopt a limited proportionality assessment requiring legitimate justification when they consider intelligence requests by foreign intelligence partners. Specifically, states should confirm that their partners would use the information for a legitimate purpose. The implementation of the proportionality requirement might not substantively differ from the requirement to meet a national security purpose. However, the articulation of justification and oversight review will ensure that the shared intelligence information is only used in a

---

[274] *See* Aldrich, *supra* note 9.

manner consistent with that state's privacy security balance. Such analyses should apply to requests for both metadata and "content" data.[275]

Before transferring information to foreign intelligence partners, government intelligence officials should explicitly account for privacy interests in addition to security and political calculations. Nevertheless, the international community would be ill-served by the adoption of a "necessity" principle for data sharing. The UN Human Rights Experts' Brief in *Kidane* provides an operational definition for necessity:

> The requirement of necessity implies that restrictions must not simply be useful, reasonable or desirable to achieve a legitimate government objective. Instead, a State must demonstrate "in specific and individualized fashion the precise nature of the threat" that it seeks to address, and a "direct and immediate connection between the expression and the threat.[276]

Such a necessity requirement would force intelligence agencies to disclose national security threats to their partners and would also require admission of domestic vulnerabilities and weaknesses in their own national security regimes. Additionally, states differ in their perceptions of necessity based on potentially private information about the nature of domestic risks. Governments would likely be unwilling to disclose such information.[277] As

---

[275] Courts have increasingly recognized that both content data and metadata invoke significant privacy concerns. *See, e.g.,* Joined Cases C-203/15 & C-698/15, Tele2 Sverige AB v. Post-Och telestyrelsen, 2016 EUR-Lex 62015CJ0203, ¶ 199 (Dec. 21 2016), https://eur-lex.europa.eu/legal-content/EN/TXT/PDF/?uri=CELEX:62015CJ0203 &from=EN ("data [that] provides the means . . . of establishing a profile of the individuals concerned, information that is no less sensitive, having regard to the right to privacy, than the actual content of communications."); United States v. Jones, 565 U.S. 400, 416 (2012) ("And the Government's unrestrained power to assemble data that reveal private aspects of identity is susceptible to abuse.").

[276] Brief of Amici Curiae United Nations Human Rights Experts in Support of Plaintiff-Appellant and Reversal at 14, Doe (Kidane) v. Fed. Rep. of Eth., 851 F.3d 7 (D.C. Cir. 2016) (No. 16-7081), 2016 WL 6476760.

[277] *See* Arar v. Ashcroft, 585 F.3d 559, 576 (2009) ("Even the probing of these [exchanges among the ministries and agencies of foreign countries on diplomatic, security, and intelligence issues] entails the risk that other countries will become less willing to cooperate with the United States in sharing intelligence resources to counter terrorism.").

such, the state requesting the information is best situated to evaluate its need of the information. While state with the information may refuse an intelligence request for any number of reasons, requiring a state to conduct a necessity test before transferring intelligence information would not serve the public world order in facilitating critical intelligence transfers.[278]

v.   Principle of Notification and Remedies

International human rights law also contains the principle of notification and remedies. Many states do not provide notifications of data use, and remedies vary widely across states. For intelligence sharing purposes, states should require notification to the originator state when the recipient state substantively accesses private information. Such provisions should also include flexibility for the state to delay notification for a limited period of time pursuant to ongoing operations. Mandatory state notifications would reduce information barriers and facilitate cooperative international self-governance. Moreover, any private right of action should be conditioned upon the principle of sovereign consent.

Procedures for individual notification should rest on the specific state laws, and the state should have discretion over the circumstances and timing of notification that personal information has been accessed. The originator state should also control the degree of disclosure, or the level of specificity of which information was accessed or by whom. Importantly, the notification procedures should be codified into law. This process will create political accountability, and the scope of government notification commitments should respond to the political process.[279]

A state-based notification system places the state as a guardian *ad litem*, charged with protecting the best interests of its citizens. In practice, intelligence sharing is policed by the understanding that violations "will be

---

[278] *See, e.g.*, UK IPT Response, *supra* note 219, at ¶208 (contending that "power to share intelligence with a foreign intelligence agency must plainly be capable of being 'necessary'").

[279] Admittedly, autocratic governments will tend to be less responsive to political pressure. However, the process of requiring even those governments to publically adopt a stance; even a zero-notification policy generates political pressure and encourages accountability.

sanctioned by reduction or cessation of future cooperation."[280]   As such, if intelligence officials have reason to believe their intelligence partners are misusing shared information, they should think twice before participating in future intelligence exchanges. While intelligence officials may have incentives to turn a blind eye to privacy intrusive practices, the presence of independent oversight bodies will lead to official compliance with domestic laws regarding sharing notification procedures.

Additionally, sovereign immunity principles weigh against allowing a private right of action absent state consent. Generally, sovereign governments are immune from lawsuits except to the extent that a government consents to a waiver of its immunity.[281] Sovereign immunity has also crystalized into a principle of customary international law forbidding suits against sovereign states in foreign jurisdictions without the states' consent.[282] Taken together, principles of state and international respect for sovereign immunity weigh against forcing a sovereign immunity waiver for an individual right of action. Nevertheless, the absence of a private right of action does not mean that individual privacy interests should remain untended. As explained above, the state has a responsibility to protect the privacy interests of its citizens. Against this backdrop, the cooperative nature of intelligence sharing leaves room for pressure and leverage through informal processes to deter future privacy violations. Finally, state oversight bodies have jurisdiction over privacy violations, and depending on the individual notification procedures, states can establish processes by which individuals or state representatives may bring claims against the government for procedural or substantive harms incurred as a result of an intelligence-sharing agreement.[283]

---

[280] BORN ET AL., *supra* note 4, at 38.

[281] *See, e.g.*, United States v. Sherwood, 312 U.S. 584, 586 (1941) ("The United States, as sovereign, is immune from suit save as it consents to be sued.").

[282] Xiaodong Yang, *Sovereign Immunity*, OXFORD BIBLIOGRAPHIES, (May 25, 2016), http://www.oxfordbibliographies.com/view/document/obo-9780199796953/obo-9780199796953-0018.xml.

[283] Ian Brown has gone so far as to suggest that "illegal surveillance should be criminalized." Brown, *supra* note 154, at 31. While states have the flexibility to criminalize surveillance activities, considerations underlying the United States' discretionary function exemption of official immunity likely applies here—namely, in

vi. Principle of Complementarity

Another important international law principle relevant for intelligence sharing concerns complementarity. The principle of complementarity "counsels deference based on both the imperatives of sovereignty and other provisions of international law, including the law of armed conflict and U.N. Security Council resolutions that require global cooperation to combat terrorism."[284] In the realm of privacy rights, complementarity encourages allowing a margin of flexibility for how states apply those rights in practice vis-à-vis security interests. The European Court of Human Rights recognized such a complementarity principle in *Leander v. Sweden*, holding that Sweden had a wide "margin of appreciation" when choosing the means for achieving the legitimate aim of protecting national security.[285]

When applied to intelligence sharing, the traditional complementarity principle receives reinforcement by the notion of international comity, or the idea that states should adjudicate their laws in a way that "respect[s] the sovereign rights of other nations by limiting the reach of its own laws and their enforcement."[286] Concerns of comity should provide states with special flexibility in arranging intelligence sharing agreements. Specifically, this principle encourages states to grant greater deference to state national security practices than they might otherwise exercise in other contexts. The principle of complementarity provides the flexibility necessary to facilitate intelligence sharing in a world of differing privacy-security tradeoffs.

vii. Principle of Good Faith

The principle of good faith must govern intelligence sharing arrangements. Namely, all information requests and request fulfillments should be carried out in good faith. Such an obligation mimics the good-faith exception to the

---

protecting the officials from "liability that would seriously handicap efficient government operations." United States v. S.A. Empresa de Viacao Aerea Rio Grandense *(Varig Airlines)*, 467 U.S. 797, 814 (1984).

[284] Margulies, *supra* note 173, at 2139.

[285] Leander v. Sweden, App No 9248/81, 9 Eur. H.R. Rep. 433 at ¶59 (1987).

[286] Kiobel v. Royal Dutch Petroleum Co., 569 U.S. 108, 128 (2013). *See generally* Jesner v. Arab Bank, 138 S. Ct. 1386 (2018) (tackling questions of international comity).

United States' Fourth Amendment exclusionary rule. United States courts generally do not permit the use of evidence collected in violation of the Fourth Amendment.[287] However, this exclusionary rule does not apply when an official conducts a search or seizure with a reasonable good faith belief that the search was consistent with the rule of law.[288] Similarly, national intelligence agencies should be able to share and utilize shared information as long as they have a reasonable good faith belief that both they and their intelligence partners have complied with the agreed-upon legal procedures.[289]

This good faith principle plays a critical role in respecting the obligation that states do not use intelligence-sharing practices to circumvent domestic safeguards through revolving door tactics. United States Executive Order 12333 establishes such a principle for U.S. conduct, and forbids members of the United States intelligence community from participating in or requesting any activities that they could not lawfully carry out themselves—including intelligence collection.[290] Similarly, good faith privacy protection motivates the tailoring of information delivered in the course of surveillance requests. To the extent that domestic regimes of a receiving state provide higher standards of protection on a given issue, such as limitations on the use of national's information, the presence of an independent oversight apparatus can also facilitate good-faith compliance.

Just as states should not request foreign intelligence agencies to engage in unlawful practices, states should also not share data that they know the partner states could not collect. Instead, foreign states should undertake a good-faith effort to avoid sharing information that, to a non-trivial degree, relies on information that their intelligence partner could not have lawfully collected. This should not impose an obligation on states to comb their

---

[287] Mapp v. Ohio, 367 U.S. 643, 657 (1961).

[288] United States v. Leon, 468 U.S. 897, 909 (1984) ("[T]he exclusionary rule be more generally modified to permit the introduction of evidence obtained in the reasonable good-faith belief that a search or seizure was in accord with the Fourth Amendment.").

[289] Of course, the good faith "use" of information here differs from the exclusionary rule context; while the exclusionary rule is concerned with evidentiary inclusion, intelligence sharing involves utilization by information by other intelligence operatives.

[290] Exec. Order No. 12,333, 3 C.F.R. 200, § 2.12 (1982).

analyzed intelligence reports to prevent any incidental disclosure of private information. Rather, the sharing states should make a good-faith effort to provide the information that the receiving state needs for implementing its access controls. For example, the United States might request a threat assessment of a particular organization from Great Britain, and that report might contain some information through a method that the receiving state could not have undertaken. The United States might not allow for foreign intelligence containing personal information on U.S. nationals in the absence of a warrant. In order for U.S. intelligence agencies to access the report, they might need to meet legislated access controls that require an independent authorizer to attest that the report does not contain information about U.S. citizens. If so, then the U.S. intelligence sharing request could request that the U.K. specify whether the report contains information about U.S. citizens so that the U.S. agency can undertake the necessary steps for authorized access. The UK should make a good faith effort to comply with such a request. If states adopt limitations that are too exacting, these exclusions could impose significant costs on each party. Including stakeholders from the intelligence agencies when designing access controls will go a long way towards minimizing the costs of such information requests.

Without good faith, state intelligence sharing cannot operate out of the public eye. The intelligence sharing system must therefore be established in a fashion that breeds public trust in the processes and procedures undergirding these covert operations shrouded in secrecy.[291] As former U.S. President Obama commented in light of United States anti-terrorism tactics, "If people can't trust not only the executive branch but also don't trust Congress and don't trust federal judges to make sure that we're abiding by the Constitution, due process and rule of law, then we're going to have some problems here."[292] Public faith in the good will of the intelligence community is foundational to a robust security establishment. However, state security interests do not require blind faith. Good faith principles combined with publically available procedural safeguards can help shore up popular legitimacy. Taken together,

---

[291] For a list of benefits that arise from maintaining the secrecy of intelligence cooperation, see Deeks, *supra* note 224.

[292] *See* Nicholas & Gorman, *supra* note 34.

these seven principles allow for public disclosure and facilitate accountability without undermining the privacy-security tradeoff.

viii. Exigency Exception for Non-Compliant States

This framework should also anticipate that not every state would immediately adopt these principles. For the reasons outlined above, an effort to completely block intelligence sharing with non-compliant states would be both impractical and highly dangerous for all states involved. So how should states approach states who lack the important safeguards outlined in this framework? First, it is clear that intelligence agencies should be limited in their ability to share information with countries that do not adopt the policies consistent with the principles above. Nonetheless, not all intelligence sharing directly implicates individual privacy rights. As such, states can still share and receive strategic and operational information with non-compliant intelligence partners as long as the information does not contain personally identifiable information. For example, important policy analyses related to foreign policy developments or general threat assessments of a particular group will not necessarily disclose personal information.[293]

One might imagine a situation in which an intelligence agency discovers information necessary to prevent a serious threat to the welfare of another state. In such circumstances, an exigency exception should prove appropriate. Specifically, this exigency exception should allow agencies to provide or receive necessary information, even if it includes personal information, in the limited scenario of a high-probability event that reasonably threatens the loss of life or substantial disruption to core operational services. Furthermore, the state must reasonably believe that the additional information presents "material" information germane to the reduction of the threat. Under these limited circumstances, non-compliant foreign partners may share intelligence information under the exigency exception. However, due to information asymmetries, the receiving state may realize that the shared information does not actually meet the exacting exigency standards. In these situations, the

---

[293] While one can make the case for a public figure exception whereby public figures enjoy diminished privacy protections, such an exploration lies beyond the scope of this Article.

receiving state should still be able to utilize the information as long as it determines that the information was shared in good faith.

The presence of exigent circumstances does not relieve a state of its responsibility to protect individual privacy. When states share information under such circumstances, they should seek to tailor the information granted to the specific request. When transferring information, states should limit sharing personally identifiable information to the extent reasonable. As part of this effort, states should avoid sharing raw intelligence data whenever feasible, and should instead convey the necessary information through analyzed "end product" intelligence. Additionally, compliant states should request that states receiving such intelligence only use this information for its intended purpose, although such an endeavor is unlikely to have any practical impact.

While this framework sets the expected standards to govern state transfers of intelligence information to non-compliant states, states may carve out additional exceptions. While recipient states would not have the ability to share intelligence information received from framework-compliant states, all states would still retain the sovereign discretion to engage in additional sharing agreements with other states. However, any information received from non-compliant states would still be subject to the procedural requirements detailed above. While deviations from this framework would likely be domestically unpopular, one could imagine popular limited exceptions, such as one that allows countries to share information related to border migration, regardless of internal governance standards.

This exigency exception should also apply to intelligence sharing among framework-compliant states. Specifically, the framework should allow the transfer of "exigent" information that would otherwise be barred due to revolving door concerns. Finally, in accordance with the principle of legality, states should undertake to codify the parameters of this exigency exception into domestic law.

D. Application

This Section seeks to concretize the above framework by testing the suggested framework against plausible scenarios. The scenarios focus on bilateral intelligence sharing. Each of the below scenarios explore the actions that State A must take to comply with the proposed intelligence-sharing framework.

i.   Scenario One: Sharing Intelligence

Suppose that State A's intelligence agency, while conducting surveillance in accordance with its domestic laws, intercepts six text message communications between two foreign nationals. The intercepted messages displays sympathies with a designated terrorist group's political goals, and mentions a willingness to further the group's cause in their home countries, States B and C. State A's intelligence agency would like to share this information with States B and C. However, State A has adopted laws implementing the proposed framework through public statutes, as required by the legality principle. How does State A proceed?

State A must initially assess whether it can share the gathered information with States B and C. This assessment raises two questions. First, States A's intelligence community will need to look to the procedural requirements that State A has legislated into domestic law to determine whether sharing this information serves a legitimate purpose. State A will have legislated public limitations on the purposes of government intelligence sharing in according with the Principle of Safeguards Against Abuse. Let us assume that the legitimate purposes include the sharing of information to prevent threats to terrorism and national security, serious crimes, and threats to public safety. As such, the proposed information sharing would meet legitimate goals under the statute.

Next, State A must assess whether States B and C have adopted this intelligence-sharing framework. Let us assume that State B has adopted the framework, but State C has not. This difference leads the analysis to diverge for the subsequent steps of the intelligence sharing process. Let us first focus on State B.

Because State B has adopted procedures consistent with the intelligence sharing framework, State A can easily assess State B's public laws to confirm that its intelligence sharing procedures provide the necessary procedural protections. Specifically, State A can confirm that State B has safe information storage procedures, has temporal limitations on the retention of shared information, and will not engage in third- party transfers, except with intelligence agencies who have adopted this same framework.

Under the sharing framework, State B will also need to conduct a proportionality test before accessing such information, balancing the nature of the data sought and the amount of data sought against the specific purpose for which the information is being accessed. Due to the fact that State B did not request the information (and therefore does not know enough to conduct the analysis), State A will need to explain the general nature of the intelligence. In this case, State A's explanation would detail the fact that State A identified text messages suggestive of a high-risk individual interested in aiding the terrorist's goals. State A would then deliver those six messages. An independent oversight officer in State B would then need to conduct a proportionality test before accessing that information. In this case, the government purpose would be to identify high-risk individuals for national security and the privacy intrusion would comprise the six messages, as well as the cell phone numbers of the communicators. Oversight officers in State B would liaise with officers in State A to ensure that State B has enough information to apply its domestic access controls.

State B, after having accessed this information and finding cause for serious concern, might believe that more of the text messages contain important information. State B might request State A to transfer all intercepted text messages by one of the communicators for a three-month time frame. However, State B can only request such information if State B believes in good faith that State B's domestic law would allow the intelligence agency to lawfully intercept these messages. Even if State B would be legally permitted to obtain such information, the Principle of Safeguards Against Abuse requires State B to condition any access to the transferred text messages in line with all legislated access controls.

The intelligence agencies in State A and State B would have the advice and counsel of their respective oversight officers as they transferred, processed, and accessed the shared information. Moreover, each agency would be subject to governmental audits to facilitate an *ex post* review. Once State B accesses the transferred intelligence data, State B must inform State A. State A will then follow its domestic laws governing the relevant notification procedures to the parties in question.

State A must take a different approach with State C. State C has not adopted the intelligence-sharing framework. As such, State A faces more limited options. State A can only share information if it falls into the exigency exception—namely, a high-probability event that reasonably threatens the loss of life or substantial disruption to core operational services. The identification of potentially dangerous terrorist sympathizers would not meet this high standard. Therefore, State A would not be able to share this intelligence information with State C (unless States A and C have negotiated a separate bilateral agreement). However, State A's inability to share the text messages does not mean that State A is completely hamstrung. State A can still warn State C without divulging any personal information. For example, State A might inform State C that they have reason to believe that State C has terrorist sympathizers in their country, and State C should exercise vigilance. In the event that State A later learned that one of the identified sympathizers has purchased explosives in preparation for a terrorist plot, State A would be able to share information with State C under the exigency exception. However, State A should avoid sharing raw intelligence information, and instead provide a report to State C identifying the suspect and the nature of the threat.

ii.   Scenario Two: Receiving Intelligence

Imagine that through the course of its lawful intelligence practice, State A's intelligence services discover that two foreign individuals, residing in State B and citizens in State C, are likely involved in a plot against State A. State A only has limited intelligence on these individuals. As such, State A contacts its intelligence partners in State B and C to learn if they can provide information related to these two individuals and assist in their threat assessment. State B has adopted the proposed intelligence-sharing framework; State C has not.

State B has also observed these two State C nationals with concern, and through an extensive bulk collection program, has pulled the raw communications data for these two suspected individuals for the last three months, and has compiled analyzed reports. State B finds that State A's request meets a permissible purpose and has established procedures in accordance with the intelligence-sharing framework. After ensuring that the shared information is reasonably tailored to State A's request, State B shares its analyzed reports and communications interceptions with State A.

State A cannot access the communications information without applying its own access controls. Imagine that State A's legislature has enacted rules that forbid its intelligence community to use bulk interception practices to gather information on any person and does not allow the access of foreign intelligence concerning any State A nationals without a judicial warrant. Before accessing the transferred information, an independent authorizer in State A would need to conduct an *ex ante* review to confirm that the transferred intelligence would not violate State A's access requirements. State A's authorizer reviews the transferred information and notices a reference to a State A national. The authorizer must then redact the information revealing personal information about the State A national. State A might ask whether the raw intelligence information was collected through bulk surveillance. State B would either have to answer State A's question or not share the bulk data. Assuming that State B explained that the information had been gathered through bulk interception, State A would then need to determine if there were a way by which State A could access the information. While State A might have an absolute rule allowing for no exceptions for bulk interceptions, it also might have a rule that permits access to a targeted subset of the bulk dataset with independent judicial authorization. Thus, State A's domestic legislation would determine State A's ability to access such information. If State A accesses personal information from State B's report, State A must notify State B. State B would then carry out notifications in line with the notification requirements outlined in its domestic legislation. State A would also need to erase the transferred data in accordance to agreed-upon retention limitations.

Unless State A has a separate intelligence sharing agreement with State C, State A would probably not be able to receive information from State C. However, if State A's preexisting intelligence leads them to reasonably believe that a) the plot against State A poses a "high-probability event that reasonably threatens the loss of life or substantial disruption to core operational services," and b) State C's intelligence could offer "material information germane to the reduction of the threat;" then State A could request such information from State C. However, any information received by State C under the exigency exception could only be used for the specific threat for which the information was requested.

VI. DEFENSE AGAINST COMMON CRITIQUES

A. Insufficient Privacy Protection

The framework above will likely raise some critiques. Most predictable is the critique from the European privacy rights camp, arguing that the proposed framework will allow intelligence sharing of information with lesser privacy protections than are mandated by the European Court of Human Rights. Substantively, this criticism is correct. If one adopts a singular approach where privacy concerns operate as the only valid interest at play, then the above framework would inexcusably disregard fundamental rights. However, such an argument stumbles once one reintroduces a critically absent component: the context. As this Article demonstrates, privacy interests operate in tension with *another fundamental right*. While privacy activists will nominally recognize that their "fundamental" privacy right is not in fact absolute, such recognition is usually just that—nominal. Take for example Hielke Hijmans's *The European Union as Guardian of Internet Privacy*. In one line during his six-hundred page tome, Hijman recognizes that "[t]hreats to security may require restrictions to the exercise of fundamental rights."[294] Even Hijmans's language is striking—"fundamental" rights connote absolute and inalienable qualities. Given the legitimate restriction of these rights, they clearly do not carry an absolute quality. If threats to security warrant the restriction of fundamental rights, then it serves to reason that threats to security also implicate fundamental rights. In short, there is a tradeoff here.

Given the presence of a tradeoff between fundamental rights, privacy advocates' implicit paradigm of "security—bad, privacy—good"

---

[294] Hijmans, *supra* note 218, at 113–14.

inappropriately misconstrues the moral considerations. By downplaying the human rights interests in adequate security, privacy advocates paint their advocacy for greater privacy protections as a unilateral quest for maximizing human rights. For example, claims proliferate founded upon the assumption that strengthening privacy at the expense of security will lead to "the establishment of a high ceiling rather than a low floor for human rights protection and accountability."[295] Similarly, this blinkered viewpoint leads to characterizations of counterterrorism practices leading to privacy limitations as "[a] race to the bottom concerning the right to privacy."[296] Such pejorative language disparages legitimate security behavior protecting fundamental rights.

The European Union, with support from privacy activists around the world, has staked out the moral high ground, declaring that their desired balance—and none others—deserve consideration or deference. As Maria Tzanou observes, "the EU has successfully constructed the image of itself as a 'moral leader of good in the fight against terrorism due to its alleged higher respect to human rights standards compared to the US."[297] Hijman reports that European Council intentionally sought to set "globalization within a moral framework."[298] Once the privacy-security balance has been 'moralized,' the heart of the question becomes whether states can legitimately strike different balances along this spectrum.

According to the European Union and privacy activists, that answer is no. The European Union has adopted its role on the basis that its values are "normatively desirable and universally applicable."[299] Hijmans provides a helpful descriptor for this practice: "regulatory imperialism."[300] The CJEU has encouraged this path towards European exceptionalism with its decision in *Kadi*: "EU concepts on fundamental rights prevail, whenever this is necessary, over international law. EU law contains principles that must be respected in

---

[295] Brown et al, *supra* note 199.

[296] Tzanou, *supra* note 144, at 101.

[297] *Id*. at 100.

[298] Hijmans, *supra* note 218, at 482–83. https://link.springer.com/content/pdf/10.1007/978-3-319-34090-6.pdf.

[299] *Id*; *see also* Bignami & Resta, *supra* note 97, at 16.

[300] Hijmans, *supra* note 218, at 488.

the international domain, are not negotiable and subject to full review of the EU Courts."[301]

If one believes the European standard offers immutable expressions of absolute morality, then my framework will be troubling. Stephen Schulhofer has explicitly embraced this approach, and strenuously opposes the effort "to find international common ground" because multilateral negotiation would create a more permissive sharing regime that would create, in his morally-infused words, "a race to the regulatory bottom."[302] Of course, for many, a major thrust of this intelligence sharing critique is that currently *no* country provides adequate privacy protections over intelligence transfers—European human rights law just provides the most promising path forward.

The proposed framework compromises on privacy absolutist ideals in a number of ways. First, the framework argues that data access controls as opposed to data collection controls should not prohibit intelligence sharing agreements. The framework also largely defers the content of such access controls to the domestic state. Second, the framework applies a watered-down proportionality test, and does not call for an independent necessity test. Instead, it would allow legitimate government intelligence requests without an inquiry or adjudication into alternative pathways for acquiring such information. Third, it does not require governments to authorize whistleblowing to the general public. Fourth, it provides for state-notification and does not mandate individual notification. Fifth, it does not demand an individual right of action. Nevertheless, the adoption of such a framework would pose a major step forward for privacy rights by legislating overdue transparency and oversight in a field long obscured by a foggy ether.[303]

Privacy concerns animated by domestic surveillance practices are also mitigated in intelligence sharing. As Schulhofer notes, "US data-collection programs pose a far greater risk of chilling political dissent within the US than of chilling political activity by Germans or Canadians critical of their own

---

[301] *Id.* at 473.

[302] Schulhofer, *supra* note 51, at 240.

[303] This framework also does not discuss control of voluntary disclosures by Internet Service Providers, an area that warrants further analysis in the future.

governments."[304]   While foreign governments are less likely to respect an individual's privacy interests, they also have limited means to suppress rights abroad. Thus, to the extent that intelligence sharing serves to provide data on foreigners, some privacy concerns are diminished.[305]

Additionally, the flexibilities of this approach make this framework practicable. The framework governs intelligence sharing practices yet places a light touch on the surveillance methods employed in each country. Privacy idealists too often ignore that a failure to grant intelligence operations special treatment will result in widespread noncompliance.[306]   After all, law as practiced within the "real world" context— operating under an operational code—are viewed as lawful by those operators.[307]   This remains true even when those operational laws deviate from the established myth system.[308] Following Asaf Lubin's lead, this Article urges a practical orientation that would shatter the "Geneva echo chamber" and reintroduce government stakeholders into the discussion.[309]   Furthermore, while some might find attractive the notion of disregarding foreign balances, the reality is that "countries with different values, . . . for instance, the BRICS countries[310] are gaining more economic power."[311] The BRIC countries are not only growing in economic power, but many also have extensive intelligence apparatuses.

---

[304] Schulhofer, *supra* note 51, at 260.

[305] This is not to say that information sharing does not cause any privacy harm. Many of the privacy concerns outlined in Part 0 still apply.

[306] *See* Deeks, *supra* note 63, at 602 ("The formalists ignore that there is something unique about intelligence activity, and that requiring intelligence services to play by precisely the same rules as law enforcement, diplomatic, and military actors is doomed to produce state noncompliance.").

[307] Lubin, *supra* note 51, at 511 (citing W. Michael Reisman, *Myth System and Operational Code*, 3 YALE STUD. WORLD PUB. ORD. 229, 230 (1977)).

[308] *Id.*

[309] *Id.* at 551–52 ("This piece proposes recognizing the legitimacy behind certain limited legal differentiations in treatment for domestic and foreign surveillance. Such recognition, quite a concession on the part of the 'Geneva echo chamber,' would bring government agencies back to the table.").

[310] *See BRIC*, CAMBRIDGE DICTIONARY, https://dictionary.cambridge.org/us/dictionary/english/bric (last visited Mar. 13, 2019) (referring to the economic pact comprised of Brazil, Russia, India and China).

[311] Hijmans, *supra* note 218, at 459.

These countries are developing the economic strength to withstand regulatory imperialism, and the need for information sharing means that their interests cannot simply be ignored. In short, this paper incorporates flexibilities, and by doing so, promulgates standards that could actually work.

B. Undermines Democratic Accountability

A similar critique suggests that an international framework undermines democratic accountability. Contrary to these complaints, this international framework will strengthen the role of civil society in holding governments accountable. Some activists have suggested that any international privacy sharing agreement would "sideline the courts, disempower legislative bodies and privacy advocates, defuse commercial pressure for strong privacy safeguards, and create a dynamic controlled almost exclusively by the executive and its national security establishment."[312] However, this fear ignores the limited control that civil society currently exerts—intelligence sharing remains a black box. By bringing (more) sunshine to the shadows of intelligence cooperation, privacy activists will receive the benefit of pushing standards and accountability into these practice areas. Even more importantly, the intelligence-sharing framework furthers transparency in far less privacy-sympathetic regimes, thereby providing an avenue for civil society to make further inroads on government accountability.

C. International Agreements Are Unrealistic

Many scholars view the notion of any international information-sharing regime as a fanciful one. While proposing international agreements might be an attractive theoretical exercise, many question the practical utility of pushing for "an international treaty forged out of pixie dust."[313] In other words, even if one accepts the principles outlined under the proposed framework, states would never agree to an international treaty. Academics provide many reasons for their skepticism: varying privacy commitments, foreign mistrust, and state sovereignty concerns.

---

[312] Schulhofer, *supra* note 51, at 240.

[313] Woods, *supra* note 59, at 781.

i. Irreconcilable Ideological Differences

Doubters suggest that states' different privacy-security balances pose an insuperable barrier to intelligence sharing. This perspective posits a "probably unbridgeable-gulf" between different states' commitment to privacy protection.[314] As one skeptic reports, "There is absence of global consensus at an aspirational level, in particular, where this approach implies agreement with countries that do not share basic democratic values."[315]

Another suggests that an international agreement "will necessarily be based on a lowest common denominator."[316] These realists are correct to recognize the different surveillance standards across countries, and an attempt to coerce all states to a uniform practices would not succeed. The proposed framework recognizes this ideological reality, and grants states significant discretion in the ways that they carry out intelligence work. Instead of prescribing an ideological viewpoint, the framework sidesteps these unyielding ideological positions by requiring unobjectionable procedural processes that facilitate the unifying interest in accessing critical intelligence.

ii. Too Much Foreign Mistrust

Another critique dismisses an intelligence-sharing agreement as unattainable due to an insufficient level of popular trust. While citizens might submit to some degree of surveillance by their own government, they would not necessarily agree to similar oversight by foreign entities. As one observer put it, "Brits may have become used to the CCTV cameras and Automatic Number Plate Recognition technology that allows their own government to monitor their travel – but they would be considerably more dubious about letting the Germans and the French do the same."[317] While some citizens will

---

[314] *See* Schulhofer, *supra* note 51, at 254 (asserting that, notwithstanding existing frameworks between the United States and other Western states, "the complexity of the issues and the diametric opposition" ensure that progress "will be arduous and slow").

[315] Hijmans, *supra* note 218, at 491.

[316] *See* Woods, *supra* note 59, at 788.

[317] Robin Simcox, *Europe, Stop Trying To Make 'Intelligence Sharing' Happen*, FOREIGN POL'Y (Apr. 14, 2016, 3:19PM), http://foreignpolicy.com/2016/04/14/europe-stop-trying-to-mak-brussels-paris-bombings.

undoubtedly find this scope unsettling, this discomfort would not likely pose a practical barrier. This is the case for several reasons. First, the procedural safeguards significantly reduce the degree of the privacy harm. States can only share information under heavily prescribed circumstances. The fact that only foreign intelligence officials can access the information would also significantly diminish citizen reticence. The average citizen is unlikely to fear that he or she will be a subject of a foreign national security investigation. As a result, most citizens will not see this law as impacting their lives. Moreover, the notification regime requiring home states to notify individuals whenever foreign intelligence agencies access their private information will further mollify citizen concerns. In short, the intelligence-sharing framework sufficiently curtails citizens' privacy risks to avoid popular resistance.

iii. Compromises State Sovereignty

Another critique questions this framework as hobbling state sovereignty. According to this argument, national governments will not submit to an agreement that limits their ownership over their privacy-security balance. Instead of the domestic national legislature determining the appropriate level of privacy intrusion, foreign states violate that national compact through sharing intelligence collected through different standards. This would be a legitimate concern, were it not for the presence of access controls. Through the exercise of access controls, states maintain control over their intelligence agencies' acceptable practices. Relatedly, it true that this framework facilitates intelligence sharing with foreign states that do not necessarily subscribe to the same privacy standards. However, it would be a mistake to consider intelligence sharing as diminishing state sovereign control. As Jennifer Daskal points out, "[T]his critique assumes a world that does not exist. It assumes that foreign governments will comply with the existing diplomatic procedures for accessing sought-after data rather than seeking out means of accessing the data unilaterally."[318] In the absence of intelligence agreements, foreign intelligence agencies would attempt to gather the same intelligence information by sweeping and privacy-invasive collection of raw data. By

---

[318] Daskal, *supra* note 50, at 497.

developing procedural limitations for the use of shared intelligence that render such invasive tactics less necessary, states reduce the incentive for costly foreign surveillance efforts. Therefore, the intelligence framework would likely allow states to exercise far *greater* sovereign control over the shared information.

Others argue that state national security branches have little interest in allowing any further limitations on their near-absolute discretion over intelligence practices. In other words, government officials have a strong interest in maintaining the status quo. However, this approach overlooks the changing norms leading to a public expectancy of greater transparency over intelligence activities.[319] Even those countries that do not face public pressure are indirectly impacted by this normative trend. The push for government accountability has jeopardized the ability for other states to receive foreign intelligence. Given the collective interest — and need — for intelligence sharing, governments have an interest in adopting procedural practices that will allow for intelligence sharing without compromising their national intelligence practices. Sovereign states enter international agreements that they view in their national interest, and adopting this framework promotes vital security interests.

VII. PATHWAYS TO IMPLEMENTATION

The proposed framework benefits from multiple avenues towards implementation. The first option is through unilateral, domestic legislation. Unlike many areas of the anarchic international arena, no collective action problem prevents unilateral adoption by individual states. As the public eye increasingly scrutinizes intelligence practices and calls for intelligence reform, states will also experience unprecedented constraints on intelligence sharing at a time when such sharing has never been more vital. The CJEU decisions in *Schrems* and *Canada PNR*[320] are only the tip of the iceberg. As states fill out their surveillance jurisprudence, they will continue to proliferate incompatible

---

[319] Deeks, *supra* note 63, at 618 ("Overall, the public now expects greater transparency about intelligence activities and some governments have begun to provide it.")

[320] *See* Opinion 1/15, ¶ 1, ECLI:EU:C:2017:592.

sharing regimes. Rather than continue their collision course with other privacy regimes, states can adopt these proposed procedures. As detailed above, states can adopt these procedures with minimal cost to their preferred privacy-security balance.

In order to be maximally effective, states would want to adopt these regulations with their closest intelligence allies. Fortunately, preexisting cooperation abounds. As Orin Kerr reports, "A complex web of global, regional, and bilateral treaties now exists addressing a wide range of crimes, such as cybercrime, corruption, transnational organized crime, narcotics, and terrorism."[321] Nations have already adopted information-sharing agreements through MLATs[322] and through financial intelligence cooperation.[323]

Bilateral agreements also provide a promising approach. A small core of states pushing this framework through bilateral agreements could quickly lead to sustained momentum. The Group of Eight (G8) countries—made up of France, Germany, Italy, the United Kingdom, Japan, the United States, Canada, and Russia might be one place to start. The G8 already has a history of coordinating regulatory efforts of a series of internet-related crimes, including industrial and state espionage.[324] The G8 states' extensive intelligence capabilities grant this group exceptional influence over promoting

---

[321] Orin S. Kerr & Sean D. Murphy, *Government Hacking to Light the Dark Web: What Risks to International Relations and International Law?*, 70 STAN. L. REV. 58, 61 (2017).

[322] *See* primer discussion on the United States' use of MLAT agreements, *supra* note 13.

[323] Mara Lemos Stein, *The Morning Risk Report: Financial-Intel-Sharing Groups Need Diversity*, WALL ST. J.: RISK & COMPLIANCE J. (Jan. 10, 2018, 7:32 AM), https://blogs.wsj.com/riskandcompliance/2018/01/10/the-morning-risk-report-financial-intel-sharing-groups-need-diversity; see also *International Programs*, U.S. DEP'T TREASURY: FINANCIAL CRIMES ENFORCEMENT NETWORK, https://www.fincen.gov/resources/international-programs (last visited Oct. 11, 2018) ("FinCEN is one of the most active FIUs in the world in terms of exchanging information with counterpart FIUs. The demand for FinCEN's services from foreign FIUs has expanded dramatically over the past decade.").

[324] Ghappour, *supra* note 159, at 1131 (citing Jack Goldsmith, *Unilateral Regulation of the Internet: A Modest Defence*, 11 EUR. J. INT'L L. 135, 147 (2000)).

such a framework.[325] This could arise through an informal agreement, or even the development of a multinational institution.

Financial intelligence cooperation shows the promise of such an approach. The effort to promote financial intelligence exchange has led to the development of a distinct international institution, the Egmont Group, comprised of 155 Financial Intelligence Units.[326] Egmont has played a role in responding to terrorist financing and provided a secure technological platform for financial intelligence exchange.[327] The long-term establishment of such an organization could help reduce information costs of monitoring intelligence-sharing which states have legislated sufficient procedural safeguards.

Formal international treaties offer another way forward. These agreements can move through the United Nations, which some have argued presents "the legitimate forum for the negotiation of a global legal framework."[328] However, others have argued that adopting an international agreement would trade efficiency for a cumbersome process that could prolong and delay adoption of new domestic legislation.[329] Nevertheless, formal international agreements could clarify the specific elements of the framework and ensure that all states are applying the same framework. As intelligence sharing becomes a more regulated practice, a treaty might help codify a widespread state practice. At this time, such an approach would likely be premature.

---

[325] American data providers' dominance over the global market gives the United States in particular tremendous leverage in facilitating an intelligence-sharing regime. *See* Daskal, *supra* note 51, at 474.

[326] *About*, EGMONT GROUP, https://egmontgroup.org/en/content/about (last visited Oct. 11, 2018).

[327] Egmont Group, Group of Financial Intelligence Units, Annual Report 2015–2016 11 (2017), https://egmontgroup.org/en/filedepot_download/1660/45.

[328] Report on the meeting of the Expert Group to Conduct a Comprehensive Study on Cybercrime, UNODC/CCPCJ/EG.4/2017/4, ¶43 (Apr. 24, 2017), http://www.unodc.org/documents/organized-crime/cybercrime/Cybercrime-April-2017/Cybercrime_report_2017/Report_Cyber_E.pdf.

[329] Koops & Goodwin, *supra* note 32, at 83..

VIII. CONCLUSION

In the early 21st century, the international community remains comprised of independent, sovereign nation states. These sovereign states will choose different privacy security tradeoffs. Governments will need to navigate a way to maintain intelligence sharing in an age when government surveillance receives increasing scrutiny. As one British parliamentarian aptly articulated, "We need to face up to the challenge —not duck, ignore, or pretend it is not there—[t]o preserve the legal safeguards that ensure that our intelligence services can do their job."[330]

The proposed intelligence framework offers a road forward; one that respects sovereign choices and also comports with international law. The proposed intelligence framework is practicable and promises unprecedented transparency in an area long devoid of legal governance. Countries implementing this framework would create unparalleled democratic accountability, without undermining intelligence officials' ability to do their jobs. Governments will be able to keep people safe and also provide meaningful privacy protection. As privacy activists demand greater transparency on intelligence sharing, both governments and privacy advocates should consider this framework as a compromise path forward. In short, this framework empowers countries to transform the impending clash of privacy-security regimes into an opportunity for a new era of global cooperation and transparency.

---

[330]15 Mar. 2018, Parl. Deb HC (2018) col. 158, https://hansard.parliament.uk/commons/2018-03-15/debates/831521d4-174f-4150-9099-7817a9e28f8b/DataProtectionBill (click PDF and HTML downloads; select "Data Protection Bill [Lords] (Fourth sitting)).

Insidious Encroachment?

Strengthening the "Crown Jewels": The 2018 Reauthorization of FISA Section 702

John F. Schifalacqua*

Abstract

This article seeks to turn a critical eye toward to the Reauthorization Act—both its development and future challenges—as a way to evaluate the current state of Section 702 since its recent reauthorization. To establish a historical context, Part II will lay out the general history of Section 702, its requirements, and the techniques the government has typically deployed under its authority. Part III will develop an account of the legislative history of the Reauthorization Act to highlight the keys issues of contention in public discourse over Section 702. Part IV will detail the key changes to Section 702 implemented by Congress. Part V will then describe the typical constitutional challenges to Section 702 prior to the Reauthorization Act and reassess the viability of in light of the key changes to the program. Finally, Part VI will conclude by offering positive developments and missed opportunities from the debates. Overall, this article seeks to emphasize that the responsibility to protect constitutional rights while simultaneously ensuring national security can at times feel like a herculean duty. But this balance is often best struck on the front end when members of Congress and are pressured to reform national security authorities rather than rely on Executive agencies to utilize its surveillance tools according to an often malleable, broad legal standard. Nevertheless, this Comment argues that there are presently substantial avenues for litigants to challenge the newest changes to Section 702 under the Fourth Amendment.

* **John F. Schifalacqua** is a May 2019 J.D. Candidate at the University of Pennsylvania Law School. He received a B.A. in History from the University of Virginia in 2014. He would like to thank David Sadoff for his guidance and valuable feedback while writing this article.

TABLE OF CONTENTS

"Experience should teach us to be most on our guard to protect liberty when the Government's purposes are beneficent. . . . The greatest dangers to liberty lurk in insidious encroachment by men of zeal, well-meaning but without understanding."

Justice Louis Brandeis

Olmstead v. United States, 277 U.S. 438, 479 (1928)

"We can't tie the hands of our national security officials at the precise moment that our enemies are taking the gloves off around the world. Terrorists don't plan to sunset their threats to our way of life, so why should our important counterterrorism tools sunset?"

Senator Tom Cotton, Speech before Congress, June 6, 2017

INTRODUCTION

The Federal Bureau of Investigation (FBI) was racing against an almost literal ticking time bomb when agents coordinated with New York City law enforcement to stop Najibullah Zazi as he crossed the George Washington Bridge just days before the 2009 anniversary of 9/11.[1] A search of Zazi's rental car was unfruitful and he grew suspicious that he was under surveillance and aborted his so-called "martyrdom operation."[2] The operation began with a 2008 visit to an al-Qaeda stronghold in Pakistan where he received weapons and bomb making training in hopes of fighting alongside the Taliban. Instead, the Taliban directed him to return to the United States—where he was a legal resident since emigrating from Afghanistan during high school—to devise a suicide attack in New York City.[3] He spent most of 2009 procuring explosive chemicals and preparing two other conspirators to carry out a coordinated bombing around 9/11's anniversary—targeting the New York City Subway, Times Square, and Grand Central Station.[4] The plan was only days away from fruition when he drove across the George Washington Bridge with hidden bomb making materials in tow. His brief encounter with law enforcement on the bridge scared him off and he fled to Colorado where he was arrested as he tried to destroy evidence to thwart any subsequent investigation.[5]

---

[1] A.G. Sulzberger & William K. Rashbaum, *Guilty Plea Made in Plot to Bomb New York Subway*, N.Y. TIMES (Feb. 22, 2010), http://www.nytimes.com/2010/02/23/nyregion/23terror.html (describing the case against Najibullah Zazi and his thwarted terrorist plot to bomb the New York Subway on the anniversary of September 11th). *See also Inside the Zazi Arrest*, NEWSWEEK (Sep. 25, 2009, 8:00 PM), http://www.newsweek.com/inside-zazi-arrest-79531 (describing the investigative details leading up to the Zazi arrest, with particular emphasis on the successful coordination between law enforcement entities).

[2] Sulzberger & Rashbaum, *supra* note 1.

[3] *Id.*

[4] Carrie Johnson & Spencer S. Hsu, *Najibullah Zazi Pleads Guilty in New York Subway Plot*, WASH. POST (Feb. 23, 2010), http://www.washingtonpost.com/wp-dyn/content/article/2010/02/22/AR2010022201916.html; Susan Candiotti, *Source: Terror plot targeted Times Square, Grand Central stations*, CNN (Apr. 12, 2010, 2:25 PM), http://www.cnn.com/2010/CRIME/04/12/new.york.plot/.

[5] *See id.*

Zazi's suspicion was certainly justified; law enforcement had been keeping a close eye on him in the months before his arrest.[6] But Zazi could not have known the full extent of the surveillance. The intelligence community (IC) had long been on his tail, deploying some of its most sophisticated surveillance methods to identify him and coordinate with the FBI. The National Security Agency (NSA) used authority granted by Section 702 of the Foreign Intelligence Surveillance Act (FISA) to monitor an email account used by an al-Qaeda operative in Pakistan.[7] That operative had received an email from a then-unknown person in the United States "urgently seeking advice regarding how to make explosives."[8] The NSA passed along this information to the FBI who used a National Security Letter[9] to rapidly identify the unknown sender as Zazi.[10] From that point forward, the FBI began a sensitive counterterrorism investigation to thwart what was considered "one of the most serious threats to the United States since 9/11."[11]

In retrospect, it was clear to the Privacy and Civil Liberties Oversight Board (PCLOB)[12]—an entity that reviews the IC—that "without the initial tip-

---

[6] *See Inside the Zazi Arrest, supra* note 1.

[7] Guide to Section 702 Value Examples, Office of the Director of National Intelligence: IC on the Record, Fact Sheet (Oct. 27, 2017), https://www.dni.gov/files/icotr/Guide-to-Section-702-Value-Examples.pdf.

[8] *Id.*

[9] *Id.* (explaining that National Security Letters are a type of administrative subpoena certain law enforcement agencies can issue to businesses without a court order). National security letters generally require the production of a narrow type of content-neutral records (e.g., information equivalent to a trap and trace list, not the content of the conversations) to aid in a national security investigation. Statutory provisions for these subpoenas range from §114(a)(5) of the Right to Financial Privacy to the extensively used Electronic Communications Privacy Act (18 U.S.C. §2709). *See* CHARLES DOYLE, *Summary*, CONG. RESEARCH SERV. RL33320, NATIONAL SECURITY LETTERS IN FOREIGN INTELLIGENCE INVESTIGATIONS: LEGAL BACKGROUND AND RECENT AMENDMENTS (2008), https://fas.org/sgp/crs/intel/RL33320.pdf#page=2.

[10] Guide to Section 702, *supra* note 7.

[11] Sulzberger & Rashbaum, *supra* note 1.

[12] Intelligence Reform and Terrorism Prevention Act, Pub. L. No. 108-458, § 1061, 118 Stat. 3638, 3684 (2004) (authorizing the PCLOB to continually review "regulations, executive branch polices, and procedures . . . related to laws pertaining to efforts to protect the Nation from terrorism, and other actions by the executive branch related to

off about Zazi and his plans, which came about by monitoring an overseas foreigner under Section 702, the subway bombing might have succeeded."[13] In other words, foreign intelligence surveillance was critical in preventing the attack. Indeed, the IC has long held that the authority for surveillance granted by Section 702 is vital to national security.[14] There are many more examples of successful counterterrorism beyond the Zazi plot to support this claim.[15] Members of the IC have testified as recently as 2017 that Section 702 is such a critical tool that some "foreign intelligence cannot be practically obtained through other methods" and the authority is a major contributor to counterterrorism and counterintelligence.[16] In fact, former FBI Director James Comey went as far as to say that Section 702 authorities are the "crown jewels" of counterterrorism, without which "we will be less safe as a country."[17]

Despite Section 702's track record of success and significance as a national security tool, it remains a contentious subject. The PCLOB recommended several reforms despite a glowing review of the program's effectiveness, citing

---

efforts to protect the Nation from terrorism to ensure that privacy and civil liberties are protected.").

[13] Guide to Section 702, *supra* note 7.

[14] *Id.* (opining that "Title VII of FISA is vital to keeping the nation safe. These authorities provide the government with a uniquely effective way to acquire information about the plans and identities of terrorists and terrorist organizations, including how they function and receive support. These authorities also enable collection of information about the intentions and capabilities of weapons proliferators and other foreign adversaries who threaten the U.S. and inform cybersecurity efforts.").

[15] *Id.* (stating that Section 702 success stories include the CIA using it "to alert[] a foreign partner to the presence within its borders of an al-Qaeda sympathizer;" the NSA collecting two years of intelligence on ISIS Finance Minister Hajji Iman; the FBI exposing Shawn Parson as a "key player" and recruiter in the ISIS network; and the U.S. helping to uncover the perpetrator of the deadly December 31, 2017 Turkish nightclub attack).

[16] *Joint Statement for the Record Before the Senate Select Committee on Intelligence*, 115th Cong. 8 (Jun. 7, 2017) (statements of Daniel Coats, DNI; Michael Rogers, NSA; Rod Rosenstein, DOJ; Andrew McCabe; FBI), https://www.intelligence.senate.gov/sites/default/files/documents/os-dcoats-060717.pdf.

[17] *Read the full testimony of FBI Director James Comey in which he discusses Clinton email investigation*, WASH. POST (May 4, 2017), https://www.washingtonpost.com/news/post-politics/wp/2017/05/03/read-the-full-testimony-of-fbi-director-james-comey-in-which-he-discusses-clinton-email-investigation/?utm_term=.944b623d6330.

"certain aspects of the Section 702 program push the program close to the line of constitutional reasonableness."[18]　Much of the concern involves incidental collection of data regarding U.S. persons that are not the target of a search at the time it is made.[19]　The broadness of Section 702's grant of authority to surveil any foreigner abroad who might possess foreign intelligence information potentially means a large swath of people can be searched, including their communications with U.S. citizens.[20]　The American Civil Liberties Union (ACLU) warns that in the process of executing a Section 702 search, the IC collects a "vast trove of data for information specifically about Americans, even though these communications were all collected without a warrant."[21]　The concern is that the government can search incidental data at a later time "to prosecute Americans for crimes" unrelated to national security, thereby doing a "backdoor" end-run around the Fourth Amendment.[22]　And there is certainly reason to believe abuse might be widespread, at least concerning the invasion of privacy.　A 2015 preliminary review found that NSA analysts "running searches on emails and other digital communications

---

[18] David S. Kris, *Trends and Predictions in Foreign Intelligence Surveillance: The FAA and Beyond*, HOOVER INST., Feb. 8, 2016, at 9, https://www.hoover.org/sites/default/files/research/docs/kris_trendspredictions_final_v4_digital.pdf#page=9.

[19] *Id.* (providing, in relevant part, "[s]uch aspects [of constitutional concern] include the unknown and potentially large scope of the incidental collection of US persons' communications, the use of 'about' collection to acquire Internet communications that are neither to nor from the target of surveillance, and the use of queries to search for the communications of specific US persons within the information that has been collected.").

[20] *See infra* Part II.B. for details on how Section 702 operates in practice.

[21] *Warrantless Surveillance Under Section 702 of FISA*, ACLU, https://www.aclu.org/issues/national-security/privacy-and-surveillance/warrantless-surveillance-under-section-702-fisa (last visited Feb. 26, 2019).　*See also* Barton Gellman, *In NSA-Intercepted Data, Those Not Targeted Far Outnumber the Foreigners Who Are*, WASH. POST (July 5, 2014), https://www.washingtonpost.com/world/national-security/in-nsa-intercepted-data-those-not-targeted-far-outnumber-the-foreigners-who-are/2014/07/05/8139adf8045a-11e4-8572-4b1b969b6322_story.html ("Nine of 10 account holders found in a large cache of intercepted conversations, which former NSA contractor Edward Snowden provided in full to The Post, were not the intended surveillance targets but were caught in a net the agency had cast for somebody else.").

[22] ACLU, *supra* note 21.

vacuumed up from undersea internet cables frequently violated Americans' privacy, albeit unintentionally."[23]

It is hard to overstate the sheer amount of information the IC can acquire under Section 702 authority. By collecting data as it runs through infrastructural switches that bring the Internet to the world—so-called "upstream backbone facility" collection—the IC can "continuously scan international internet traffic in bulk, looking for communications associated with tens of thousands of 'targets.'"[24] Such collection only requires a surface-level system of judicial oversight. The Foreign Intelligence Surveillance Court (FISC) need only approve a reasonable set of targeting procedures and minimization standards designed to reduce the potential of surveilling Americans.[25] As such, civil libertarians fear a process ripe for abuse.[26] Critics paint an Orwellian picture that "broad, warrantless collection of data under Section 702 creates an understandable fear that private messages may be read or used by the government."[27] This issue is particularly acute when activists and critics of the program feel targeted as they pursue advocacy to challenge government practices under Section 702.[28] Intelligence collection is one thing,

---

[23] Jenna McLaughlin, *Report: NSA Analysts Frequently Broke Rules on Intelligence Collection*, FOREIGN POLICY, (May 12, 2017), https://foreignpolicy.com/2017/05/12/report-nsa-analysts-frequently-broke-rules-on-intelligence-collection/.

[24] ACLU, *supra* note 21. *See also* Kris, *supra* note 18, at 9–10.

[25] 50 U.S.C. §§ 1881a(d)–(e) (providing, in relevant part, "[t]he Attorney General, in consultation with the Director of National Intelligence, shall adopt minimization procedures that meet the definition of minimization procedures under section 1801(h) of this title . . . [and] ensure that any acquisition authorized under subsection (a) is limited to targeting persons reasonably believed to be located outside the United States; and prevent the intentional acquisition of any communication as to which the sender and all intended recipients are known at the time of the acquisition to be located in the United States.").

[26] *See, e.g.*, ACLU, *supra* note 21. *See also, e.g.*, Andrea Peterson, *LOVEINT: When NSA Officers Use Their Spying Power on Love Interests*, WASH. POST (Aug. 23, 2013), https://www.washingtonpost.com/news/the-switch/wp/2013/08/24/loveint-when-nsa-officers-use-their-spying-power-on-love-interests/?utm_term=.94b715045371.

[27] ACLU, *supra* note 21.

[28] *See, e.g.*, Clapper v. Amnesty Int'l USA, 568 U.S. 398, 406 (2013) (stating in relevant part, "Respondents are attorneys and human rights, labor legal, and media organizations Respondents are attorneys and human rights, labor, legal, and media organizations whose work allegedly requires them to engage in sensitive and sometimes

but law enforcement later searching data without restriction—data initially collected for intelligence purposes—is quite another. It is not unfounded to ask whether Section 702 permits the government to undermine the Constitution on the pretense of national security.

At the core of the issue is the reoccurring "tension between privacy and national security."[29] No amount of Zazis captured fully mitigate the history of governmental abuse of counterterrorism tools. One court reminds us that "in the 1960s and 1970s, the public was outraged over the revelation that the government conducted domestic surveillance—in the name of national security—of Dr. Martin Luther King, Jr., Vietnam War protesters, and other domestic groups the government labeled 'subversive.'"[30] And whether such a history repeats itself, as the court warns, is a specter haunting the debates over Section 702.[31]

Nowhere has this tension been more apparent recently than in the debates preceding the passage of the FISA Amendments Reauthorization Act of 2017 (Reauthorization Act).[32] The original statutory authority for Section 702 derives from the FISA Amendments Act (FAA), which was set to expire by the end of 2017. With both its usefulness and dangers in mind, Congress debated the efficacy of Section 702. The result was a renewal of the FAA and Section 702 authority until 2023—with some key changes—that was signed into law by President Trump on January 19, 2018.[33] The debates preceding the reauthorization of Section 702 and the changes to the program provide an opportunity to take a fresh look at its value and constitutionality.

---

privileged telephone and e-mail communications with colleagues, clients, sources, and other individuals located abroad.... Respondents claim that § 1881a compromises their ability to locate witnesses, cultivate sources, obtain information, and communicate confidential information to their clients.").

[29] United States v. Hasbajrami, No. 11-CR-623, 2016 WL 1029500, at *1 (E.D.N.Y. Mar. 8, 2016).

[30] Id. (citing DAVID S. KRIS & J. DOUGLAS WILSON, 1 NATIONAL SECURITY INVESTIGATIONS AND PROSECUTIONS § 3.1 (2d ed. 2012)).

[31] Id.

[32] FISA Amendments Reauthorization Act of 2017, Pub. L. 115-118, 132 Stat. 4 (2018).

[33] Statement by the President on FISA Amendments Reauthorization Act of 2017, THE WHITE HOUSE: STATEMENTS AND RELEASES (Jan. 19, 2018), https://www.whitehouse.gov/briefings-statements/statement-president-fisa-amendments-reauthorization-act-2017/.

This article seeks to turn a critical eye toward to the Reauthorization Act—both its development and future challenges—as a way to evaluate the current state of Section 702 since its recent reauthorization. To establish a historical context, Part II will lay out the general history of Section 702, its requirements, and the techniques the government has typically deployed under its authority. Part III will develop an account of the legislative history of the Reauthorization Act to highlight the keys issues of contention in public discourse concerning Section 702. Part IV will detail the key changes to Section 702 implemented by Congress. Part V will then describe the typical constitutional challenges to Section 702 prior to the Reauthorization Act and reassess the viability of those challenges in light of the key changes to the program. Finally, Part VI will conclude by offering positive developments and missed opportunities from the debates. Overall, this article seeks to emphasize that the responsibility to protect constitutional rights while simultaneously ensuring national security can at times feel like a herculean duty. However, this balance is often best struck on the front end when members of Congress are pressured to reform national security authorities rather than rely on Executive agencies to utilize their surveillance tools according to a broad and often malleable legal standard. Nevertheless, this article argues that there are presently substantial avenues for litigants to challenge the newest changes to Section 702 under the Fourth Amendment.

I.   ORIGIN AND AUTHORITIES OF SECTION 702

A. Background of FISA and Section 702

It is useful to begin by differentiating between the two statutes under which the government can conduct electronic surveillance: Title III and FISA. Generally, Title III concerns electronic surveillance the government may deploy for criminal law enforcement purposes. FISA exists within the realm of foreign intelligence operations and was enacted much later. But the clear line between the two is more an ideal than a reality.[34] Some of the core

---

[34] *USA Patriot Act Amendments to Foreign Intelligence Surveillance Act Authorities: Hearing Before the S. Select Comm. on* Intel., 109th Cong. (2005) (statements of U.S.

constitutional issues with Section 702 arise from the blurring of this boundary between foreign intelligence gathering and criminal investigation.[35] Unsurprisingly then, the onus for passing FISA—and ultimately expanding it under Section 702—develops out of the interplay between the boundaries set by Fourth Amendment electronic surveillance case law and flexibility needed to protect the nation.

The first case setting a substantive boundary was *Katz v. United States*. In that seminal case, the government introduced evidence obtained by "attach[ing] an electronic listening and recording device to the outside of the public telephone booth from which [the defendant] had placed his calls."[36] In a critical passage, Justice Stewart declared that "the Fourth Amendment protects people, not places" and that a physical intrusion into a protected area was not necessary to constitute a Fourth Amendment violation—privacy would be the new compass rose directing the analysis.[37] By overruling long-standing property-based precedent established in *Olmstead v. United States*,[38] the government could no longer conduct electronic surveillance without conforming to the privacy limits implied by the Fourth Amendment.[39] A court

---

Attorney General Alberto R. Gonzales & Robert S. Mueller, III, Director, FBI), https://www.govinfo.gov/content/pkg/CHRG-109shrg24983/html/CHRG-109shrg24983.htm ("the USA PATRIOT Act helped to bring down this 'wall' separating intelligence and law enforcement officials. They erased the perceived statutory impediment to more robust information sharing between intelligence and law enforcement personnel. They also provided the necessary impetus for the removal of the formal administrative restrictions as well as the informal cultural restrictions on information sharing").

[35] *See infra* Part IV.

[36] Katz v. United States, 389 U.S. 347, 348 (1967).

[37] *Id.* at 351.

[38] *See* Olmstead v. United States, 277 U.S. 438, 475 (1928) (stating "[i]t is not the breaking of his doors, and the rummaging of his drawers, that constitutes the essence of the offense; but it is the invasion of his indefeasible right of personal security, personal liberty and private property . . . ").

[39] Coincidentally, the Supreme Court would once again reintroduce the topic of property into its Fourth Amendment analysis with United States v. Jones, 565 U.S. 400 (2012). However, for all intents and purposes, absent a violation of an individual's property rights, the *Katz* two-pronged test remains the main way to evaluate whether a Fourth Amendment "search" occurred. Given that most electronic surveillance

would be forced to focus on personal privacy by asking: 1) Did a person intend their effects to be private? (subjective question); and 2) Is society prepared to recognize that subjective expectation of privacy as reasonable? (objective question)[40] If both questions can be answered in the affirmative, a constitutionally recognized "search" occurs, implicating the Fourth Amendment.

These questions were much more onerous for law enforcement to answer than whether a physical intrusion of property occurred. Consequently, Congress passed Title III of the 1968 Omnibus Crime Control and Safe Streets Act to hedge investigative misconduct by requiring more particularized judicial warrants to obtain electronic surveillance for law enforcement purposes.[41] As such, these warrants were much more thorough than a regular search warrant would require.[42] But it was not until 1967 that these higher standards were put to another test when the Supreme Court was presented with the question of electronic surveillance in the national security context. In *United States v. U.S. District Court (Keith)*,[43] the Court recognized that national security cases often "reflect a convergence of First and Fourth Amendment values not present in cases of 'ordinary' crime. Though the investigative duty of the Executive may be stronger in such cases, so also is there greater jeopardy to constitutionally protected speech."[44] In balancing interests, the Court rejected any arguments about an exception for special circumstances,[45]

---

neither physically intrudes on property nor impairs an individual's use of such property, electronic surveillance remains wholly within the realm of *Katz*.

[40] *See Katz*, 389 U.S. at 361.

[41] Omnibus Crime Control and Safe Streets Act of 1968, Pub. L. No. 90-351, §§ 801–804, 82 Stat. 197 (1968).

[42] SCOTT M. MATHESON, JR., PRESIDENTIAL CONSTITUTIONALISM IN PERILOUS TIMES 109 (2009) (citing 18 U.S.C.A. §§ 2516, 2518 (West 2000 & Supp. 2007)).

[43] 407 U.S. 297 (1972).

[44] *Id.* at 313.

[45] *Id.* at 320 (providing, in relevant part, that "[t]he Government argues that the special circumstances applicable to domestic security surveillances necessitate a further exception to the warrant requirement. . . . The circumstances described do not justify complete exemption of domestic security surveillance from prior judicial scrutiny. Official surveillance, whether its purpose be criminal investigation or ongoing intelligence gathering, risks infringement of constitutionally protected privacy of speech. Security surveillances are especially sensitive because of the

holding instead that "Fourth Amendment freedoms cannot properly be guaranteed if domestic security surveillances may be conducted solely within the discretion of the Executive."[46] A judicial warrant would be required to electronically surveil *domestic* targets, even for national security purposes.

But the Court explicitly reserved judgement "on the scope of the President's surveillance power with respect to the activities of *foreign powers*, within or without this country" (emphasis added).[47] The Court stressed that the President had a duty under Article II, Section 1 of the Constitution "to protect our Government against those who would subvert or overthrow it by unlawful means."[48] This passage left open the possibility that the government need not be constrained when surveilling foreign targets. In absence of any direction, a number of lower courts looked to fill out the doctrine. The Third, Fourth, Fifth, and Ninth Circuits all held that a warrant was not necessary when surveilling foreign targets so long as the Executive branch could certify that foreign intelligence was the object of the surveillance.[49]

The *Troung Dinh Hung* court explained that "because of the need of the Executive branch for flexibility, its practical experience, and its constitutional competence, the courts should not require the Executive to secure a warrant each time it conducts foreign intelligence surveillance."[50] But there were three conditions: 1) "the object of the search or surveillance [had] to be a foreign power" because in those circumstances the need for stealth and speed were so great that the judiciary would have difficulty with the "subtle judgements

---

inherent vagueness of the domestic security concept, the necessarily broad and continuing nature of intelligence gathering, and the temptation to utilize such surveillances to oversee political dissent. We recognize, as we have before, the constitutional basis of the President's domestic security role, but we think it must be exercised in a manner compatible with the Fourth Amendment. In this case we hold that this requires an appropriate prior warrant procedure.").

[46] *Id.* at 316.

[47] *Id.* at 308.

[48] *Id.*

[49] *See* United States v. Troung Dinh Hung, 629 F.2d 908, 913 (4th Cir. 1980); United States v. Buck, 584 F2d 871, 875 (9th Cir. 1977); United States v. Butenko, 494 F.2d 593, 604–605 (3d Cir. 1974) (en banc); United States v. Brown, 484 F.2d 418, 426 (5th Cir. 1973).

[50] *Truong Dinh Hung,* 629 F.2d at 914.

about foreign and military affairs"; 2) the primary purpose of the search had to be to collect foreign intelligence (as opposed to prosecution), otherwise "courts are entirely competent to make the usual probable cause determination"; and 3) the search had to be reasonable according to the facts and circumstances of the case.[51]   Behind this reasoning was an acknowledgement—similar to the theoretical underpinnings of the political question doctrine[52]—that courts are not competent to evaluate the intricacies of Executive branch policies, and in this context, the Executive branch's needs and methods for collecting foreign intelligence. Courts could not make a judgement on a warrant in this context, even if *Katz* factors were implicated to protect citizens' privacy interests.

The tension between trusting judges to make a warrant evaluation for surveillance of domestic intelligence gathering (i.e., *Keith*), but not trusting them in the foreign intelligence context (i.e., *Troung Dinh Hung*) was not lost on the D.C. Circuit in *Zweibon v. Mitchell*.[53] One would assume that if national security concerns are implicated in both cases, a judge would be either competent or incompetent in both, even if citizen privacy concerns are arguably more significant in the former than the latter.[54] The *Mitchell* court posited that the explanation for the incongruity originates from an argument that the "President's preeminent power over the conduct of foreign affairs" under Article II, Section 2 permits surveillance without a warrant.[55] But the

---

[51] *Id.* at 915–16.

[52] *See* Baker v. Carr, 369 U.S. 186, 211 (1962) (providing, in relevant part, "Foreign relations: There are sweeping statements to the effect that all questions touching foreign relations are political questions. Not only does resolution of such issues frequently turn on standards that defy judicial application or involve the exercise of a discretion demonstrably committed to the executive or legislature; but many such questions uniquely demand single-voiced statement of the Government's views.").

[53] 516 F.2d 594 (D.C. Cir. 1975).

[54] *Id.* at 624 (providing, in relevant part, "'Judicial competence': Although the judicial competence factor arguably has more force when made in the foreign rather than the domestic security context, the response of *Keith* to the analogous argument is nevertheless pertinent to any claim that foreign security involves decisions and inform-ation beyond the scope of judicial expertise and experience.").

[55] *Id.* at 615–16 (providing, in relevant part, that "[t]o be sure, the fact that the *Keith* Court found the President's powers with respect to domestic affairs   insufficient to justify an exception to the warrant requirement when the domestic aspects of national

court refused to hold that this power necessarily "preordain[s] the procedures [or lack thereof] with which the President must comply in exercising that authority."[56] The court laid out the numerous arguments against judicial competence,[57] rejecting them all by relying on *Keith* for the notion that even in the foreign intelligence context, courts so regularly deal in complex domestic matters that such surveillance issues cannot be too complicated for judges to comprehend.[58] "If the threat is too subtle or complex for our senior law enforcement officers to convey its significance to a court, one may question whether there is probable cause for surveillance."[59] The court went on to discuss the possibility of security leaks, the nature of ongoing foreign surveillance, the possibility of dangerous delay in following a warrant process, and the administrative burden on the Executive branch when applying for these warrants.[60] None of these were considered compelling.[61]

This circuit split over Title III authority in the context of foreign intelligence surveillance embodied two broad debates. First, would complying with Fourth Amendment requirements so substantially handicap the Executive as to seriously infringe on the effectiveness of Article II, Section 1 and 2 powers? This debate was the objective dispute between courts in *Troung Dinh Hung* and *Mitchell*, which disagreed over the extent to which the warrant process would lead to leaks, delays, and administrative burdens that would undercut the ability of the government to collect critical foreign intelligence.[62] Second, the more subjective and theoretical issue dealt with the

---

security are involved, yet refused to specify what   procedures would be entailed if the national security threat had its origin with foreign powers, indicates that any difference in result must turn on the   President's peculiar powers in the field of foreign affairs.").

[56] *Id.* at 616.

[57] *Id.* at 641 (describing security leaks, the ongoing nature of foreign surveillance, administrative burden, etc.)

[58] *Id.* at 641–46.

[59] *Id.* at 641 (citing United States v. United States District Court (Keith), 407 U.S. 297, 320 (1972)).

[60] *Id.* at 641.

[61] *Id.*

[62] *Compare Truong Dinh Hung*, 629 F.2d at 913 (providing that, for example, "[a] warrant requirement would add a procedural hurdle that would reduce the flexibility of executive foreign intelligence initiatives, in some cases delay executive response to

possibility that even if such handicapping were to occur, civil liberties should nonetheless prevail over national security effectiveness in the foreign intelligence context, even where an exception for special circumstances to the Fourth Amendment might be present. This was the view that the *Keith* court refused to address. These two debates remain relevant for Section 702 today.

At the time, the Supreme Court did not have to work through these boundaries because Congress stepped to the fore.[63] A series of stunning political developments indicated that pure deference to national security concerns in the foreign surveillance context might be dangerous. In 1975, the Church Committee began investigating instances where "warrantless electronic surveillance ostensibly deployed for national security had been seriously abused. For decades Executive agencies had been secretly monitoring American citizens."[64] For example, President Nixon's White House spied on political opponents as part of the Watergate Scandal and the CIA conducted intelligence collection against domestic dissidents opposing the Vietnam war.[65] These overt abuses were punctuated by subtler—but no less sinister—intrusions for the sake of gathering foreign intelligence.

---

foreign intelligence threats, and increase the chance of leaks regarding sensitive executive operations.") *with Mitchell*, 516 F.2d at 641 (finding that being "mindful of the fact that the existence of presidential powers . . . does not preclude a finding that the legitimate exercise of those powers would in no way be frustrated by subjecting them to prior judicial approval," and that of the factors that had been asserted —judicial competence, leaks, intelligence gathering not implicating the Fourth Amendment, delay that would result in substantial harm to the national security, or undue administrative burden—none were compelling).

[63] "Whether Congress has considered and authorized [an action] . . . is not irrelevant to its constitutionality. The endorsement of the Legislative Branch of government provides some degree of comfort in the face of concerns about the reasonableness of the government's assertions [about a program.]" ACLU v. Clapper, 785 F.3d 787, 824 (2d Cir., 2015). This suggests that when Congress acts before the judiciary to permit an Executive action in the national security space, the judiciary is more likely to honor it. This is especially pertinent in the FISA context, as it is often the case that Congress responds to negative public opinion or negative dicta with legislative changes before judicial review.

[64] MATHESON, *supra* note 42, at 109.

[65] ELIZABETH GOITEIN & FAIZA PATEL, BRENNAN CENTER FOR JUSTICE, WHAT WENT WRONG WITH FISA 13 (2015).

"Between 1953 and 1973, the CIA checked more than 28 million letters (mostly to and from the Soviet Union) against a watch list, and opened 200,000."[66] A program called Project Shamrock, lasting 30 years, featured the NSA acquiring telegrams sent by American citizens—up to 150,000 messages a month.[67] These revelations precipitated the passage of FISA in 1978 as a solution to the problem.[68]

Congress seemed to reject the notion that the Executive's Article II, Section 1 and 2 authorities gave it unilateral ability to conduct foreign surveillance. Rather, "Congress agreed that a special scheme was necessary for foreign intelligence surveillance conducted at home, but placed strict limits on such surveillance to ensure that it would not be used to suppress domestic dissent or to evade the warrant requirement in ordinary cases."[69] The procedural framework of FISA's protections are detailed below, but it cut the difference between substantially handicapping the Executive with a full range of procedural requirements and awarding maximal flexibility to further the IC's collection goals.[70] Consequently, a full criminal warrant would not be required for foreign intelligence surveillance, but less onerous oversight would be imposed. Under FISA, the government needs to obtain a FISC order in an ex parte proceeding, which certifies that there is probable cause that a

---

[66] *Id.*

[67] *Id.*

[68] *See* MATHESON, *supra* note 42, at 109 (providing, in relevant part, that "[t]he Church Committee stressed the lack of congressional guidelines for agencies such as the NSA. Responding to the need for a statutory framework, Congress passed the FISA in 1978 to regulate electronic surveillance of foreign intelligence information in the United States.").

[69] GOITEIN & PATEL, *supra* note 65, at 14. The Chairman of the Church Committee cautioned that "[i]f the government ever became a tyranny, if a dictator ever took charge in this country, the technological capacity that the intelligence community has given the government could enable it to impose total tyranny, and there would be no way to fight back because the most careful effort to combine together in resistance to the government, no matter how privately it was done, is within the reach of the government to know. Such is the capability of this technology." *Id.* (quoting NBCUniversal Archives, *The Intelligence Gathering Debate – www.NBCUniversal Archives.com,* YOUTUBE (Jan. 23, 2014), https://www.youtube.com/watch?v=YAG1N4a84Dk (statement of Sen. Frank Church)).

[70] *See generally* Part II.

target of surveillance is a "foreign power" or "agent of a foreign power" and that the specific site being electronically surveilled is equally connected to a foreign power.[71] With this nexus to foreign powers established by such an individualized probable cause standard, the government need only demonstrate a "significant purpose" of collecting foreign intelligence to be awarded a surveillance order.[72] Such a test does not preclude the government from seeking a surveillance order to also pursue criminal prosecution, but the framework's requirement that the government demonstrate probable cause that the target is linked to a foreign power was probable cause requirement linked to foreign powers initially enough to permit flexible use of FISA while preventing its abuse to easily prosecute American citizens. Yet with changes in technology since 1978, the boundaries broke down. Scholars note that:

> Although the Supreme Court in *Keith* attempted to distinguish between surveillance of domestic organizations and surveillance of foreign powers, the demarcation was never clean and has become even more strained. Advances in technology mean that the exercise of authorities aimed at foreigners abroad inevitably picks up swaths of information about Americans who should enjoy constitutional protections. But rather than develop additional safeguards for this information, the law has developed in the opposite direction: the government's authority to collect communications pursuant to its foreign intelligence gathering authorities has expanded significantly.[73]

Indeed, the very act of differentiating the surveillance of foreign powers from Title III eventually exacerbated the above issue. Drawing on *Troung Dinh Hung*, FISA "allowed the government to obtain surveillance orders if it certified that the 'purpose' of surveillance was the acquisition of foreign intelligence."[74] This primary purpose test created a "strong perception within

---

[71] 50 U.S.C. § 1805(a)(2)(B) (2012). FISA was amended to include physical searches, pen registers/trap and trace, and the seizure of other "tangible things" for the purpose of foreign intelligence collection, *see* 50 U.S.C. §§ 1821–29 (physical searches); §§ 1841–46 (pen register/trap and trace); §§ 1861 (access to business records for foreign intelligence investigations) (2008).

[72] 50 U.S.C. § 1804(a)(6)(B).

[73] GOITEIN & PATEL, *supra* note 65, at 19.

[74] *Id.* at 23.

the government that the procedures erected a 'wall' between intelligence and law enforcement that inhibited robust cooperation."[75] Incidental intelligence gathered through primary purpose FISA surveillance could not be shared with law enforcement to prosecute citizens, who are guaranteed robust Fourth Amendment protections detailed in Title III. Not only did advances in technology mean the government was inadvertently (or intentionally) collecting more information about Americans—information that would otherwise be protected in a Title III search—but law enforcement could not access information under the primary purpose test that could lead to the prosecution of terrorists.[76]

In the aftermath of 9/11, many in the government viewed this wall as unacceptable. President Bush responded by authorizing a counterterrorism program called the Terrorist Surveillance Program (TSP) in 2002. The New York Times broke the story detailing how the TSP permitted the "interception (i.e., wiretapping), without warrants, of telephone and email communications where one party to the communication is located outside the United States" and the NSA has a good reason to believe a connection to al-Qaeda existed.[77] To many, the program completely contravened even the minimal procedures of FISA and arguably violated the Fourth Amendment because it scrapped the foreign power requirement.[78] Instead, the government began surveilling without judicial review any U.S. person it believed was communicating with

---

[75] *Id.* at 24.

[76] *See* GOITEIN & PATEL, *supra* note 65, at 24 (providing, in relevant part, "There was a strong perception within the government that the [FISA] procedures erected a 'wall' between intelligence and law enforcement that inhibited robust cooperation"). This wasn't necessarily the impression of the 9/11 report, *see* THE NAT'L COMM'N ON TERRORIST ATTACKS UPON THE U.S., THE 9/11 COMMISSION REPORT 266–72 (2004). But it was enough for the DOJ to modify its procedures to allow FISA surveillance to be conducted under the laxer standard of "significant purpose" instead of "primary purpose" for acquiring foreign intelligence. The rationale was that the lower standard would allow more cooperation between law enforcement and the IC. This standard was challenged and upheld by the FISCR. *See* In re Sealed Case, 310 F.3d 717, 746 (FISA Ct. Rev. 2002).

[77] ACLU v. Nat'l Sec. Agency, 493 F.3d 644, 648 (6th Cir. 2007) (citing James Risen & Eric Lichthlau, *Bush Lets U.S. Spy on Callers Without Courts,* N.Y. TIMES (Dec. 16, 2005)).

[78] *See* ERIC LICHTBLAU, BUSH'S LAW 144, 226 (2008). *See also* ACLU v. Nat'l Sec. Agency, 438 F. Supp, 2d 754 (E.D. Mich. 2006).

a member of al-Qaeda abroad. Understandably, people feared a return to the pre-FISA days of government abuse; the public could not easily ascertain the extent any unreviewed foreign intelligence was being shared with law enforcement. And while the President reauthorized the program many times until 2007, the administration did not disclose much of the legal and operational components of the program—even to the PCLOB.[79] It later came to light that the government was again relying on Article II (harkening back to the question reserved in *Keith*) to argue the President had the authority to conduct this program under the Executive's responsibility to protect the country.[80] Even after the Bush administration assented to FISC oversight of the TSP, public outcry over the administration's specious arguments led to FISA Amendments precipitating Section 702.[81]

The administration convinced a Democratically-controlled Congress in 2007 and 2008 to create the FAA's system of "programmatic surveillance" by arguing that the rapidly digitalizing nature of communication required broader authorities for electronic communication in the war on terror.[82] Section 702 was created as a result. Under its authority, "government may conduct a program to collect any communications 'targeting' a person or entity's communications with Americans in the United States. In other words, the government no longer needs an individualized court order to acquire Americans' international calls and emails, as long as the American is not the 'target' of the surveillance."[83] While programmatic limits exist, Section 702's is the statutory version of the TSP and a paring back from FISA's original procedural safeguards against government abuse by foregoing the need for individualized orders focused on surveilling agents of foreign powers. Now,

---

[79] MATHESON, *supra* note 42, at 111.

[80] See DEP'T OF JUSTICE, LEGAL AUTHORITIES SUPPORTING THE ACTIVITIES OF THE NATIONAL SECURITY AGENCY DESCRIBED BY THE PRESIDENT 7–10 (2006), https://www.epic.org/privacy/terrorism/fisa/doj11906wp.pdf.

[81] *See, e.g.*, James Risen & Eric Lichtblau, *Bush Lets U.S. Spy on Callers Without Courts*, N.Y. TIMES (Dec. 16, 2005), https://www.nytimes.com/2005/12/16/politics/bush-lets-us-spy-on-callers-without-courts.html (describing pressure from inside and outside the administration to curtail the program).

[82] GOITEIN & PATEL, *supra* note 65, at 25–26.

[83] *Id.*

communicating with a foreigner abroad is enough to be caught up in the IC's foreign intelligence programs.

Consequently, the history of FISA embodies competing interests weighed by the case law of electronic surveillance. On the one hand, harkening back to *Keith* and *Troung Dinh Hun*, "different standards may be compatible with the Fourth Amendment if they are reasonable both in relation to the legitimate need of Government for intelligence information and the protected rights of our citizens."[84] But on the other hand, and in the context of uncertainty and government abuses, "FISA was essentially enacted to create a secure framework by which the Executive branch may conduct legitimate electronic surveillance for foreign intelligence while meeting our national commitment to the Fourth Amendment."[85] The issue can be distilled from the original *Keith* framework. There the Court believed that the *Katz* concerns about personal privacy were implicated much more significantly when a domestic person was the target of electronic surveillance compared to a foreign person.[86] As such, Executive responsibilities to provide for the nation's safety and direct foreign affairs were significant enough to recognize flexible oversight requirements in the foreign intelligence context. Courts and Congress were comfortable comporting them with the Fourth Amendment. However, when technology advances and massive amounts of data can be collected in the process, the line blurs to such an extent that citizen privacy concerns may be equally implicated when foreign powers are targeted. The *Keith* framework begins to crumble, but not concerns about giving the Executive flexibility to accomplish its Article II responsibilities. This trend is embodied by the push toward the original FISA's restrictions designed to combat abuse (while maintain government flexibility) and the pull from the Bush administration's TSP (that ultimately

---

[84] United States v. United States District Court (Keith), 407 U.S. 297, 322–23 (1972).

[85] ACLU v. Nat'l Sec. Agency, 438 F. Supp. 2d 754, 773 (E.D. Mich. 2006), *vacated*, 493 F.3d 644 (6th Cir. 2007) (reversed on standing grounds).

[86] *See* United States v. U.S. District Court (Keith), 407 U.S. 297, 308, 312 (1972) (holding that while "the instant case requires no judgment on the scope of the President's surveillance power with respect to the activities of foreign powers, within or without this country . . . [t]here is, understandably, a deep-seated uneasiness and apprehension that this capability will be used to intrude upon cherished privacy of law-abiding citizens.").

morphed into Section 702) to require more flexibility to adequately protect national security. This history is useful because it frames these conceptual battles ebb and flow concerning the nature of electronic intelligence surveillance for national security and its demands from competing interests. Section 702's development is therefore critical for understanding the stakes in the constitutional battles over the program's adherence to the First Amendment, Fourth Amendment, and Separation of Powers principles. And these stakes are increasingly higher as the nature of war and intelligence evolves. The core question is whether Section 702's new authorities tip the constitutional balance.

B. Authorities Under Section 702

Before addressing these new authorities, it is helpful to detail Section 702's original authorities to set a baseline for understanding its changes. Section 702 is programmatic, not individualized. Put differently, "the government no longer needs an individualized court order to acquire Americans' international calls or emails, as long as the American is not the 'target' of surveillance."[87]   Indeed, this is a major difference from typical FISA surveillance under which the government can only surveil foreign powers or agents of foreign powers (not just any foreigner abroad) for intelligence information under some semblance of probable cause.[88] The statute authorizes electronic surveillance of non-U.S. persons "reasonably believed" to be located outside the country.[89] The Attorney General (AG) and Director of National Intelligence (DNI) can jointly authorize such targeting for up to a year by procuring an order from the FISC (renewal is possible).[90] If the two determine

---

[87] GOITEIN & PATEL, *supra* note 65, at 26.

[88] 50 U.S.C. §§ 1801(a), et seq. (requiring a traditional FISA search to render some showing of probable cause that the target is a foreign power or agent   of a foreign power — including the specific facilities and/or persons to be searched. Section 702 does away with this specificity and individualized   determinations.   Rather, a major restriction is that the target of a Section 702 search has to be reasonably believed to be a foreigner abroad.).

[89] 50 U.S.C. § 1881a(a) (1978).

[90] *Id.*

exigent circumstances exist, then they can proceed without an order.[91] This exigency is limited to those situations where "without immediate implementation of an authorization . . . intelligence important to national security of the United States may be lost or not timely acquired . . . ."[92] In this case, surveillance can begin without a FISC order, but must be submitted to the FISC within no more than seven days.[93] If it becomes known that a non-U.S. person enters the country, the government has 72 hours to continue surveillance under a current order if discontinuing surveillance would threaten real harm.[94] In any case, when the government applies to the FISC for a Section 702 order, they are asking to implement a surveillance program, which must not intentionally target any person within the U.S.; target any U.S. person located outside the U.S.; or "acquire any communication as to which the sender and all intended recipients are known at the time of the acquisition to be located in the United States."[95] Finally, the program must comport with the Fourth Amendment and the Constitution.[96] To ensure these limits, the government must attest to certain targeting and minimization procedures that will decrease the likelihood of capturing the information of U.S. persons or those who reside in the U.S. First, the government must certify that a "significant purpose" of the surveillance is to capture foreign intelligence information.[97] Second, that this intelligence is being captured with the cooperation of electronic service providers with whom the government must coordinate.[98] Third, "the targeting procedures must ensure that the program's targets are indeed 'reasonably believed' to be foreigners overseas, while the minimization procedures must be 'reasonably designed' to minimize the collection and retention—and prohibit the sharing—of Americans'

---

[91] *Id.* § 1881a(c)(2).

[92] *Id.*

[93] *Id.* § 1881a(g)(1)(B).

[94] 50 U.S.C. § 1805(f) (1978).

[95] EDWARD C. LIU, CONG. RESEARCH SERV., R44457, SURVEILLANCE OF FOREIGNERS OUTSIDE THE UNITED STATES UNDER SECTION 702 OF THE FOREIGN INTELLIGENCE SURVEILLANCE ACT (FISA) 2 (2016); § 1881a(b).

[96] *Id.* § 1881a(b)(6).

[97] *Id.* § 1881a(h)(2)(A)(v).

[98] *Id.* § 1881a(h)(2)(A)(v)(i).

information."[99] All of this is to prevent so-called "reverse targeting" whereby the government uses Section 702 to collect information about a foreigner abroad, but really wishes to target a particular known person in the U.S.[100]

The tools at the disposal of the government under Section 702 are both astonishing in scale and in technological development. In 2013, a FISC report detailed that the NSA "collected 250 million Internet communications per year under Section 702."[101] The government can collect this information using many methods. First, the government can tap into "upstream" facilities.[102] These facilities are the infrastructural "backbone" of the Internet and telephone networks.[103] They include fiber cables, switches, undersea cables, and other critical junctions.[104]

As data passes through them, the NSA applies complex algorithms to determine if they contain certain targeted information (while applying minimization standards).[105] For example, the NSA could filter for an email address from a foreigner abroad. It would pick up emails sent to and from that email address (i.e., To/From Collection) and emails between non-targets who mention the target (i.e., "About" Collection).[106] "About" Collection is highly controversial because it can pick up the contents of U.S. person communications that are simply about or mention a target foreigner located abroad. This collection method was eventually (and perhaps only temporarily) ended by the NSA despite the government arguing for its

---

[99] GOITEIN & PATEL, *supra* note 65, at 26; §§ 1881a(d)(1)(A), 1881a(e)(1), 1801(h)(1).

[100] GOITEIN & PATEL, *supra* note 65, at 26.

[101] LIU, *supra* note 95, at 1.

[102] *See* Memorandum Opinion, No. [REDACTED], slip op. at 22–23 (FISA Ct. Oct. 3, 2011), http://www.dni.gov/files/documents/0716/October-2011-Bates-Opinion-and%20Order-20140716.pdf.

[103] *See* Kris, *supra* note 18, at 9 (discussing ". . . the international switches or other backbone facilities . . ." through which communications transit).

[104] *See* Kris, *supra* note 18, at 9–10, 24–45 (discussing the network of cables that makes up the backbone of telecommunications networks).

[105] *See* Kris, *supra* note 18, at 9–10 (discussing how the NSA finds targeted information during "upstream" collection and applies minimization standards.)

[106] Kris, *supra* note 18, at 9.

permissibility under the Constitution.[107] Controversy also exists as to whether the government can store and later search unminimized data (i.e., before the approved search algorithms are applied). This storage could allow the government to search incidental data for related (or unrelated) law enforcement purposes—all without adequate Fourth Amendment procedures. This technique is colloquially known as "backdoor searching."[108] It is possible to conduct backdoor searches with U.S. persons data obtained using "about" collection.[109]

The government can also use Section 702 for "downstream" collection, colloquially known as PRISM collection.[110] Here the government works with Internet Service Providers (ISPs), like Google, to retrieve data that likely contains foreign intelligence information. ISPs will either send this data along on their own fruition or respond periodically based on search algorithms the government gives them which are pre-approved by the FISC. This is especially helpful for data that passes through upstream facilities encrypted

---

[107] The NSA stopped "about" collection "to resolve problems it was having complying with special rules imposed by the [FISC] in 2011 to protect Americans' privacy. . . . The problem stemmed from certain bundled messages that internet companies sometimes packaged together and transmitted as a unit. If even one of them had a foreign target's email address somewhere in it, all were sucked in. . . . The NSA was having technical difficulties figuring out a way to deal with bundled packages" and so stopped collection to comply with the goals set out by the FISC with regard to the bundles. *See* Quinta Jurecic, *NSA Stops "About" Collection, Lawfare* (Apr. 28, 2017, 2:14 PM), https://www.lawfareblog.com/nsa-stops-about-collection.

[108] Kris, *supra* note 18, at 12–13.

[109] *See* Neema Singh Guliani, *Congress Just Passed a Terrible Surveillance Law. Now What?* ACLU (Jan. 18 2018), https://www.aclu.org/blog/national-security/privacy-and-surveillance/congress-just-passed-terrible-surveillance-law-now (suggesting that "the NSA conducts over 30,000 of these "backdoor" searches a year and, while the FBI refuses to report their number, we know they perform these searches routinely when investigating a crime, assessing whether they should open an investigation, or even just hunting for information about foreign affairs.").

[110] LIU, *supra* note 95, at 1. PRISM was the program revealed by Edward Snowden's disclosures, *see supra* note 107.

but becomes unencrypted upon reaching an ISP.[111]   Most Section 702 intelligence comes from this type of collection method.[112]

C. Separating Theory from Practice

On the surface, the authority under Section 702 is designed to capture Signals Intelligence (SIGINT)[113] communications from foreigners abroad. It echoes the original differentiation focus in *Keith*: by only concentrating on foreigners abroad, American constitutional privacy concerns are not heavily implicated, and the government is afforded maximum flexibility. As such, the government does not need an individualized court order every time it chooses to surveil a foreigner abroad, even if such surveillance incidentally picks up on a U.S. person's communications. Rather, the FISC need only approve of the programmatic design of a SIGINT program—it does not need to know who

---

[111] *See* Siobhan Gorman & Jennifer Valentino, *New Details Show Broader NSA Surveillance Reach*, WALL ST. J. (Aug. 13, 2013), https://www.wsj.com/articles/new-details-show-broader-nsa-surveillance-reach-1377044261 (describing the process of NSA downstream collection and queries involved); *see also* Barton Gellman & Ashkan Soltani, *NSA Infiltrates Links to Yahoo, Google Data Centers Worldwide, Snowden Documents Say*, WASH. POST (Oct. 30, 2013), https://www.washingtonpost.com/world/national-security/nsa-infiltrates-links-to-yahoo-google-data-centers-worldwide-snowden-documents-say/2013/10/30/e51d661e-4166-11e3-8b74-d89d714ca4dd_story.html?utm_term=.9dcb79c831da (describing what the Snowden leaks revealed about NSA surveillance programs).

[112] LIU, *supra* note 95, at 1 ("The NSA collected 250 million Internet communications per year under 702. Of these communications, 91% were acquired 'directly from Internet Service Providers,' using a mechanism referred to as PRISM collection. The other 9% were acquired through what the NSA calls "upstream collection," meaning acquisition while Internet traffic is in transit from one unspecified location to another."). Note how staggering this number is—if only 1% of the 250 million included communications with Americans, that would be 2.5 million Americans indirectly surveilled.

[113] LIU, *supra* note 95, at 2 ("Acquisitions under Section 702 are also geared towards electronic communications or electronically stored information. This is because the certification supporting acquisition . . . requires the AG and DNI to attest that, among other things, the acquisition involves obtaining information from or with the assistance of an electronic communication service provider.").

or what specifically the government plans to surveil.[114] At its framing, this design was viewed as sufficient to prevent the government from abusing its foreign surveillance authorities to spy on Americans as they did in the pre-FISA era. Theoretically, the balancing seems correct. There should be a lot of flexibility for a type of surveillance that does not per se pose much harm to American privacy interests.

In practice, collection of electronic communications to or from Americans is increasingly beyond incidental.[115] Section 702 represents such a stark change from original FISA authority because it "eliminates [an individualized] court order requirement for the domestic capture of foreigners' communications with Americans."[116] So long as the surveillance has a significant purpose (how big is "significant"?), of acquiring foreign intelligence from a foreigner abroad, it would seem that any communications to or from a U.S. person is fair game to be collected without an individualized warrant typical of the Title III process. For any particular SIGINT program, the government might have another "significant purpose" of prosecuting terrorists. Under this framework, the warrantless intelligence collected under Section 702 could theoretically be used to prosecute an American whose communications were "incidentally" collected. Indeed, some argue that "the legislative history makes clear that facilitating the capture of communications to, from, or about U.S. persons was a primary purpose, if not the primary purpose of the FAA."[117] The potential for these end-runs around the Fourth Amendment are only exacerbated by the fact that unlike previous iterations of

---

[114] GOITEIN & PATEL, *supra* note 65, at 27 ("Under Section 702 . . . the court has no role in approving individual instructions at all.").

[115] *Id.* at 26 ("The existence of targeting and minimization requirements, as well as a reverse targeting prohibition, has enabled the government to portray Section 702 as a program designed to capture the communications of non-U.S. persons abroad . . . . With the exception of e-mails stored in the United States, [Section 702] had no impact on the government's ability to collect the communications of foreigners with other foreigners. The sea change that the statute brought about was the elimination of the court order requirement for the domestic capture of foreigners' communications with Americans.").

[116] *Id.*

[117] *Id.*

FISA, the government can surveil any non-U.S. person overseas, not just those reasonably believed to be an agent of a foreign power.[118]

With the sheer amount information collectable under the program, the efficacy of 702 was certainly on the mind of Congress as Section 702 was set to expire in 2017 without reauthorization.

II. REAUTHORIZATION DEBATES

The debates to reauthorize and amend Section 702 embodied a fundamental question. Representative Barbara Lee (D-CA) framed it by quoting Alexander de Tocqueville, saying "the reason democracies invariably prevail in military conflict is because democracy is the governmental form that best rewards and encourages those traits that are indispensable to success: initiative, innovation, courage, and love of justice."[119] The extent that Section 702 could be improved to forward these ends was the conceptual dispute at the heart of the reauthorization debates. Indeed, the opportunity for disagreement on this front was varied—at least four different bills and various individual amendments were proposed.[120] All sought to provide its own theory. Is a more flexible, extensive Section 702 the answer to promoting the innovation and initiative of the IC to keep our country safe? Or should the country have the courage and love of justice to handicap the useful tools of foreign surveillance to ensure our liberties were preserved? How would Congress strike a balance "between our cherished liberties and smart security?"[121] The

---

[118] *Id.* at 27 (["The court's] substantive role is limited to determining whether generic sets of targeting and minimizations procedures comply with the statute . . . and with the Fourth Amendment. The Court is not even informed of the specific targets of surveillance or the facilities to be surveilled, let alone asked to approve them. And the court may not review the substance of the government's certifications, including its certification of a significant foreign intelligence purpose, even for 'clear error.'"). This review should be compared with the more robust Title III and regular FISA authorities.

[119] 164 CONG. REC. H146 (daily ed. Jan. 11. 2018) (statement of Rep. Jackson Lee).

[120] *See* USA Liberty Act of 2017, H.R. 3989, 115th Cong. (2017); FISA Amendments Reauthorization Act of 2017, S. 2010, 115th Cong. (2017); FISA Amendments Reauthorization Act of 2017, H.R 4478, 115th Cong. (2017); USA Rights Act, S. 1997, 115th Cong. (2017); USA Rights Act, H.R. 4124, 115th Cong. (2017).

[121] 164 CONG. REC. H146–47 (daily ed. Jan. 11, 2018) (statement of Rep. Lee).

answers were far from clear. The reauthorization debates were so pivotal because it was not evident that Section 702 would be reauthorized—let alone expanded—given the above privacy concerns. A focus on the legislative history illuminates the critical considerations at play.

Debates over reauthorizing Section 702 began to foment with the 2017 nomination of then-Congressman Mike Pompeo (R-KS) to be the CIA Director. Congress was already acutely aware that the 2012 reauthorization for Section 702 was set to sunset at the end of the year. Additionally, Section 702 had been "the focus of ceaseless criticism from a politically diverse group of opponents who insist[ed] that it transcends constitutional bounds and represents the harbinger of an Orwellian surveillance state: charges that reached a crescendo in the aftermath of the disclosures by Edward Snowden in 2013."[122] With this context in mind, Congress took the nomination as an opportunity to have "an open discussion about the future of the CIA," which included the IC's intelligence collection capabilities, even though Section 702 has much more to do with the NSA's collection methods than the CIA.[123] In a long speech, Senator Ron Wyden (D-OR), who would later introduce The USA Rights Act, criticized the Pompeo nomination—detailing his support for wide ranging metadata and "about" collection programs.[124] Troubled by Representative Pompeo's belief in a "broader and more flexible [standard of surveillance] than the standard that currently applies to Section 702," Senator Wyden keyed up his issue with Section 702 as one concerned with the primary purpose standard and backdoor searches.[125] Other senators who opposed Representative Pompeo did so on similar grounds. Senators Tom Udall (D-NM), Jon Tester (D-MT), and Chris Van Hollen (D-MD) all spoke out, using the nomination debates as a proxy to voice their concern about backdoor searches and how "the Constitution limits how much intelligence agencies

---

[122] George W. Croner, *Terrorists, America is Still Listening: Section 702 is Alive and Well*, FOREIGN POL'Y RESEARCH INST. (Jan. 22, 2018), https://www.fpri.org/article/2018/01/terrorists-america-still-listening-section-702-alive-well/#_ftn8.

[123] 163 CONG. REC. S367–84 (daily ed. Jan. 23, 2017).

[124] *Id* at S373–76 (statement of Sen. Wyden).

[125] *Id.*

and the government can intrude into the lives of Americans."[126] Senator
Bernie Sanders (D-VT) even described Section 702 as a tool for "Big Brother"
to abuse, and called for amending the program to keep its effectiveness, but
"without invading the privacy rights of the American people."[127] Those who
supported Representative Pompeo did so on typical grounds—citing his
background and accomplishments.[128]   Others chose to engage with their
colleagues' concerns. Notably, Senator James Lankford (R-OK) reminded his
colleagues that the "CIA has strict prohibitions from gathering data on U.S.
persons"—implying that the issue lies with the information sharing of
warrantless intelligence between the IC and law enforcement, not on the scope
by which the IC can collect intelligence.[129] Narrowing the issue on backdoor
searches seemed pervasive across the aisle.

Although Representative Pompeo was confirmed relatively easily,[130] the
surveillance issues through which many opposed his nomination were just
beginning to brew. By March 1, 2017 the full Judiciary Committee was hearing
testimony on Section 702 from various IC agencies.[131] Again, Senator Wyden
led the floor discussion, this time highlighting concerns about "targeting
mistakes," "about" collection, and the implications of upstream/downstream
collection—namely "you don't even have to be communicating with one of
the government's targets to be swept up . . . law abiding Americans who have
done absolutely nothing wrong, both overseas and in the United States can
have their communications collected."[132] Ultimately, Senator Wyden called
for more information to assess the privacy impact of Section 702 and whether
"liberty and security are not mutually exclusive":[133]

> Should there be safeguards against reverse targeting?   Should
> Congress legislate on "upstream" collection and collection of

---

[126] *Id.* at S379–81.

[127] *Id.* at S382–83 (statement of Sen. Sanders).

[128] *Id.* at S385 (statement of Sen. Wyden).

[129] *Id.* at S383 (statement of Sen. Lankford).

[130] 164 CONG. REC. S385 (daily ed. Jan. 23, 2017) (passed 66 to 32 with bipartisan
support).

[131] 163 CONG. REC. D212 (daily ed. Mar. 1, 2017).

[132] 163 CONG. REC. S1814–17 (daily ed. Mar. 15, 2017) (statement of Sen. Wyden).

[133] *Id.* at S1817.

> communications about targets which raises unique concerns about
> the collection of the communications of law-abiding Americans? Are
> the rules related to dissemination, use, and retention of these
> communications adequate? Should there be limits on the use of these
> communications by the FBI for non-intelligence purposes?[134]

With the debate keyed up along these lines, Congress began to experiment. In the House, Representative Tulsi Gabbard (D-HI) introduced legislation to amend FISA to "codify the prohibition on the acquisition of 'about' communications under Section 702."[135] Her bill, H.R. 2588, never made it out of committee.[136] Conversely, Senator Tom Cotton (R-AR)—long a supporter of FISA—introduced a bill "that would reauthorize Section 702 permanently, as it is, with no changes."[137] In his view, concerns about Section 702 were exaggerated: "we can't tie the hands of our national security officials at the precise moment that our enemies are taking the gloves off," suggesting that "if you are concerned about protecting Americans' privacy rights, then you should support extending 702 [given its host] of privacy protections."[138] His bill, S. 1297, also never made it out of committee.[139] Clearly, neither a band-aid fix nor the status quo would do, even though AG Jeff Sessions and DNI Daniel Coats requested reauthorization "without amendment beyond removing the sunset provision."[140] In the months preceding reauthorization, a flurry of proposals flooded Congress.

The USA Liberty Act (H.R. 3989) was first introduced by the House Judiciary Committee. The bill "proposed a new framework of protections and transparency requirements to ensure that the government's use of Section 702

---

[134] *Id.*

[135] 164 CONG. REC. H4423 (daily ed. May 22, 2017).

[136] Summary: H.R. 2588 — 115th Congress (2017–2018), https://www.congress.gov/bill/115th-congress/house-bill/2588.

[137] 163 CONG. REC. S3296 (daily ed. Jun. 6, 2017) (statement of Sen. Cotton).

[138] *Id.*

[139] Summary: S. 1297 — 115th Congress (2017–2018), https://www.congress.gov/bill/115th-congress/senate-bill/1297.

[140] Letter from Attorney General Jefferson B. Sessions III and Director of National Intelligence Daniel R. Coats to Congressional Leadership (Sep. 7, 2017), https://www.justice.gov/opa/press-release/file/995661/download.

accords with principles of privacy and due process."[141] Among many reforms, the bill would require: a national security purpose to query data collected; law enforcement to receive individualized court orders based on probable cause to view the content of communications collected on a Section 702 program (excluding metadata), logging queries, and strengthening oversight. The bill would also ban "about" collection programs, improve the PCLOB and whistleblowing protections, and encourage the IC to share information among themselves and foreign allies.[142]

The FISA Amendments Reauthorization Act of 2017 (S. 2010) was introduced in the Senate within weeks of the USA Liberty Act. It took the opposite approach to scaling back Section 702. It would give permission to the IC to conduct "about" collection, pending a review of a formal DNI report and FISC certification for any resumed programs.[143] Nevertheless, the bill would prohibit the use of Section 702 intelligence for law enforcement purposes, except for certain serious enumerated offenses, mainly related to terrorism.[144] Perhaps most importantly, it would extend the ability to temporarily surveil U.S. citizens abroad without a FISC order in emergency situations if there was related exigency to surveil a connected non-U.S. person.[145]

The USA Rights Act (S. 1997) was Senator Wyden's proposed solution (a companion legislation was introduced in the House by Representative Zoe Lofgren (D-CA)) and featured perhaps the most radical paring back of Section 702. The bill would end backdoor searches by requiring a warrant for law enforcement to search for Section 702 intelligence.[146] Moreover, it would ban

---

[141] The USA Liberty Act of 2017, H.R. 3989, 115th Cong. (2017), https://judiciary.house.gov/wp-content/uploads/2017/10/100517-USA-Liberty-Act.pdf.

[142] *Id.*

[143] S. 2010, 115th Cong. § 3 (2017).

[144] *Id.* § 5.

[145] *Id.* § 6.

[146] The USA Rights Act One Pager, https://www.wyden.senate.gov/imo/media/doc/102017%20USA%20RIGHTS%20Act%20one-pager.pdf; *see also* Lawrence Husick, *The USA Rights Act: What's in There?* FOREIGN POLICY RESEARCH INSTITUTE (Nov. 1, 2017), https://www.fpri.org/2017/11/usa-right-act-what-in-there/ ("The bill reforms the present law by losing the "back door searches" loophole by prohibiting the government from searching through communications collected under

"about" collections in non-terrorism investigations and clarify that "reverse targeting" is prohibited (i.e., using Section 702 to target a foreigner, but really with the intention to access communications with a U.S. person).[147] The bill sought to "place stronger statutory limits on the use of unlawfully collected information" and require the FISC to have an appointed Constitutional Advocate to argue against the government.[148]

The FISA Amendments Reauthorization Act of 2017 (H.R. 4478) tracked closely with Senate version of the same name. In addition, it would require annual approval of querying procedures, publication of minimization procedures, "new procedures for unmasking Americans' names in intelligence reports," additional reporting requirements to Congress, and the temporary suspension of "about" collection pending Congressional review.[149] But it differed in its approach to querying procedures. Whereas the Senate bill would require the FBI to inform the FISC of any query hitting on U.S. persons as a way to guarantee consistency with the Fourth Amendment, the House bill would not require such an individualized approval but would provide the FBI with the opportunity to receive a FISC order based on standard probable cause.[150] Despite these differences, commentators were surprised that the bill also mirrored The USA Liberty Act in its minimization declassification

---

702 to deliberately conduct warrantless searches for the communications of specific Americans.").

[147] *Id.*

[148] *Id.*

[149] Loren Blinde, *House Intel Committee Introduces Section 702 Reauthorization Bill,* INTELLIGENCE COMMUNITY NEWS (Dec. 1, 2017),

http://intelligencecommunitynews.com/house-intel-committee-introduces-section-702-reauthorization-bill/.

[150] *See* George W. Croner, *The Gun Lap: FISA Renewal in the Homestretch* FOREIGN POLICY RESEARCH INSTITUTE (Dec. 6, 2017), https://www.fpri.org/article/2017/12/gun-lap-fisa-renewal-homestretch/ ("The SSCI bill, for example, includes a provision requiring that the FBI inform the FISC (within one business day) of any query that "returns information that concerns a known United States person . . .. The HPSCI bill takes a somewhat different route. There is no requirement that any form of individual query be cleared by the FISC; however, in those instances where a query of the Section 702 database is not designed to extract foreign intelligence information (i.e., is undertaken for law enforcement inquiries), the HPSCI bill furnishes the FBI with the option of applying for an order from the FISC . . ..").

procedures and mandating "specific procedures regulating the 'unmasking' of U.S. person identities [caught up in Section 702 surveillance] as part of a broadening of existing statutory minimization requirements."[151]

Between these four proposals, Congress had plenty of options for reforming Section 702 before its expiration date. Many other floor amendments were proposed,[152] but conceptually the USA Liberty and the USA Rights Act stood for a paring back of Section 702 authority whereas the dually named FISA Reauthorization Act bills arguably stood for the opposite.[153] Ultimately, the bill that became law was the product of reconciliation of the two FISA Reauthorization Act bills by the House and Senate Judiciary and Intelligence Committees. But given the Congresspersons' concerns about Fourth Amendment violations from "about," backdoor, and reverse targeting collection, what accounts for the ratcheting up of Section 702?

The legislative history suggests a complex story and hardly a partisan one.[154] The possibility for reform was most possible in the House where 58 Republicans and 125 Democrats voted for the USA Rights Act, whereas 65 Democrats joined 178 Republicans to vote for the bill (S. 139) that would become law.[155] Republicans who supported S. 139 believed that the USA Rights Act "would begin resurrecting the information-sharing walls between national security and law enforcement that the 9/11 Commission identified as a major factor in the failure to identify and thwart the 9/11 plot."[156] They believed S. 139 was "drafted in the spirit of the USA Liberty Act" and,

---

[151] *Id.*

[152] *See* Sarah Tate Chambers et. al., *FISA Section 702 Reauthorization Resource Page,* LAWFARE (Jan. 9, 2018), https://lawfareblog.com/fisa-section-702-reauthorization-resource-page.

[153] For a good comparison of the four bills, *see* George Croner, *The FISA Section 702 Saga: With Section 702 Expired, Where Do Things Go From Here?,* FOREIGN POL'Y RESEARCH INST. (Jan. 3, 2018), https://www.fpri.org/wp-content/uploads/2018/01/Croner-FISA-Bills-Table-2017-18.pdf.

[154] Indeed, the bill that became law, S. 139, began as the Rapid DNA Act—"a bill to expand the use of DNA in law enforcement." *See* GovTrack Summary of S. 139 (Jan. 14, 2018), https://www.govtrack.us/congress/bills/115/s139/summary (supporting that legislation evolves in complex ways).

[155] Croner, *supra* note 122.

[156] 164 CONG. REC. H143 (daily ed. Jan. 11, 2018) (statement of Rep. Stewart).

consequently, was a bipartisan solution that allayed privacy concerns.[157] For example, one Congressman thought the bill struck the right balance — "rather than ending 'abouts' [sic] collection . . . if NSA wants to reestablish 'abouts [sic] communication' collection, [the] NSA would first need to go back to court, [and] convince the judge that it has satisfied the court's concern."[158] Most Democrats did not agree. They argued that:

> S. 139 fails to address the core concerns of Members of Congress and the American public — the government's use of Section 702 information against United States citizens investigations that have nothing to do with national security. The warrant "requirement" contained in the bill is riddled with loopholes and applies only to fully predicated, official FBI investigations, not to the hundreds of thousands searches the FBI runs every day to run down a lead or check out a tip. S. 139 exacerbates existing problems with Section 702 by codifying so-called "about collection," a type of surveillance that was shut down after it twice failed to meet Fourth Amendment scrutiny. S. 139 is universally opposed by technology companies, privacy, and civil liberties groups across the political spectrum from the ACLU to FreedomWorks.[159]

A significant number of Republicans were apt to agree. Libertarian conservatives, some part of the House Freedom Caucus, were equally concerned about backdoor searches and "about" collections, urging their colleagues to force the government "to get a warrant [and] stay out of the house of communications."[160] Nevertheless, some Democrats believed "[they had] to come down in favor of honoring our Constitution and our civil liberties, but [could not] do that completely at the expense [of national security].[161] "They believed the USA Rights act "would disable 702."[162] Despite a last minute effort by Representatives Justin Amash (R-MI) and Zoe

---

[157] *Id.* at H145 (statement of Rep. Goodlatte).

[158] *Id.* at H143 (statement of Rep. Conaway).

[159] *Id.* at H146 (statement of Rep. Lee).

[160] *Id.* at H145 (statement of Rep. Poe).

[161] *Id.* at H148 (statement of Rep. Pelosi).

[162] *Id.* at H154 (statement of Rep. Goodlatte).

Lofgren (D-CA) to save the USA Rights Act, S. 139 prevailed to preserve most of the status quo and reject the best chance of Section 702 reform.[163]

Proceedings in the Senate followed in a similar fashion despite initial uncertainty resulting from a tweet by President Trump as to whether he supported S. 139.[164] Overall, the failure of major reform efforts is likely the result of a few trends. First, leadership in both the House and Senate opposed FISA reform. Notably, House Speaker Paul Ryan (R-WI) and Minority Leader Nancy Pelosi (D-CA) opposed the USA Rights Act, which likely helped whip up support for S. 139.[165] Second, of the 28 freshman Republicans elected to the House in the 2016 Trump wave, 24 voted for S. 139 in line with the White House's direction, which now seemed to give credence to the belief that the current Executive branch embraced Section 702 as a critical tool rather than

---

[163] *Id.* at H160 (recording failure to pass the Amash-Lofgren amendment).

[164] Martin Matishak, *Trump Undercuts White House Stance Hours before Critical Surveillance Vote*, POLITICO (Jan. 11, 2018, 9:21 AM EST; updated Jan. 11, 2018, 1:43 PM EST), https://www.politico.com/story/2018/01/11/trump-surveillance-fisa-vote-279321 (detailing how Trump made two contradictory tweets before the reauthorization vote, one indicating his desire for reforms to Section 702 and the other indicating he would like to proceed with the status quo. The confusions almost completely derailed the reauthorization vote.). In the Senate, 43 Republicans and 23 Democrats voted for S. 139. Despite discussion of potential filibuster, the Senate vote was far less contentious, *see* Ashley Killough & Ted Barrett, *After Unexpected   Scare, Senate Overcomes Filibuster and Advances FISA Extension Bill*, CNN (Jan. 16, 2018), https://www.cnn.com/2018/01/16/politics/senate-fisa-bill/index.html.

[165] Gopal Ratnam, *With House Passage of FISA Measure, Action Moves to Senate*, ROLLCALL (Jan. 11, 2018, 3:11 PM), https://www.rollcall.com/news/politics/house-passage-fisa-measure-action-moves-senate ("In an unusual alignment, House Speaker Paul D. Ryan   and Minority Leader Nancy Pelosi opposed the Amash-Lofgren amendment, saying that it would weaken intelligence agencies' ability to stop terror plots in a timely fashion.").

something to be feared.[166] Of the 27 freshman Democrats, 14 voted for S. 139.[167] Clearly, the 2016 elections ushered in new Congresspersons across the aisle who were sympathetic to a robust Section 702. Whereas the old guard, particularly Tea Party Republicans, were more sympathetic to the USA Rights Act. These new views might not have been dispositive to the result, but they certainly made the margin greater, perhaps to an extent that mounting a realistic reform effort was out of the question. Third, and relatedly, there is reason to believe that the last-minute vote on the USA Rights Act was engineered by Speaker Ryan as part of a compromise with more conservative Republicans. By allowing "one amendment with the changes the bill's opponents wanted to get a vote," but knowing full well the vote would fail, Speaker Ryan likely converted some Congresspersons on the fence to approve S. 139 "by at least giv[ing] these members the chance to say they got something," (i.e., floor time to speak their grievances to constituents and bemoan the failure of their preferred reform plan, while still letting them support national security with an affirmative vote on S. 139).[168] It does seem that members were flipped in this way when the roll-call votes for the USA Rights Act and S. 139 are compared.[169] At least in the Senate, members

---

[166] *See* White House Statement of Administration Policy – House Amendment to S. 139 (Jan. 9, 2018), https://www.whitehouse.gov/wp-content/uploads/2017/11/saps139hr_20180109.pdf (stating that "[i]f the House Amendment to S. 139 were presented to the President in its current form, his advisors would recommend that he sign the bill into law."). *Compare Newly elected members to the 115th Congress*, BALLOTPEDIA, https://ballotpedia.org/Newly_elected_members_to_the_115th_Congress *with* S. 139 Roll Call Vote (Jan. 11, 2018), http://clerk.house.gov/evs/2018/roll016.xml (showing the number of new members of Congress and comparing that to the roll call for votes on S. 139).

[167] S. 139 Roll Call Vote (Jan. 11, 2018), http://clerk.house.gov/evs/2018/roll016.xml.

[168] Deirdre Walsh & Ashley Killough, *House Passes FISA Reauthorization Despite Trump Tweet Criticizing the Program*, CNN (Jan. 11, 2018, 1:53 PM), https://www.cnn.com/2018/01/11/politics/fisa-house-vote-congress/index.html.

[169] Fifty-eight Republicans voted for the USA Rights Act when it was introduced. Only 45 voted against S. 139. This reduction suggests that 13 members both voted for The USA Rights Act and then voted for S. 139 after the USA Rights Act failed, or at least abstained in the S. 139 vote. *Compare* S. 139 Roll Call Vote, http://clerk.house.gov/evs/2018/roll016.xml, *with* The USA Rights Act Roll Call Vote, http://clerk.house.gov/evs/2018/roll014.xml.

switched positions on Section 702 easily, with Senator Feinstein being a notable example.[170]

Politics certainly matters. And the political currents of the 2016 election undoubtedly shaped Section 702's ultimate fate. But conceptually, the failure of major reform efforts can be placed into the historical push and pull of electronic surveillance described above. Not unlike the rhetoric deployed at the time the TSP was instituted, Congress was thinking about reforming Section 702 at a specific moment when terroristic threats seemed to be evolving. Frequently, Congresspersons reminded the public that the bombing "attacks like that in London are the new normal, [and] we have to be proactive . . . one way to be proactive and keep our country safe is to reauthorize section 702."[171]   Indeed, the democracy destroying purpose of ISIS featured prominently in the legislative debates—the example of Hajii Iman and Shawn Parsons's threat to civilian lives were highly relevant cases studies featuring the efficacy of robust Section 702.[172]   And against a threat which seeks to eliminate the very existence of democracy, not the typical foreign state actor, the reauthorization debates implicitly place a robust foreign surveillance tool like Section 702 as necessary, *a priori*, to ensuring a state even exists to create forum for civil liberties.[173]   But this view is one that is historically influenced.

---

[170] Evan Halper, *After Calling for Surveillance Reform, Democrats Help Kill It*, L.A. TIMES (Jan. 17, 2018, 11:40 AM PST), http://www.latimes.com/politics/la-na-pol-fisa-democrats-20180117-story.html ("Feinstein broke with privacy advocates from the right and left to cast a crucial vote in favor of leaving the program largely unchanged for the next six years. Feinstein's retreat back to a hawkish posture on Section 702 of the Foreign Intelligence Surveillance Act (FISA) gave supporters of the status quo the vote they needed to quell a growing movement in the Senate for more privacy protections.").

[171] 163 CONG. REC. S5826 (daily ed. Sep. 19, 2017) (statement of Sen. Cornyn).

[172] 164 CONG. REC. S227 (daily ed. Jan. 17, 2018) (statement of Sen. Cornyn).

[173] Indeed, this was a consideration of the *Keith* court when contemplating the efficacy of warrantless surveillance for domestic national security purposes: "Unless the Government safeguards its own capacity to function and preserve the security of its people, society itself could become so disordered that all rights and liberties might be endangered." *Keith*, 407 U.S. at 312; *see also* Cox v. New Hampshire, 312 U.S. 569, 574 (1941) ("Civil liberties, as guaranteed by the Constitution, imply the existence of an organized society maintaining public order without which liberty itself would be lost in the excesses of unrestrained abuses."). Nevertheless, the "recognition of these

When government abuses national security tools to make that forum impossible, *a posteriori*, the focus of the debate shifts to ask what principles the nation is actually protecting. To put it differently—and to paraphrase Benjamin Franklin—if we sacrifice liberty for national security, do we get neither? Or, if we sacrifice national security for liberty, do we also get neither? These questions are essentially the same but framed differently. And yet in different historical moments, the question is often asked in one way or another. This framing matters because it tilts the balance toward that which is being potentially sacrificed. The threat of ISIS, global terrorism, and the success of Section 702 placed civil liberty advocacy in the tough position of having to address the second framing: is national security worth sacrificing given these clear threats? But if these tools get abused, these advocates will benefit from being able to reframe the question and better reform Section 702 authorities. In the face of its enormous potential and success as a surveillance tool, 2017 was a difficult historical moment to push for major reform, even with credible concerns about abuse.[174] The fluidity of this historical framing is a constant feature of electronic surveillance debates. But regardless of this changing context, whether the reformed Section 702 complies with the Constitution will remain a standard question.

---

elementary truths does not make the employment of by the Government of electronic surveillance a welcome development" disregarding completely the Bill of Rights. *Keith*, 407 U.S. at 313.

[174] Although, "in the post-Snowden revelations era [there is an] absence of credible allegations of political or venal use of 702 authorities. In essence, the public evidence confirms that the problems that used to bedevil secret electronic surveillance through the Hoover/Nixon era—namely, senior political figures deploying intelligence agencies and tools for inappropriate, abusive political purposes—have been resolved by a robust legal regime of oversight and reporting." Jack Goldsmith & Susan Hennessey, *The Merits of Supporting 702 Reauthorization (Despite Worries About Trump and the Rule of Law)*, LAWFARE (Jan. 18, 2018, 9:20 AM), https://www.lawfareblog.com/merits-supporting-702-reauthorization-despite-worries-about-trump-and-rule-law. In other words, absence of credible abuse may have helped kill the major reform efforts more than anything else—the historic moment did not compare to the abuse of electronic surveillance in the 20th Century. *See id.*

III.   THE REAUTHORIZATION ACT'S REFORM TO SECTION 702

Section 702 has withstood frequent constitutional challenge. Whether it continues to succeed as a constitutionally viable law will depend on its recent changes. When President Trump signed S. 139 into law, Section 702 changed in the following ways:

- **Querying Procedures:** The AG and DNI must now adopt certain procedures that will regulate how intelligence analysts search databases of raw Section 702 intelligence. These querying procedures are subject to FISC review for compliance with the Fourth Amendment.[175] Additionally, procedures must be adopted which keep "record of each 'United States person query term' used."[176] The FBI must get a court order on grounds of probable cause to access Section 702 intelligence communications "responsive to U.S. person search terms where the query 'was not designed to find and extract foreign intelligence information' and instead is performed 'in connection with a predicated criminal investigation' unrelated to national security."[177] Here, predicated criminal investigation likely means one that is beyond its initial stage, but already has some semblance of probable cause of illegality.[178] But an order may not be required if there is a reasonable threat of serious harm or death.[179]

- **Criminal Proceedings.** The reforms go on to detail the circumstances where a U.S. person's data collected by a Section 702 surveillance can

---

[175] Emma Kohse, *Summary: The FISA Amendments Reauthorization Act of 2017*, LAWFARE (Jan. 18, 2018, 4:29 PM), https://www.lawfareblog.com/summary-fisa-amendments-reauthorization-act-2017.

[176] *Id.*

[177] *Id.*

[178] *See* Croner, *supra* note 122 ("It would have been helpful to have defined "predicated criminal investigation," but the statute is silent, so one is left to   assume that it is an investigation that has moved beyond a preliminary assessment of suspected criminal activity that is unrelated in any way to national security; i.e., your garden variety criminal investigation conducted through the FBI's criminal investigative division.").

[179] *See* Kohse, *supra* note 173.

be used in a criminal investigation. The FBI must otherwise get a court order described above or the criminal proceeding must "involve one of an enumerated list of conduct, including death, kidnapping, serious bodily injury, crimes against minors, incapacitation of critical infrastructure, cybersecurity, and transnational crime."[180] Regardless, reporting requirements to Congress now exist to mandate disclosure of the use of Section 702 intelligence for law enforcement investigations against U.S. persons.[181]

- **"About" Collection.** The new reforms do not ban "about" collection but allow the IC to resume such collection if it so chooses (i.e., should the NSA so choose since voluntarily ceasing such activities in 2017 amidst compliance concerns).[182] However, the DNI and AG must inform Congress prior to restarting the program and provide a FISC opinion approving any specific program and "a summary of the protections in place to detect any material breach."[183] The IC can begin "about" collection after the period of Congressional notice if any exigency exists. Anytime a material breach occurs in the program's protections, Congress must now be notified.[184] Finally, because restarting about collection on approval of the FISC will likely "present a novel or significant interpretation of the law," amici briefs will be considered as to this question.[185]

Overall, there were many more reforms made to Section 702, especially for transparency, including: publication of minimization procedures after declassification, increased whistleblower protections, review of applicable classification systems, strengthening of the PCLOB, increased capacity in civil liberties offices across the FBI and NSA, and clarification of the Section 705 emergency provision.[186] However, the reforms to querying procedures and

---

[180] *Id.*

[181] *Id.*

[182] *See* Jurecic, *supra* note 107 (explaining why the NSA stopped "about" collections).

[183] *Id.*

[184] *Id.*

[185] *Id.*

[186] *Id.*

"about" collection are most relevant to a re-evaluation of the Section 702's constitutional compliance. The querying reforms might help assuage concerns about backdoor searches, but Gregory Croner has noticed that the FBI still has significant leeway. He points out that the querying reforms are merely a:

> Political gesture offered to appease critics rather than seriously constrict access to the Section 702 database for foreign intelligence purposes. For example, after creating this new 'querying' limitation in purely criminal cases, the FISA Reauthorization Act hastens to point out that the FBI is relieved of any obligation to seek a FISC order: (1) where the FBI is conducting lawful queries of the Section 702 database (i.e., queries directed to producing foreign intelligence information); or (2) where the results of an FBI query are "reasonably designed to find and extract foreign intelligence information, regardless of whether such foreign intelligence information would also be considered evidence of a crime;" or (3) where the FBI query is initiated to evaluate "whether to open an assessment or predicated investigation relating to the national security of the United States;" or (4) where the query is initiated upon reasonable belief that the content of Section 702 communications "could assist in mitigating or eliminating a threat to life or serious bodily harm."[187]

Consequently, the strength of Section 702's fundamental authorities, pending "about" collection re-evaluation, has been left intact notwithstanding the transparency reforms enacted.

IV. REEVALUATING POINTS OF CONSTITUTIONAL CONTENTION

There are open questions in the aftermath of Section 702's reauthorization — not least of which is whether Congress was even aware of the full-extent of Section 702's use to make an informed decision.[188] Regardless, the program's

---

[187] Croner, *supra* note 122.

[188] Some commentators argue that "we don't know how the government is using Section 702 data, but we do know that it is singling out communities for increased scrutiny based on country of origin, faith, and race. The administration has deemed illegal immigration as a leading national security threat, and President Trump has even said that legal immigration poses a national security threat." Robyn Greene, *Americans Wanted More Privacy Protections. Congress Gave Them Fewer*, SLATE (Jan. 26, 2018;

expansion reopens the viability of constitutional challenge in areas where litigation has previously failed. Namely, the program's changes to querying procedures and the possibility of restarting "about" collection are arguable violations of the Fourth Amendment. While the "course of true law pertaining to the [Fourth Amendment] . . . has not . . . run smooth[ly]"[189] because it suffers from "both the virtue of brevity and the vice of ambiguity,"[190] a few basic requirements are clear. First, only government surveillance that meets the *Jones-Katz* requirements[191] will count as a "search" implicating the Fourth Amendment. Second, any such searches must be "reasonable." And third, a warrant must be obtained to carry out these searches, unless an exception applies. Querying and "about" collection arguably violates each of these three requirements.

First, given the amount of incidental information that can be acquired in Section 702 surveillance (particularly "about" surveillance), it is no longer plausible under the *Katz* factors to claim the program does not amount to a Fourth Amendment search because it only targets foreigners abroad. Nevertheless, this question has not been directly addressed by the Supreme Court, and its resolution might greatly narrow the government's ability to carry out the program.

Second, assuming Section 702 does involve Fourth Amendment searches, there is a strong argument that such searches are unreasonable. Trends in case law involving government searches using technology imply an uneasiness with technology that can acquire large amounts of information on a person. With increased collection ability, courts are becoming concerned that the government can acquire a mosaic of information that penetrates the most private aspects of a person's life.[192] As Section 702 collects more incidental

---

7:45AM), https://slate.com/technology/2018/01/congress-reauthorization-of-section-702-of-the-fisa-is-an-expansion-not-a-reform.html.

[189] Chapman v. United States, 365 U.S. 610, 618 (1961) (Frankfurter, J., concurring).

[190] JACOB W. LANDYNSKI, SEARCH AND SEIZURE AND THE SUPREME COURT: A STUDY IN CONSTITUTIONAL INTERPRETATION 42 (1966).

[191] *See supra* PART II.A. for a discussion of *Katz* and *Jones*.

[192] *See, e.g.*, Carpenter v. United States, 138 S. Ct. 2206, (2018) (citing United States v. Jones, 565 U.S. 400, 416–420 (2012) and Kyllo v. United States, 533 U.S. 27, 34 (2001)).

information on U.S. persons, it surely triggers the same concerns that courts are increasingly striking down as unreasonable Fourth Amendment searches.

Third, even if Section 702 searches are considered reasonable, it is not clear that current Section 702 FISC orders can be considered warrants as contemplated by the Fourth Amendment. If they are not, then the government can only conduct such searches if an exception to the warrant requirement applies. Here, the special needs exception and the incidental overhear exception (the -often-cited exceptions justifying warrantless FISA searches) do not easily apply for Section 702's new querying procedures and for "about" collection.

In sum, the new querying procedures and "about" collection authorizations are susceptible to constitutional challenge on just about every front of Fourth Amendment jurisprudence. The following discussion lays out the applicable doctrine for each of the three Fourth Amendment requirements and previews the legal analysis that might soon be presented to courts reviewing the Reauthorization Act.

A. *Querying and "About" Collection are Fourth Amendment Searches*

As mentioned above, the foreign intelligence surveillance doctrine established in *Keith* lays the foundation for FISA surveillance under a theory that surveillance targeting foreigners implicates less privacy concerns than domestic surveillance. As such, this surveillance does not amount to a Fourth Amendment search. But as commentators note, by passing Section 702 Congress "specifically authorized programmatic warrantless foreign intelligence surveillance in a manner almost guaranteed to sweep up a substantial volume of communications involving U.S. persons."[193] And so the debate between courts like *Troung Dinh Hung* and *Zweibon v. Mitchell* remains a continuous issue: is it really the case today that foreign intelligence surveillance targeting foreigners abroad does not implicate privacy concerns of U.S. persons caught up in the surveillance? And would requiring

---

[193] Steve Vladeck, *More on Clapper and the Foreign Intelligence Surveillance Exception,* LAWFARE (May 23, 2012, 3:32 PM), https://www.lawfareblog.com/more-clapper-and-foreign-intelligence-surveillance-exception.

compliance with the Fourth Amendment frustrate the Executive's Article II power?

As to the first, it seems hard to believe that individuals do not have a recognizable expectation of privacy over the content of their communications that are increasingly swept up, and subject to review, by Section 702:

> [T]he collection of foreign intelligence surveillance today involves Americans' communications at a volume and sensitivity level Congress never imagined when it enacted FISA. If the government wished to acquire the communications of a non-citizen overseas in 1978, any collection of exchanges involving Americans could plausibly be described as "incidental." Today, with international communication being a daily fact of life for large numbers of Americans, the collection of their calls and e-mails in vast numbers is an inevitable consequence of surveillance directed at a non-citizen overseas. The volume of information collected on U.S. persons makes it difficult to characterize existing foreign intelligence programs as focused solely on foreigners and thus exempt from ordinary Fourth Amendment constraints.[194]

As to whether complying with the Fourth Amendment will frustrate the Executive, that does not seem to be the case with the current operation of the FISC. While the FISC rarely rejects FISA or Section 702 applications,[195] the process of approving such generalized requests has hardly reduced the amount of people the government has surveilled under these programs.[196] The Supreme Court has explicitly rejected arguments that lack of resources or

---

[194] GOITEIN & PATEL, *supra*, note 65, at 21.

[195] "From 1996 to 2013, less than 0.032 percent of applications were denied, even though requests grew by more than 200 percent." *Id.* at 37 (citing ADMIN. OFF. OF THE U.S. CTS., WIRETAP REP. tbl. 7 (2013); ADMIN. OFF. OF THE U.S. CTS., WIRETAP REP. tbl. 7 (2002)).

[196] *See generally* Statistical Transparency Report Regarding the Use of National Security Authorities—Calendar Year 2017, *Office of the Director of National Intelligence*, https://www.dni.gov/files/documents/icotr/2018-ASTR-CY2017-FINAL-for-Release-5.4.18.pdf (while exact numbers may be hard to specify with certainty, the ODNI lays out a steady increase in the estimated targets of Section 702 orders, increasing from roughly 89,000 in 2013 to about 129,000 in 2017. These numbers likely to do not account for the number of individuals incidentally caught up in the surveillance.).

strain on the Executive automatically obviates the warrant requirement.[197] Thus, as a matter of operation, FISA surveillance does constitute "searches" under the Fourth Amendment—particularly because the government has done just fine complying with procedural restrictions enacted by Congress. Even if such searches focus on metadata or individual information not subject to privacy protections, courts are "tak[ing] a more holistic and less formalistic view of the government's actions and examin[ing] what the government is really learning about us when it collects and processes massive amounts of data."[198] Enough "non-searches" can amount to a constitutionally recognized search when a government program is viewed holistically.[199]

As discussed above, the Supreme Court never had to explicitly address the *Katz* framework left open by *Keith* in the foreign intelligence space because Congress essentially assumed foreign surveillance did constitute a Fourth Amendment search by creating FISA procedures which mimic Title III warrant processes.[200] Nevertheless, if the Supreme Court were to wholly review Section 702, it might be compelled to once and for all declare such foreign surveillance as Fourth Amendment searches when U.S. persons are involved. Such a finding would hardly be surprising given FISA's development. But how the Supreme Court—or even lower courts—opine on the scope of these searches, and its interaction with Article II powers, will have ramifications on how "reasonable" they are when conducted by increasingly

---

[197] *See* United States v. Karo, 468 U.S. 705, 718 (1984) (rejecting the Government's argument that an obligation to obtain warrants for monitoring beepers withdrawn from public view would lead to the Government obtaining warrants in a large number of cases as unpersuasive); *see also Zweibon*, 516 F.2d at 636-37 (recognizing the U.S. Supreme Court's warning that arguments regarding the foreign intelligence warrant exception cannot be based on the length of time needed to obtain the warrant or the potential amount of warrants necessary to comply).

[198] JOSHUA DRESSLER ET AL., UNDERSTANDING CRIMINAL PROCEDURE: VOL. I: INVESTIGATION 104 (7th ed., 2017).

[199] Indeed, this is the general theory of the mosaic theory: government acquisition of seemingly inconsequential personal information can, when added together, amount to such an intrusive holistic picture into an individual's life that it can implicate the Fourth Amendment. For a full explanation, including criticism, *see generally* Orin Kerr, *The Mosaic Theory and the Fourth Amendment*, 111 MICH. L. REV. 311 (2012).

[200] *See supra* Part II.A.

intrusive and advanced surveillance methods. Here is where future litigants have room to argue, particularly for "about" searches. Not only do these collection methods count as Fourth Amendment searches, but they are so broad that no argument can make them reasonable, even when interacting with the Executive's Article II powers related to foreign affairs and national security. The scope of these Article II powers in this space will undoubtedly influence the means by the government can continue to adapt its surveillance methods under Section 702. Indeed, courts seem to care about the mode by which the government intrudes as part of the search analysis.[201] Consequently, litigation against Section 702 might proceed by challenging specific types of surveillance (e.g., upstream) as not only searches, but unreasonable per se by nature of its technology alone.

B. Newly Authorized Section 702 Searches are Unreasonable

Litigants need not focus too much on the scope of whether a search occurred because current case law suggests courts are increasingly amendable to finding overbroad technological collection as unreasonable, even in the metadata space. "A search is not beyond Fourth Amendment scrutiny; for it must be reasonable in its scope and manner of execution."[202] Scholars have pointed to the D.C. District Court in *Klayman v. Obama* as portending a shift among courts to reign in the definition of reasonableness in the intelligence collection context, particularly with new trends in the Supreme Court's Fourth Amendment jurisprudence.[203] *Klayman* was a successful challenge to the FISA Section 215 metadata program on unreasonableness grounds, but its

---

[201] *See, e.g.*, State v. Bonnell, 856 P.2d 1265, 1276–77 (Haw. 1993) (finding that the mode of government intrusion matters as to whether government surveillance　counts as a Fourth Amendment search).

[202] Maryland v. King, 569 U.S. 435, 448 (2013).

[203] *See* Patrick Walsh, *Stepping on (or over) the Constitution's Line: Evaluating FISA Section 702 in a World of Changing Reasonableness under the Fourth Amendment*, 18 N.Y.U. J. Legis. & Pub. Pol'y 741, 783 (2015) (discussing the effect of the U.S. Supreme Court's interpretation of a reasonable expectation of privacy in Klayman v. Obama, 957 F. Supp. 2d 1 (D.D.C. 2013)).

implications are far reaching.[204] "The *Klayman* court emphasized that one of the driving purposes behind the Fourth Amendment is to prevent the government from acquiring a significant amount of private information without a judicial determination of probable cause." This concern is equally implicated with Section 702, particularly regarding incidental "about" collection. Instructive too is how the FISCR treated the predecessor to Section 702 in *In re Directives*.[205] The court determined that the special needs exception to warrant requirement applies "when surveillance is conducted to obtain foreign intelligence for national security purposes *and* is directed against foreign powers or agents of foreign powers reasonably believed to be located outside the United States."[206] Again, scholars note that "a strict reading of the *In re Directives* foreign intelligence exception would result in a determination that Section 702 does not qualify for this exception to the warrant requirement."[207] The court in *In re Directives* upheld the Section 702 predecessor on reasonableness grounds but based on protections that were not replicated when Section 702 was updated in 2008 and in subsequent years.[208]

These cases demonstrate a willingness for FISA courts and district courts to strike down provisions of statues similar to Section 702 on Fourth Amendment reasonableness grounds and a narrower conception of the special

---

[204] *See generally* Klayman, 957 F. Supp. 2d 1, 41 (D.D.C. 2013) (holding that the phone record metadata collection constituted a search under the Fourth Amendment and that Klayman was likely to succeed in demonstrating that the government's searches were unreasonable under the Fourth Amendment).

[205] *See In re* Directives Pursuant to Section 105B of the Foreign Intelligence Surveillance Act, 551 F.3d 1004, 1016 (FISA Ct. Rev. 2008) (reviewing the identical predecessor to Section 702 under the 2007 short-lived Protect America Act and holding that directives issued to the petitioning service provider under the Protect America Act satisfied the Fourth Amendment's reasonableness requirement).

[206] *Id.* at 1012 (emphasis added).

[207] Walsh, *supra* note 200, at 786.

[208] *See id.* at 787 ("Unlike the PAA, section 702 does not require a determination that "probable cause existed to believe that the targeted person is a   foreign power or an agent of a foreign power." This negatively affects both sides of the balancing test as applied to section 702. Without a   connection to a foreign power, the government interest in national security is reduced. . . . " (quoting *In re* Directives Pursuant to Section 105B of the Foreign Intelligence Surveillance Act, 551 F.3d 1004, 1014 (FISA Ct. Rev. 2008)).

needs exception described below. They also portend precedent that does not quite match with the increasingly expansive Section 702. The FISC court will have to squarely face this issue if the government decides to reactivate "about" collection programs as part of the recent reauthorization. Whether "about" collection passes reasonableness muster might very well hinge on the changing privacy implications at the core of the third-party doctrine. In *United States v. Jones*, the concurring opinions contemplate the fact that "it may be that [long-term surveillance] through electronic means, without an accompanying trespass, is an unconstitutional invasion of privacy."[209] Indeed, the surveillance data collected via the third-party doctrine is so much more intrusive in the information era than the phone records which spawned the creation of the doctrine in *Smith v. Maryland*.[210] A mosaic of data points can pierce one's private life in intricate detail, even when incidentally collected.[211] The reasonableness prong of the Fourth Amendment turns on a balancing test between privacy interests and security interests that has frequently favored an expansive interpretation of Section 702. But if the Court amends the reach of the third-party doctrine based on "technological advances that have made possible non-trespassory surveillance techniques" courts may very well lean on cases like *Klayman* and *In re Directives* to preserve "the evolution of societal privacy expectations."[212] Future cases might address the so-called equilibrium-adjustment theory whereby the Court does and should update Fourth Amendment rules to maintain the balance of government power as technology changes. The idea that is that some technological shifts so transform the level of government investigative power (whether expanding it

---

[209] United States v. Jones, 565 U.S. 400, 412 (2012).

[210] *See* Smith v. Maryland, 442 U.S. 735, 742–43 (1979) (holding that a pen register does not constitute a search under the Fourth Amendment because individuals do not have a subjective or societal reasonable expectation of privacy in regard to their phone numbers).

[211] *See, e.g.*, Carpenter v. United States, 138 S. Ct. 2206, 2213–14 (2018) (citing United States v. Jones, 565 U.S. 400, 405–06 (2012) and Kyllo v. United States, 533 U.S. 27, 34 (2001)).

[212] *Jones*, 565 U.S. at 414–15 (Sotomayor, J., concurring).

or restricting it) that they justify new rules to restore the prior level of government power.[213]

The outcome of *Carpenter v. United States*, which evaluated the bulk collection of cell-site data, seems to confirm this theory by recognizing that "seismic shifts in digital technology" which produce "deeply revealing" amounts of information can constitute a search, regardless of the third-party doctrine.[214] In other words, people have a cognizable privacy interest in the information they give to third parties, particularly when this information reveals more as its collected and evaluated in bulk. Each individual data point may not violate any privacy interests. But when technology permits the government to put together a complex mosaic made of these individual points, the resulting picture can implicate Fourth Amendment protections. While the Court clarified that its holding "does not consider other collection techniques involving foreign affairs or national security," *Carpenter* will provide ammunition for those who will argue that bulk collection programs constitute protected searches. These arguments might restrict the government's ability to search unminimized data or the breadth of "about" collection.

C. Exceptions to the Warrant Requirement Do Not Apply

Even assuming Section 702's newest authorities are considered reasonable searches, they still need go through a warrant process to comply with the Fourth Amendment. Whether or not current Section 702 FISC orders are considered permissible warrants is still an open question. In the regular FISA context—where the FISC approves individualized orders to surveil agents of foreign powers—the answer is clearer. *In re Sealed Case* held that the pre-2008 FISA "did not itself violate the Fourth Amendment, at least largely because FISA warrants were probably still effectively 'warrants' within the meaning of

---

[213] Orin Kerr, *Four Thoughts on the Briefing in Carpenter v. United States*, LAWFARE (Nov. 17, 2017, 3:06 PM), https://www.lawfareblog.com/four-thoughts-briefing-carpenter-v-united-states.

[214] *See generally Carpenter*, 138 S. Ct. at 2217 (holding that the Government usually must obtain a search warrant in order to request cell location information from a wireless carrier).

the Warrant Clause."[215]   The alternative argument was that the *Keith* and *Troung Dinh Hung* line of cases creates a foreign intelligence surveillance exception to the warrant requirement because of the strain such a warrant would place of the Executive's Article II responsibilities and due to the minimal privacy implications.[216]   But as discussed above, both of these arguments seem operationally unpersuasive, and *In re Sealed Case* refused to "endorse a categorical foreign intelligence surveillance exception" to warrant requirement by effectively holding traditional FISA warrants as in compliance with the Fourth Amendment.[217]

But with Section 702, FISA warrants are no longer necessary for surveilling foreigners abroad, just programmatic FISC orders. If *In re Sealed Case* did not opine on pre-Section 702 compliance with the foreign intelligence exception, then whether Section 702 complies with the exception is an open question. This question is especially important considering that the exception is based on the *Keith* rationale that foreign surveillance does not require a warrant because privacy interests are not as implicated compared to domestic surveillance.   Given Section 702's expansion, that is an assumption worth reevaluating, particularly as it relates to the reasonableness of searches. This question was one the plaintiffs sought to address in *Clapper v. Amnesty International*.[218]   As that case was dismissed on standing grounds, the issue remains a live question that could upend Section 702 in favor of the government.[219]

---

[215] Steve Vladeck, *More on Clapper and the Foreign Intelligence Surveillance Exception*, LAWFARE (May 23, 2012, 3:32 PM), https://www.lawfareblog.com/more-clapper-and-foreign-intelligence-surveillance-exception.

[216] *See id.* (discussing the origins of the foreign intelligence exception to the Fourth Amendment's warrant requirement).

[217] *Id.*

[218] *See generally* Clapper v. Amnesty International, 568 U.S. 398, 401 (2013) (determining that plaintiffs failed to illustrate that FISA surveillance against them would impose an impending, future injury).

[219] *Id.* at 402 (holding that "respondents cannot manufacture standing by choosing to make expenditures based on hypothetical future harm that is not certainly impending. We therefore hold that respondents lack Article III standing."); *id.* at 422 (preserving the core of the merits by noting that "any dissatisfaction that respondents may have about the Foreign Intelligence Surveillance Court's rulings—or the congressional

Nevertheless, many commentators proceed on the assumption that notwithstanding the uncertainty about the foreign intelligence exception, the special needs and incidental overhear exceptions are more than enough to permit warrantless Section 702 searches.[220] But in this space, litigants have the strongest arguments to challenge the new provisions of Section 702 because neither of the exceptions seem to permit querying of incidentally collected data or "about" collection.

Griffen v. Wisconsin made clear that "when special needs, beyond the normal need for law enforcement, make the warrant and probable cause requirement impracticable," court-issued warrants are unnecessary.[221] Promoting public safety is often considered one such exigency and the FISCR has permitted FISA under these grounds, remarking that such foreign intelligence surveillance "goes well beyond any garden-variety law enforcement objective," even with the incidental collection of a U.S. person's data.[222] Although the Supreme Court has never directly endorsed foreign surveillance under the special needs analysis, it would likely accept the FISC's rationale that there is a "high probability that requiring a warrant" could harm "vital national security interests" that depend on the time sensitive information Section 702 is able to acquire.[223] This view seems especially likely given the holding of *City of Indianapolis v. Edmond*, where the Court recognized stopping a terrorist attack as justification for a suspiciousness search.[224] But the new Section 702 authorities might go beyond this broad exception. Under

---

delineation of that court's role—is irrelevant to our standing analysis" and therefore remains a live question.).

[220] *See Section 702 of the Foreign Intelligence Surveillance Act: Hearing Before the* H. Judiciary Comm., 115th Cong. 2 (2017) (statement of Jeff Kosseff).

[221] Griffin v. Wisconsin, 483 U.S. 868, 873 (1987) (citing: New Jersey v. T.L.O., 469 U.S. 325, 351 (1985) (Blackmun, J., concurring in judgment)).

[222] *In re* Directives Pursuant to Section 105B of the Foreign Intelligence Surveillance Act, 551 F.3d at 1011 (FISA Ct. Rev. 2008); [Redacted Case Name], 68–69 (FISA Ct. 2011) (Bates, J., mem.).

[223] *Id.* at 69.

[224] City of Indianapolis v. Edmond, 531 U.S. 32, 44 (2000) ("The Fourth Amendment would permit an appropriately tailored roadblock set up to thwart an imminent terrorist attack or to catch a dangerous criminal who is likely to flee by way of a particular route." (citing Edmond v. Goldsmith, 183 F.3d 659, 662–63 (7th Cir. 1999)).

the reauthorized Section 702, backdoor searches of incidentally collected data on U.S. persons seem permissible when the investigations are related to foreign intelligence, national security, or imminent threat of injury.[225] Moreover, it seems like law enforcement can search this data at any point, for any purpose, before a fully "predicated" investigation—i.e., before they suspect a particular U.S. person has committed a crime in question, they can query Section 702 databases looking for any connections on which to establish probable cause.[226] The ability for law enforcement to undertake these warrantless fishing expeditions arguably stretches beyond the special needs exception.

In *City of Los Angeles v. Patel*, the Court clarified the special needs exception as applying in situations where there is a special need _and_ "where the primary purpose of the searches is distinguishable from the general interest in crime control."[227] Consider too some crucial points in *Edmond*. The Court cited *Delaware v. Prouse* for the proposition that discretionary roadblocks set for public safety were unconstitutional extensions of the special needs exception primarily because "discretionary, suspicionless stop[s]" constituted an "exercise of standardless and unconstrained discretion"— discretion which could be abused.[228] If warrantless roadblock searches could be permitted under the special needs exception, they would have to apply to all cars or be randomized to prevent abuse of discretion. Additionally, "the Court must consider the nature of the interests threatened and their connection to the particular law enforcement practices at issue."[229] In *Edmond*, roadblocks designed to stop cars for drug searches were impermissible

---

[225] *See* Croner, *supra* note 149 (explaining how a reading of the statute arguable permits backdoor searches where the FBI query is initiated to evaluate "whether to open an assessment or predicated investigation relating to the national security of the United States;" or where the query is initiated upon reasonable belief that the content of Section 702 communications "could assist in mitigating or eliminating a threat to life or serious bodily harm.").

[226] *Id.*

[227] *See* City of Los Angeles, Calif. v. Patel, 135 S. Ct. 2443, 2452 (2015); *see also* Ferguson v. City of Charleston, 532 U.S. 67, 81–86 (2001).

[228] City of Indianapolis v. Edmond, 531 U.S. 32, 39 (2000) (citing Delaware v. Prouse, 440 U.S. 648,661 (1979)).

[229] *Id.* at 33.

because searching for drugs is not a law enforcement practice connected to the public safety interest in promoting safe driving (whereas, stopping cars to prevent DUIs is much more clearly connected to promoting safe driving).[230] Applying these principles, the Reauthorization Act's backdoor provisions seem dubious. In the first instance, the significant purpose standard for FISA searches permitted by *In Re Sealed Case*[231] seems to conflict with the *Patel* court's clarification that the special needs exception must have a primary purpose distinct from law enforcement. *In Re Sealed Case* upheld the congressional decision under Fourth Amendment grounds to require only a "significant purpose" of collecting foreign intelligence to receive a FISC surveillance order.[232] Unlike the previous standard, law enforcement could also be a significant purpose so long as collecting foreign intelligence remained significant. It is important to notice the incongruity between the more permissive significant purpose test to begin foreign surveillance and what is permitted under the special needs exception for warrantless searches of U.S. persons in the public safety context. When incidental data on U.S. persons is collected under the significant purpose collection, there might be a problem in later using this information under the more restrictive primary purpose *Patel* standard. For example, if foreign intelligence is collected with the main aim of prosecuting a foreign terrorist—but nevertheless meets the threshold for a significant foreign intelligence aim—there is an issue if incidental information is picked up. Suppose a potential U.S. person is caught up in this surveillance as a co-conspirator. Because the initial aim of the surveillance had a significant purpose of prosecuting a foreign terrorist, the primary purpose of later using incidental information to prosecute a U.S. co-

---

[230] Whereas, stopping cars to prevent DUI's is much more clearly connected to promoting safe driving. *Id.* at 43 ("Nor can the narcotics-interdiction purpose of the checkpoints be rationalized in terms of a highway safety concern similar to that present in Sitz . . . only with respect to a smaller class of offenses, however, is society confronted with the type of immediate, vehicle-bound threat to life and limb that the sobriety checkpoint in Sitz was designed to eliminate.").

[231] 310 F.3d 717 (FISA Ct. Rev. 2002) ("The FISA as amended is constitutional because the surveillances it authorizes are reasonable [under the significant purpose test].").

[232] *Id.*

conspirator is indistinguishable from the crime control purpose in *Patel* if the special needs requirement underpins Section 702. Without a separate warrant/probable cause determination, the very act of conducting a query triggers Fourth Amendment concerns. To conduct a warrantless special needs search, the primary purpose must be distinguishable from crime control. In many cases this requirement is impossible to meet because the data is collected *ex ante* via a FISC order which applies a standard that allows law enforcement purposes to be a substantial reason to implement foreign intelligence surveillance.

Much of the complexity arises from the meaning (or lack thereof) of the "significant purpose" test required for the collection of foreign intelligence. Nevertheless, as the wall between foreign intelligence and law enforcement continues to weaken, an argument can be made that backdoor searches—or even Section 702 surveillance generally—stretches the limit of the special needs exception. This is not the case because the national security interests implicated are not special needs within the doctrine—promoting national security squarely falls under the purview of public safety recognized as the classic exigency within the doctrine. It stretches the limit because the use of the information collected is increasingly tied up in the crime control which the special needs analysis excludes from its purview under *Patel*.

More clearly problematic is the ability for law enforcement to query Section 702 databases before a predicated investigation. To the extent that law enforcement queries data in an unrandomized or exclusive fashion, it would seem no different than the contexts held unconstitutional in *Prouse* or *Edmond*. It might just be data in this situation, but the same abuse of discretion and privacy concerns are still relevant. The implication in *Prouse* was that if officers had full discretion to make any suspicionless stop grounded in public safety reasons, they could use this authority to search people based on race, gender, or any immutable characteristics. Likewise, in *Edmond*, the implication was that impermissible profiling could also be deployed in the drug stop situation. Whether someone is carrying drugs is much less obvious compared to drunkenness. Officers might rely on stereotyping or animus in subjecting individuals to an invasion of privacy to conduct searches. These concerns are present with the pre-predicated backdoor searches: unless the querying is conducted in the same randomized or all-encompassing way, nothing stops law enforcement from abusing its discretion in similar ways.

There are undoubtedly some caveats to these cases. For one, it can be argued that querying can be conducted in a randomized way. Plus, when law enforcement seeks to prosecute under terrorism statutes, there might be enough of a connection to the special need of national security to pass muster under *Prouse/Edmond*. Not to mention the *Patel* case was decided in the administrative search context (i.e., ordinance compliance), so it is not completely clear its clarification of the special needs analysis maps onto the foreign intelligence surveillance context.[233] Additionally, some courts have held that "subsequent querying of a Section 702 collection, even if U.S. person identifiers are used, is not a separate search" which "does not make Section 702 surveillance unreasonable under the Fourth Amendment."[234] But many courts have found in other contexts that "subsequent querying of the information after acquisition is a search requiring a warrant."[235] Thus, it is an open question whether Section 702 querying by law enforcement is a separate search from that of the initial intelligence collection. If so, Fourth Amendment concerns are heavily implicated. Regardless, the Reauthorization Act extends Section 702 authority far enough to at least allow reasonable grounds for litigation in this area. And the Supreme Court's decisions in "*United States v. Jones* and *Riley v. California* show that at least some Justices recognize the heightened potential for governmental overreach in an age when digital records are kept on nearly every aspect of our lives . . . now more than ever, because of their heightened vulnerability to government abuse in the Information Age."[236] Indeed, some suggest that technological advancement

---

[233] *See, e.g.*, MacWade v. Kelly, 460 F.3d 260, 263–64 (2d Cir. 2006) (explaining that lower courts have endorsed the applicability of the special needs doctrine, at least in the national security context).

[234] United States v. Mohamud, 2014 WL 2866749, at *26 (D. Or. Jun. 24, 2014), aff'd, 843 F.3d 420 (9th Cir. 2016).

[235] *Id.* at *24 (citing United States v. Sedaghaty, 728 F.3d 885, 910–13 (9th Cir. 2013) (computer search)); United States v. Young, 573 F.3d 711, 720–21 (9th Cir. 2009) (searching a backpack after accessing a hotel room); United States v. Mulder, 808 F.2d 1346, 1348 (9th Cir. 1987) (laboratory testing of pills).

[236] Maximilian Sladek de la Cal, *City of Los Angeles v. Patel: The Fourth Amendment's Special Needs in the Information Age*, 31 BERKELEY TECH. L. J. 1137, 1137 (2016).

can actually help reduce the use of the special needs exception—with one suggestion calling on courts to "use statistical forecasting to measure whether continued surveillance is necessary to address the special needs of law enforcement."[237]

As to the potential application of the so-called "incidental overhear" exception, similar doctrinal concerns are implicated. Before reauthorization, three district courts—*United States v. Mohamud, United States v. Muhtorov,* and *United States v. Hasbajrami*—heard cases challenging Section 702, all of which upheld the program citing the foreign intelligence exception to the warrant requirement and its reasonableness after a balancing of interests.[238] But these cases failed to appreciate the incidental overhear arguments that defendants were making about incidental collection under Section 702. The incidental overhear doctrine was established in the Title III context where "defendants argued that their own communications were acquired unlawfully because they were not identified by name in [search] orders."[239] Essentially, law enforcement placed a wiretap on a suspect that incidentally caught incriminating evidence on bystanders, who were never targeted in the initial warrant. Nevertheless, the Supreme Court held that it was not unlawful to introduce this incidentally overheard evidence so long as the warrant in dispute was sufficiently particularized: "identify[ing] the phone line to be tapped and the conversations to be acquired, and the government followed rigorous 'minimization' procedures to avoid the collection of 'innocent conversation.'"[240] In many ways, FISA's own procedural requirements map onto these same restrictions. But if the courts conceive of these protections as

---

[237] Justin W. Whitney, *FISA's Future: An Analysis of Electronic Surveillance in Light of the Special Needs Exception to the Fourth Amendment,* 47 WASHBURN L. J. 127, 129 (2007).

[238] *See generally* United States v. Mohamud, 2014 WL2866749, (D. Or. Jun. 24, 2014); United States v. Muhtorov, 187 F. Supp. 3d 1240 (D. Colo. 2015); United States v. Hasbajrami, 2016 WL 1029500 (E.D.N.Y. Mar. 8, 2016).

[239] Elizabeth Goitein, *Another Bite out of Katz: Foreign Intelligence Surveillance and the Incidental Overhear Doctrine,* 55 AM. CRIM. L. REV. 105, 115 (2018) (citing United States v. Donovan 429 U.S. 413, 416-20 (1977) (examining the doctrine in the context of an FBI wiretap under Title III and United States v. Khan, 415 U.S. 143, 144–47 (1974) (addressing the doctrine in the context of a Dept. of Justice application under Title III related to an illegal gambling investigation)).

[240] *Id.*

something more—as creating an exception to the warrant requirement for incidentally collected communications—then Section 702 seems further insulated from constitutional challenge.

Indeed, this jump is what the *Mohamud, Muhtorov,* and *Hasbajrami* courts have assumed by including incidental U.S. person data within the foreign intelligence exception.[241] Yet they are two different issues. It is one thing to say Section 702 surveillance is permitted without a warrant due to the *Keith* foreign intelligence exception. Yet is quite another to say incidental data are swallowed by this exception because the Supreme Court has permitted such an overlap in the criminal investigation context. Elizabeth Goeitein frames the issue accordingly:

> If Americans have a reasonable expectation of privacy in their communications with foreigners overseas, then the 'incidental overhear' cases would justify dispensing with a warrant only if they established an exception to the warrant requirement. This follows from the basic rule . . . that warrantless searches and seizures are per se unreasonable unless an established exception applies.[242]

Yet courts have made a flawed assumption. It may be that "when surveillance is lawful in the first place . . . the incidental interception of non-targeted U.S. persons' communications with the targeted persons is also lawful."[243] But this does not mean that subsequent querying of the incidental communications does not require a warrant. In Goeitein's words: the cases establishing the incidental overhear doctrine did not "hold or suggest that no warrant was necessary to collect the defendants' conversations, as long as there was a warrant for the person with whom the defendants were

---

[241] *See generally* United States v. Hasbajrami, 2016 WL 1029500 (E.D.N.Y. Mar. 8, 2016) (rejecting motion to suppress evidence collected under FISA §702 and rejecting the assertion that incidental collection triggers the warrant requirement of the Fourth Amendment); United States v. Muhtorov, 187 F. Supp. 3d 1240 (D. Colo. 2015); United States v. Mohamud, 2014 WL2866749 (D. Or. Jun. 24, 2014) (rejecting a motion for dismissal and reversal of a conviction and suppression of evidence predicated on an argument that the introduction of §702 evidence had violated a notice requirement).

[242] Goitein, *supra* 236, at 120.

[243] United States v. Mohamud, 843 F.3d 420, 440–41 (9th Cir. 2016).

communicating."[244] To the contrary, the warrants questioned in these cases had been broad to anticipate the capture of incidental incriminating information because the warrant had detailed the phone line and conversations it sought to pick up.[245] Moreover, exceptions to the warrant requirement are "jealously and carefully drawn" to an extent that it is hard to imagine the Supreme Court has created an incidental overhear exception without expressly saying so.[246] Additionally, with Section 702's increased collection and querying authorities, it is hard to argue that the Title III incidental overhear doctrine is as easily applicable in the FISA context—where incidental collection is magnified tenfold. If anything, the incidental overhear doctrine stands for the proposition that a "small number of innocent conversations" [picked up] does not invalidate a warrant. This is a far cry from holding that the government can warrantlessly acquire the communications of anyone in contact with a lawfully surveilled target."[247] And yet this is the position held by many district courts as well as the FISC for FISA applications. Consequently, the point of contention is that incidentally collected information on U.S. persons may not invalidate the foreign intelligence exception to the warrant requirement (if it is recognized), but that does not mean such incidental information can be searched by the government in any meaningful way without judicial review. Such an argument could challenge the FBI's new ability to search incidentally collected Section 702 data to fish for information to establish probable cause.

All this analysis highlights a shaky foundation for Fourth Amendment authority to query incidental data collected about U.S. persons under the Reauthorization Act. The government's reliance on the special needs exception and the incidental overhear doctrine are open to substantial challenge given Section 702's expansion. And the reasonableness of the searches conducted—particularly regarding "about" collection—exist in an

---

[244] Goitein, *supra* note 236, at 122.

[245] *Id.*

[246] *See* United States v. Donovan, 429 U.S. 413, 416–20 (1977); United States v. Kahn, 415 U.S. 143, 144–47 (1974).

[247] Goitein, *supra* note 236, at 123.

era where courts are increasingly finding ways to rollback principles like the third-party doctrine to protect privacy interests in an intrusive digital age.

In short, these areas of constitutional contention are a few among many open issues that have been made viable by the expansion of Section 702. Notwithstanding narrow cases challenging the vagueness of statutory phrases in the Reauthorization Act (e.g., what does "predicated" mean?), these contention points are places where courts are most likely to restrain Section 702—something Congress could not manage to do. It is unlikely any court will find the program completely unconstitutional, but it will not be surprising if certain querying procedures or "about" collection (which now likely just require a "reference" to the target) are restricted given trends in the precedent discussed above.[248] Nevertheless, *Clapper v. Amnesty International* serves as warning that justiciability will be a difficult issue to surmount because it is often difficult for plaintiffs subject to surveillance to prove injury in fact caused by a specific Section 702 search. In the future, the best chance for justiciable challenges may come from the ISPs who cooperate with the government and are increasingly required to provide more and more technical assistance to carry out downstream surveillance imposed by the NSA.

V.   CONCLUSION

It is easy to find many missed opportunities for reform with the Reauthorization of Section 702. The concerns of privacy advocates were not meaningfully addressed, including clarification on unmasking. Some of the more complicated issues that will face FISA in the next decade were seemingly unanticipated. For example, the role of international data sharing, whether service providers will be compelled to provide increasingly complicated technical assistance to de-encrypt Section 702 data, and the growing ability to exploit smart technology connected the Internet for surveillance purposes.[249]

---

[248] *See, e.g.,* 50 U.S.C. § 1881a (2018) (defining "[t]he term "abouts communication" means a communication that contains a reference to, but is not to or from, a target of an acquisition authorized under subsection.").

[249] Examples of smart technology connected to the internet, commonly known as the internet of things, include doors, appliances, and cars.

These are all open issues that Section 702 is unprepared to explicitly address.[250] Nevertheless, ideas abound for reforming FISA and Section 702. Some propose an "inextricably intertwined test" to replace the significant purpose test such that FISA material would be admitted in court only if it is intertwined with national security related crimes.[251] The idea would prevent the use of incidental FISA data on U.S. person's to be used in prosecutions for ordinary crime. Others push for procedural protections, such as "expand[ed] opportunities for appellate review of FISC and FISCR cases."[252] Additionally, "increased public reporting, mandatory disclosure of FISC opinions, and more adversarial briefing at the FISC" have frequently been proposed.[253] Relatedly, many propose that "querying procedures should provide for some independent periodic auditing of the queries and the recorded justifications for them" to ensure maximum accountability and to provide litigants with a record to challenge searches.[254]

There is no shortage of ideas for improving FISA and Section 702. But there is often a shortage of political capital which is almost always contingent on the historical moment in which changes to FISA are considered. Broadly speaking, the history of electronic surveillance is one of ebb and flow. Evolving threats to national security demand evolving tools for staying ahead of those threats. But the government's long history and record of abusing these tools often causes a cyclical curtailing of those instruments. Depending on the moment, the issue of balancing liberty and safety gets framed in the alternative ways discussed above.

The least nuanced—but perhaps truest—explanation for Section 702's expansion in 2018 is that the question was framed as liberty reducing security rather than the alternative. In this narrative—with the threat of ISIS and a

---

[250] *See* Kris, *supra* note 18, at 13-27

[251] Wesley S. McCann, *Addressing the Balance: Restructuring CIPA and FISA to Meet the Needs of Justice and the Criminal Justice System*, 80 ALB. L. REV. 1131, 1166 (2016).

[252] *Id.* at 1171.

[253] *Id.* at 1166.

[254] *See generally* Elizabeth Goitein and Robert Litt, *A Way Forward on Section 702 Queries*, LAWFARE (Feb. 20, 2018, 12:30 PM), https://www.lawfareblog.com/way-forward-section-702-queries.

program that has not yet compared to the government abuses of surveillance emblematic of the mid-20th century—Congress was not willing to cripple the crown jewel of the IC. But because history tells us that it is certainly possible Congress does not know the full extent of Section 702 or has been confused about the extent of its success, courts must remain vigilant. The power of Section 702 belongs to the flexibility at which it can be used. Congress has likely relinquished its power to amend the program until it again faces renewal six years from now. But the courts have several avenues to hear constitutional litigation against the program. Perhaps the greatest obstacles are justiciability doctrines like standing, which prevent cases from easily being brought before Article III courts. Nevertheless, one hopes that as the government continues to expand its electronic surveillance programs, the probability of a case and controversy increases so courts can adequately weigh in. And lest courts give a blank check to the government, we can expect that the judicial drama surrounding the heightened strength of Section 702 is far from over.

Treason in the Age of Terrorism: Do Americans Who Join ISIS 'Levy War' Against the United States?

Stephen Jackson

Abstract

Treason is a crime often considered archaic and unnecessary in the modern era. In the post-9/11 world, however, treason is a viable legal instrument available for use against a ruthless enemy known as the Islamic State in Iraq and Syria ("ISIS"). To combat this floundering but still formidable foe, the U.S. government must consider how the crime applies to those Americans who actively or previously supported ISIS. To be sure, terrorism statutes will remain the main weapons in a U.S. prosecutor's legal arsenal. but for those cases where an American ISIS member commits the heinous acts of a traitor, for example murdering his fellow citizen in cold blood, treason is the most apparent crime committed.

The only crime defined in the U.S. Constitution is treason. The Founding Fathers understood the gravity of the crime and sought to limit its scope to avoid its use in those "doubtful cases." The arguments in this manuscript aim to respect this notion by exploring the genesis of the Treason Clause and applying legal precedent to today's war against ISIS. Although treason has a place in the War on Terror, certain legal ambiguities must be eliminated to ensure its proper utilization. Only by addressing these difficult issues directly can U.S. prosecutors hope to avoid maneuvering in the shadows similar to how the American betraying his nation for ISIS operates.

* **Stephen Jackson** received his juris doctor from George Mason University School of Law in 2016 and is licensed to practice law in Virginia. Stephen is currently a Senior Policy Analyst with SAIC supporting the U.S. Air Force. The views and arguments expressed in this manuscript are solely the author's and do not represent the views of either SAIC or the U.S. Air Force. The author would like to thank Jamil Jaffer for all his help and guidance during the drafting process.

TABLE OF CONTENTS

> *As there is no crime which can more excite and agitate the passions of men than treason, no charge demands more from the tribunal before which it is made a deliberate and temperate inquiry. Whether this inquiry be directed to the fact or to the law, none can be more solemn, none more important to the citizen or to the government; none can more affect the safety of both.*[1]

---

[1] *Ex parte* Bollman, 8 U.S. 75, 125 (1807).

INTRODUCTION

The crime of treason carries an emotional response unlike any other.[2] Its severity is second to none because one who commits treason aims to support the enemies his government, betray his own nation, and wage war against his own people. Infamous traitors such as Benedict Arnold[3] conjure a near-unanimous feeling of disdain and anger amongst Americans, while others like John Brown do not so easily create the same uniform negative perception.[4] Such is the nature of treason: those convicted of betraying their nation receive the designation of "traitor," arguably the most severe, polarizing, and stigmatic title law can provide, which may partially explain why the last case of treason occurred in 1952.[5] However, the centuries-old crime of treason is still as relevant as it was during the establishment of the United States. America currently faces a stateless enemy which operates in the shadows using unconventional warfare. This enemy engages in terrorism and promotes small-scale attacks against civilians.[6]

---

[2] *See* Joseph Story, *3 Commentaries on the Constitution § 1791* (1833), *in* 4 THE FOUNDERS' CONSTITUTION 467 (Philip B. Kurland & Ralph Lerner eds., 2000)) (stating "[t]reason is generally deemed the highest crime, which can be committed in civil society, since its aim is the overthrow of the government. . . . Its tendency is to create universal danger and alarm; and on this account it is peculiarly odious, and often visited with the deepest public resentment.").

[3] *See* WALTER L. POWELL, BENEDICT ARNOLD: REVOLUTIONARY WAR HERO AND TRAITOR 81–85 (2004) (noting in the fall of 1780, Benedict Arnold instructed John Andre to travel to West Point, New York in an effort to assist the British in capturing the West Point forts).

[4] *See* DAVID S. REYNOLDS, JOHN BROWN, ABOLITIONIST: THE MAN WHO KILLED SLAVERY, SPARKED THE CIVIL WAR, AND SEEDED CIVIL RIGHTS 1 (2005) (stating "John Brown planted seeds for the civil rights movement by making a pioneering demand for complete social and political equality for America's ethnic minorities.").

[5] *See* Kawakita v. United States, 343 U.S. 717, 744–45 (1952).

[6] *See, e.g.,* Faith Karimi, et al., *ISIS, San Bernardino Shooters 'Supporters' of ISIS, Terrorist Group Says*, CNN (Dec. 5, 2015), http://www.cnn.com/2015/12/05/us/san-bernardino-shooting/index.html; *Paris Attacks: What Happened on the Night*, BBC NEWS (Dec. 9, 2015), http://www.bbc.com/news/world-europe-34818994.

This enemy is named the Islamic State of Iraq and Syria ("ISIS"), a Sunni terrorist organization[7] that views the United States as an enemy with which it is at war.[8] Since the outbreak of the Syrian civil war in 2011, ISIS has sought to overthrow the Assad regime and establish an Islamic caliphate that traverses Iraqi and Syrian borders.[9] Led by Abu Bakr al- Baghdadi, ISIS is notorious for brutally beheading journalists,[10] burning its enemies alive,[11] and slaughtering innocent civilians.[12] Notwithstanding major defeats over the past several years in Iraq and Syria, the terror group continues to disrupt daily life in the Middle East and poses a direct threat to Western Europe and the United States.[13]

---

[7] *See* Press Release, U.S. DEP'T OF STATE, Foreign Terrorist Organizations, http://www.state.gov/j/ct/rls/other/des/123085.htm (last visited March 9, 2016) (designating ISIS as a foreign terrorist organization on December 17, 2004).

[8] *See* Ahmed Tolba & Sylvia Westall, *Islamic State Urges Jihad Against Russians, Americans: Audio*, REUTERS (Oct. 13, 2015, 1:58 PM), https://www.reuters.com/article/us-mideast-crisis-islamicstate/islamic-state-urges-jihad-against-russians-americans-audio-idUSKCN0S72DH20151013 (reporting that ISIS calls for Muslims to wage a "holy war" against Russia and America for fighting a "crusaders war" in the Middle East).

[9] *See* Sylvia Westall, ISIS Declares Islamic 'Caliphate' and Calls on Groups to Pledge Allegiance, WORLD POST (June 29, 2014, 1:44 PM), http://www.huffingtonpost.com/2014/06/29/isis-declares-caliphate_n_5541634.html.

[10] *See, e.g.*, Chelsea J. Carter, *Video Shows ISIS Beheading U.S. Journalist James Foley*, CNN (Aug. 20, 2014), http://www.cnn.com/2014/08/19/world/meast/isis-james-foley/ (beheading of American journalist James Foley).

[11] *See* Jordanian Pilot's "Obscene Burning Death by ISIS Sparks Outrage in Mideast*, CBS NEWS (Feb. 4, 2014, 9:40 A.M.), http://www.cbsnews.com/news/jordanian-pilots-obscene-burning-death-by-isis-sparks-outrage-in-mideast/ (burning alive Jordanian pilot Muath al-Kasaesbeh).

[12] *See* Will Worley, *ISIS 'Kidnaps 400 Civilians' After Mass Slaughter of Civilians in Syrian City of Deir al-Zor*, THE INDEPENDENT (Jan. 17, 2016), http://www.independent.co.uk/news/world/middle-east/isis-kidnaps-400-civilians-after-mass-slaughter-of-civilians-in-syrian-city-of-deir-al-zor-a6817081.html (evidence of ISIS slaughtering 150 civilians in Syria).

[13] *See* Rukmini Callimachi, *Fight to Retake Last ISIS Territory Begins*, N.Y. TIMES (Sept. 11, 2018), https://www.nytimes.com/2018/09/11/world/middleeast/isis-syria.html.

On November 13, 2015, ISIS successfully executed a coordinated attack in Paris, where 129 people were killed.[14] Less than a month later, two people affiliated with ISIS murdered 14 people in San Bernardino, California.[15] The horrific attack was magnified by the realization that one of the attackers was an American.[16] As a result, Americans drew their attention to the emerging threat posed by fellow citizens engaging in terrorism both at home and abroad. The bloodshed continued on March 22, 2016, when ISIS cells successfully executed coordinated terrorist attacks in Brussels, Belgium killing 32 victims and injuring 340 others.[17] Later that year, the United States witnessed the deadliest terror attack on American soil since September 11, 2001,[18] when Omar Mateen slaughtered 49 people at the Pulse nightclub in

---

[14] *See* Andrew Higgins & Kimiko de Freytas-Tamura, *Paris Attacks Suspect Killed in Shootout had Plotted Terror for 11 Months*, N.Y. TIMES (Nov. 19, 2015), https://www.nytimes.com/2015/11/20/world/europe/paris-attacks.html.

[15] *See* Richard Winton & James Queally, *FBI is Now Convinced that Couple Tried to Detonate Bomb in San Bernardino Terror Attack*, L.A. TIMES (Jan. 15, 2016), http://www.latimes.com/local/lanow/la-me-ln-fbi-san-bernardino-bombs-20160115-story.html.

[16] *See* Michael S. Schmidt, *F.B.I. Treating San Bernardino Attacks as Terrorism Case*, N.Y. TIMES (Dec. 4, 2015), http://www.nytimes.com/2015/12/05/us/tashfeen-malik-islamic-state.html (reporting that Syed Rizwan Farook was born in Illinois).

[17] *See Brussels Explosions: What We Know about Airport and Metro Attacks*, BBC NEWS (Apr. 9, 2016), http://www.bbc.com/news/world-europe-35869985.

[18] On October 1, 2017, Stephen Paddock shot and killed 58 people while injuring over 500 others during a concert on the Las Vegas strip, making it the worst mass shooting in the United States. The Department of Homeland Security has not deemed the shooting an act of terror. However, MGM Resorts is seeking a declaratory judgment in federal court to find the attack to be an act of terrorism under the SAFTEY Act in order to shield the corporation from any legal liability resulting from the shooting. *See* Dep't of Homeland Sec., Press Release – DHS Statement on Las Vegas Shooting (Oct. 2, 2017), https://www.dhs.gov/news/2017/10/02/dhs-statement-las-vegas-shooting; Serge F. Kovaleski & Richard A. Oppel Jr., *A Man Stashed Guns in His Las Vegas Hotel Room. 3 Years Later, a Killer Did the Same*, N.Y. TIMES (Sep. 28, 2018), https://www.nytimes.com/2018/09/28/us/las-vegas-shooting-mgm-lawsuits.html.

Orlando, Florida.[19] Prior to executing the attack, Omar pledged allegiance to ISIS during a 911 phone call.[20] Following these devastating attacks, ISIS continued to execute successful terror attacks around the world over the next two years, notwithstanding losing most of its territory held in Syria and Iraq.[21]

To combat terrorism, the U.S. government has traditionally used counterterrorism laws found in Title 18, Chapter 113B of the U.S. Code.[22] The U.S. government also holds another legal tool at its disposal: treason. Treason is the only crime defined in the U.S. Constitution and may be used in prosecutions against Americans who join ISIS.[23] As stated by the late Justice Antonin Scalia, "[w]here the Government accuses a citizen of waging war against it, our constitutional tradition has been to prosecute him in federal court for treason or some other crime."[24] The U.S. government could argue that Americans who join ISIS and wage war against the United States or support its combat efforts necessarily engage in treason.

Terrorism is a relatively new and unique form of warfare. For the purpose of the Treason Clause, terrorism must be analyzed differently than warfare conducted against the United States by a sovereign nation.[25] Sovereign nations with standing armies have few issues with the loyalty of their troops or the intent of those troops to fight Americans in times of conflict with the United States.

---

[19] See Ralph Ellis et al., *Orlando Shooting: 49 Killed, Shooter Pledged ISIS Allegiance*, CNN (June 13, 2016), https://www.cnn.com/2016/06/12/us/orlando-nightclub-shooting/index.html.

[20] See id.

[21] See Tom O'Connor, *What Did ISIS Do in 2017? Islamic State Reveals Its Favorite Terror Attacks and Calls for More*, NEWSWEEK (Nov. 18, 2017), https://www.newsweek.com/what-isis-do-2017-islamic-state-reveals-favorite-terror-attacks-calls-more-715867; Sara Malm, *A Worldwide State of Terror: Map Shows How ISIS Continues to Wreak Carnage Across the Globe, Despite Losing its Caliphate*, DAILY MAIL (July 12, 2018), https://www.dailymail.co.uk/news/article-5945599/ISIS-terror-attacks-2018-Map-Islamic-States-continued-carnage-not-defeated.html.

[22] See generally Terrorism, 18 U.S.C. Ch. 113B (2015).

[23]U.S. CONST. art. 3, § 3, cl. 1; United States v. Greathouse, 26 F. Cas. 18, 21 (C.C.N.D. Cal. 1863) (No. 15,254).

[24] Hamdi v. Rumsfeld, 542 U.S. 507, 554 (2004) (Scalia, J., dissenting).

[25] *Terrorist Groups*, TERRORISM RESEARCH, http://www.terrorism-research.com/groups/ (last visited Mar. 3, 2016).

Terrorists do not function in the same way. Terrorist organizations such as ISIS are often comprised of smaller cells and subgroups.[26] When terror cells form in the United States, the question of whether those cells commit treason against the United States is hard to answer. Terror cells must hold a duty of loyalty to the United States and engage in actual hostilities on behalf of an enemy of America to commit treason.[27] An assessment of actual Americans who act on behalf or in support of ISIS is imperative to assess and apply the elements of treason to this modern threat.[28] In analyzing the merits of any treason claim against these Americans, the inquiry must first examine the history of the Treason Clause. Treason derives from British common law and was carefully defined by the Founding Fathers in the Constitution.[29]

The inquiry must then outline U.S. case law, following the evolution of the treason convictions deemed important by the U.S. government throughout later criminal proceedings. This examination will necessarily delve into the "Levying War" and "Aid and Comfort" provisions of the Treason Clause and apply them to Americans who join ISIS.[30]

An examination and application of the Treason Clause to American ISIS members will lead to the conclusion that treason is a viable option for the U.S. government in combating ISIS. The conclusion is not all-encompassing, but

---

[26] *See id.* (explaining that terrorist groups are often organized either in a hierarchy or network structure).

[27] *See* U.S. CONST. art. III, § 3, cl. 1 (stating, in relevant part, "[t]reason against the United States, shall consist only in levying war against them, or in adhering to their enemies, giving them aid and comfort.").

[28] The government must prove a purported traitor's intent to commit treason against the United States to receive a guilty verdict. *See* Cramer v. United States, 325 U.S. 1, 31 (1945) (stating "to make treason the defendant not only must intend the act, but he must intend to betray his country by means of the act.").

[29] *See* JAMES W. HURST, THE LAW OF TREASON IN THE UNITED STATES: COLLECTED ESSAYS 25 (1945) (stating Lord Coke cited the common law in outlining what constituted an overt act); J. Taylor Mcconkie, *State Treason: The History and Validity of Treason Against Individual States*, 101 KY. L. J. 281, 286 (2013) (stating "[i]n seeking to restrict the content of the crime [of treason], the drafters of the resolution evidenced an awareness that existing treason laws in the colonies had expanded dangerously beyond recognition.").

[30] *See* Tim Lister et al., *ISIS Goes Global: 143 Attacks in 29 Countries Have Killed 2,043*, CNN (Feb. 12, 2018), https://www.cnn.com/2015/12/17/world/mapping-isis-attacks-around-the-world/index.html.

distinguishes between those American supporters of ISIS who are eligible and ineligible for treason prosecution. Because treason should be used as one of many weapons in the U.S. government's legal arsenal in the fight against ISIS, this crime is best applied to those Americans who fit legal precedents found throughout American history.

Treason is not an obsolete and ancient crime, but one that can be useful and relevant today when combating organizations like ISIS. Though treason convictions are rare in U.S. history, they have been effective in putting traitors behind bars and signaling the gravity of betraying one's nation.[31] In a time where numerous Americans seek to join a group that is avidly waging war against the United States, treason prosecutions may help battle this threat, which has penetrated the U.S. border and successfully executed attacks on American soil.[32]

I.   THE HISTORY OF THE TREASON CLAUSE

Since the dawn of America's experiment with democracy, treason has played an important role in efforts to administer the rule of law.[33] The original American colonists understood the severity of the crime due to its use against both common citizens and royalty throughout English history.[34] The American colonies adopted the concept when drafting the Treason Clause of the U.S. Constitution, in large part because of English influence in the colonies.[35] While English law played a vital role in constructing the Treason

---

[31] *See, e.g.*, Kawakita v. United States, 343 U.S. 717, 737–41 (1952).

[32] *See, e.g.*, Ellis, et al., *supra* note 19.

[33] *See, e.g., Laws of Maryland at Large 1638, in* 4 THE FOUNDERS' CONSTITUTION 408 (Philip B. Kurland & Ralph Lerner eds., 2000) (including "compass or conspire the Death of the King," "levy War against his Majesty," to counterfeit the King's Great or Privy Seal," and "to join or adhere to any foreign Prince or State" within the scope of treason).

[34] *See* Kristen E. Eichensehr, *Treason in the Age of Terrorism: An Explanation and Evaluation of Treason's Return in the Democratic States*, 42 VAND. J. TRANSNAT'L L. 1443, 1448 (2009) (explaining King Charles I was put to death for levying war against the "Parliament and Kingdom.").

[35] *See* Joseph Story, *Commentaries on the Constitution* §§ 1791–94, 1796 (1833) *in* 4 THE FOUNDERS' CONSTITUTION 409, 467–68 (Philip B. Kurland & Ralph Lerner eds., 1987).

Clause, the Founding Fathers sought to safeguard against arbitrary use of the crime.[36] These concerns led to the inclusion of the Treason Clause in the Constitution, a tactical maneuver that sought to restrain subsequent American leaders from expanding its meaning.[37] Understanding the history and intent of the Treason Clause is important for determining whether it may be used against Americans who join ISIS or conduct terrorist attacks in its name.

A. The Treason Act of 1351

The American concept of treason is rooted in England's Treason Act of 1351, implemented during the reign of King Edward III.[38] The Treason Act of 1351 provided English courts a much-needed definition of the high crime.[39] Until the passage of the Act, English courts held much latitude in construction of the ill-defined crimes.[40] In the Act, "treason" was defined as "compassing the Death of the King, Queen, or their eldest son," "levying War," "adhering to the King's Enemies," and "killing the Chancellor, Treasurer, or Judges in Execution of their Duty."[41] The passage of this act signified a new restrictive nature to treason jurisprudence.[42] As Sir Matthew Hale explained, "there should be some fixed and settled boundary for this great crime of treason, and

---

[36] See THE FEDERALIST NO. 43, at 436 (James Madison) (Philip B. Kurland & Ralph Lerner eds., 1987) (explaining the Treason Clause's purpose in eliminating "new-fangled and artificial treasons.").

[37] See Treason Act of 1351, 25 Edw. III (Eng.).

[38] See HURST, supra note 29, at 4, 16–17 (explaining King Edward III's intentions to resolve uncertainties in the common law regarding treason); Eichensehr, supra note 33, at 1447 (discussing the enactment of the Treason Act).

[39] See Note, Historical Concept of Treason: English, American, 35 IND. L. J. 70, 71 (1959).

[40] Id. (stating "[the Treason Act of 1351] attempted to define the law and abolish the latitude for construction which the local courts had exercised up to that time.").

[41] See Treason Act of 1351, 25 Edw. III, c. 2 (Eng.). See also James Wilson, Of Crimes Immediately Against the Community Lectures on Law 2:663–69 (1791), in 4 THE FOUNDERS' CONSTITUTION 436–47 (Philip B. Kurland & Ralph Lerner eds., 1987) (outlining the history of the Treason Clause).

[42] See HURST, supra note 29, at 17 (stating "the general terms of [Lord] Coke's analysis are all such as to stress that the distinguishing mark of the Statute of Edward III is its limitation of the scope of the crime [of treason].").

of what great importance the [Treason Act of 1351] was, in order to that end."[43] While commentators applauded the restrictions inherent in the Treason Act of 1351, the scope of the crime fluctuated over the course of several centuries, garnering much debate.[44]

Perhaps the most significant clarification in the statute was the requirement of an overt act. As Lord Coke explained, "a compassing or conspiracy to levy war is no Treason, for there must be a levying war *in facto*."[45] Without an actual, overt act, a person cannot commit treason. The Treason Act of 1351 attempted to codify an invaluable procedural safeguard against arbitrary criminal convictions: the requirement for a court to find that a purported traitor *actually* committed an act against the State with treasonous intent.[46] Though English leaders often abused use of the crime after the passage of the Treason Act of 1351,[47] its text served as the foundation for the United States' clearer and more narrowly defined Treason Clause.[48]

B. The Treason Clause – Article III, Section 3 of the U.S. Constitution

In deciding to secede from the British Empire, the American colonies listed numerous "despotic" wrongdoings committed by Great Britain in the Declaration of Independence as support for their secession.[49] Many of these grievances related to arbitrary and unlawful acts committed by King George

---

[43] Matthew Hale, 1 *History of the Pleas of The Crown* 83, 86–87, 115–16, 119, 122 *in* 4 THE FOUNDERS' CONSTITUTION 409, 410 (Philip B. Kurland & Ralph Lerner eds., 1987).

[44] *See generally* D. ALAN ORR, TREASON AND THE STATE: LAW, POLITICS, AND IDEOLOGY IN THE ENGLISH CIVIL WAR 15–28 (2002); Eichensehr, *supra* note 34, at 1447 (explaining the role of the Tudor monarchs in expanding the reach of the Treason Act of 1351).

[45] HURST, *supra* note 29, at 28.

[46] *See* EDWARD COKE, THIRD INSTITUTE 38 (1641), *in* 4 THE FOUNDERS' CONSTITUTION 408–09 (Philip B. Kurland & Ralph Lerner eds., 1987) (stating that "besides [] confederacy, compassing, conspiracy, or imagination, there must be some other over act or deed tending thereunto, to make it treason within the [Treason Act of 1351]").

[47] *See generally, Historical Concept of Treason: English, American, supra* note 39, at 73–76.

[48] *See id.* at 76–77 (noting the similarities between the text of the Treason Act of 1351 and that of Article III, Section 3 of the U.S. Constitution).

[49] *See generally* THE DECLARATION OF INDEPENDENCE ¶¶ 6–29 (1776).

III and the British Parliament.[50] Several drafters of the Constitution were perturbed by what appeared to be rampant arbitrariness in the administration of the law.[51] The drafters of the Treason Clause considered these concerns and added several new procedures to protect potential defendants.[52] In particular, the drafters added the qualifying phrase "giving them Aid and Comfort" to restrict the phrase "adhering to their Enemies."[53] They also included the requirement that two witnesses must present testimony to the same overt act, adding more procedural safeguards during treason prosecutions.[54]

Several of the drafters, such as James Madison, were wary of making the clause too restrictive and sought to grant the legislative branch more latitude in defining treason.[55] They believed congressional oversight over how treason is defined would offer sufficient protections.[56] The drafters also determined that the terms "levying war" and "adhering to their enemies" should be separated by the conjunction "or" instead of "and" to signify both were separate overt acts of treason.[57] Upon ratification, the new United States adopted Article III, Section 3, which reads:

> Treason against the United States, shall consist only in levying War against them, or in adhering to their Enemies, giving them Aid and Comfort. No Person shall be convicted of Treason unless on the Testimony of two Witnesses to the same overt Act, or on Confession in open Court. The Congress shall have Power to declare the Punishment of Treason, but no Attainder of Treason shall work

---

[50] *See id. See also* Story, *supra* note 35, at §§ 1791–94, 1796.

[51] *See* HURST, *supra* note 29, at 142–44.

[52] *See* THE FEDERALIST NO. 43, at 436 (James Madison) (Philip B. Kurland & Ralph Lerner eds., 1987). *See generally Records from the Federal Convention, in* 4 THE FOUNDERS' CONSTITUTION 435 (Philip B. Kurland & Ralph Lerner eds., 1987).

[53] George Mason proposed this restrictive phrase because he thought without it, the provision would be too indefinite. *See Records from the Federal Convention, supra* note 52.

[54] U.S. CONST. art. III, § 3, cl. 1.

[55] *See Records From The Federal Convention, supra* note 52, at 435.

[56] *Id.*

[57] *See id.* The use of "or" provides for two distinct overt acts instead of one. This is in line with James Madison's view of avoiding an overly restrictive Treason Clause, outlined in the beginning of the paragraph.

Corruption of Blood, or Forfeiture except during the Life of the Person attainted.[58]

As the only crime defined in the Constitution, treason became solidified in the bedrock of American law. The statutory definition of "Treason," states "[w]hoever [] ow[es] allegiance to the United States" commits treason if he "levies war against them or adheres to their enemies, giving them aid and comfort within the United States or elsewhere . . .."[59] The statute clarifies the Treason Clause by explaining that a treason charge may only be invoked against someone who owes allegiance to the United States.[60] The term allegiance, which the Second Continental Congress defined in its "Committee on Spies,"[61] caused debate as to the extent of its reach.[62]

Treason cases are often surrounded by controversy due to the lack of uniformity in definition. Calls to utilize the treason statute in the post-9/11 "War on Terror" only add to this controversy. In light of successful attempts by Americans to join ISIS and enter Syria and Iraq to fight on the group's behalf, this constitutional crime may benefit the government in potential prosecutions while also protecting those who owe allegiance to the United States. For example, Hoda Muthana, an American woman who seeks to return to the United States after joining ISIS in 2014, may have committed treason by

---

[58] U.S. CONST. art. III, § 3.

[59] *See* Treason, 18 U.S.C. § 2381 (2018). This crime carries either the death penalty or a prison term of no less than five years and includes a fine of no less than $10,000. *Id.* Someone convicted of treason also relinquishes his ability to hold any office in the United States. *See* U.S. CONST. art. 3, § 3.

[60] Treason, 18 U.S.C. § 2381 (2018).

[61] John Adams, et al., *Continental Congress, "Committee on Spies"* (June 5, 1776), *in* 4 THE FOUNDERS' CONSTITUTION 430 (Philip B. Kurland & Ralph Lerner eds., 2000) (stating that "all persons abiding within any of the United Colonies, and deriving protection from the laws of the same, owe allegiance . . . [including] all persons passing through, visiting, or mak[ing] a temporary stay in any of the said colonies, being entitled to the protection of the laws . . .."). *See also* An Act for the Punishment of Certain Crimes Against The United States, 1 Stat. 112, § 1 (1790) (including the "allegiance" provision).

[62] *See, e.g.,* Carlisle v. United States, 83 U.S. 147, 148 (1872) (stating "[t]hose aliens who, being domiciled in the country prior to the [Civil War], gave aid and comfort to the rebellion, were, therefore, subject to be prosecuted for violation of the laws of the United States against treason and for giving aid and comfort to the rebellion.").

tweeting her support for ISIS atrocities across the globe and urging Americans to join the jihadist cause.[63] The crime may provisions of the Treason Clause may protect Kimberly Gwen Polman, a Canadian-American citizen who traveled to the former Islamic State, may be protected by the restricted nature of the Treason Clause because she did not tweet her support of terror attacks or propagandize on behalf of ISIS.[64]

Similar to the Treason Act of 1351, the Treason Clause evolved over time in U.S. courts.[65] To properly understand the evolution of treason and its role in the age of terrorism, reference to major American treason cases is beneficial. This inquiry is timely because treason is no longer merely a historical aspect of American law. The common assumption that the clause had all but disappeared from American legal practice are no longer warranted after the indictment of Adam Gadahn, known as Azzam al-Amriki (Azzam the American).[66] In 2006, a federal grand jury indicted Gadahn for treason because he joined al Qaeda and participated in propaganda videos.[67] Though Gadahn never faced trial,[68] this indictment serves as precedent for potential future indictments against American members of ISIS. An analysis of previous treason cases is necessary to better understand the legitimacy of any action against an American ISIS member, mirroring the Gadahn example.

---

[63] *See* Rukmini Callimachi & Catherine Porter, 2 American Wives of ISIS Militants Want to Return Home, N.Y. TIMES (Feb. 19, 2019), https://www.nytimes.com/2019/02/19/us/islamic-state-american-women.html.

[64] *See id.*

[65] See Hurst, *supra* note 29, at 10–11, 186–92.

[66] *See* First Superseding Indictment, at 2–8, United States v. Gadahn, SA CR 05-254(A) (D.C.C. Cal. 2006) [hereinafter Gadahn Indictment].

[67] *Id.*

[68] In early 2015, President Obama reported that a CIA drone strike near the Pakistan-Afghanistan border killed Gadahn. *See* Jim Miklaszewski et al., *Americans Warren Weinstein and Adam Gadahn Killed in U.S. Drone Strikes*, NBC NEWS (Apr. 23, 2015, 6:29 PM), http://www.nbcnews.com/news/us-news/warren-weinstein-adam-gadahn-killed-u-s-operation-n346861.

II. TREASON IN THE COURTS: AN ANALYSIS OF THE TREASON CASE LAW

When debating over which provisions would comprise the Treason Clause, the drafters of the U.S. Constitution attempted to define which overt acts and what sort of intent constituted a betrayal of one's nation.[69] Though they added language to clarify aspects of treason and narrow its scope, ambiguities remained.[70] As the young nation faced various conflicts and rebellions, U.S. courts had to interpret the intent of the drafters and the terms and provisions of the Treason Clause. This arduous process resulted in a series of court decisions which shaped the "Levying War" and "Aid and Comfort" provisions.[71]

Though there are fewer than thirty instances of treason charges in U.S. history,[72] an examination of these cases is useful in determining whether joining ISIS warrants a treason indictment. This section outlines the most prominent historical cases of treason in the United States, beginning with the Whiskey Rebellion and ending with the World War II cases. These cases show that the charge of "levying war" essentially disappeared in the 20th century, leaving the charge of "adhering to their Enemies" as the favored option for prosecutors.[73] In the current conflict against ISIS, the levying war charge should be considered for use against Americans who wage war in the name of ISIS jihad.

---

[69] *See generally*, HURST, *supra* note 29, at 129–38 (outlining the debates, examinations, and discussions of the Constitutional Convention of 1787).

[70] *See id.* at 190–92 (noting the early legal debate over the extent to which British precedent could be used in American treason cases).

[71] *See generally id.* at 196–210 (outlining U.S. court cases related to both provisions of the Treason Clause).

[72] See Pamela J. Podger, *Few Ever Charged or Convicted of Treason in U.S. History/Many Americans Fought for other Religious, Political, Cultural Beliefs*, SF GATE (Dec. 9, 2001), http://www.sfgate.com/crime/article/Few- ever-charged-or-convicted-of-treason-in-U-S-2843242.php.

[73] *See, e.g.*, Haupt v. United States, 330 U.S. 631, 635 (1947).

A. Early Rebellions and the Case of Aaron Burr

Within ten years of the ratification of the Constitution, the first overt act of treason occurred on American soil. After the Washington administration implemented a whiskey excise tax in 1791, the United States witnessed an uprising by farmers in rural Pennsylvania, known as the Whiskey Rebellion.[74] The uprising occurred because these farmers experienced a major shortage of credit and hard currency as well as waves of foreclosures.[75] The Pennsylvania farmers viewed the whiskey tax, one they opposed since at least 1783, as a violation of the U.S. Constitution and a betrayal of their efforts during the Revolutionary War.[76] As the rebellion began to spiral out of control in 1794,[77] President Washington led an army against the farmers and quelled the opposition.[78]

As a result of this rebellion, twenty-four farmers were indicted in the Circuit Court for the Federal District of Pennsylvania for committing treason, the first such instance in U.S. history.[79] Of these twenty-four, only two, Philip Vigol and John Mitchell, were convicted of treason for levying war against the United States.[80] During these trials, Justice William Paterson accepted the prosecution's argument that since Vigol and Mitchell intended to force Congress to repeal the tax, the tax *"would* be suppressed throughout the Union," which would accomplish the goal of levying war against their

---

[74] *See* CHRISTIAN G. FRITZ, AMERICAN SOVEREIGNS: THE PEOPLE AND AMERICA'S CONSTITUTIONAL TRADITION BEFORE THE CIVIL WAR 153 (2008).

[75] *See id.* at 158.

[76] *See id.* at 162 (stating those opposed to the Whiskey Excise Tax of 1791 believed U.S. constitutionalism embraced the idea of the "People" over the state and federal governments, including their right to resist taxes deemed unjust and unequal).

[77] Protestors burned chief tax collector John Neville's home to the ground. *See* Michael Hoover, *The Whiskey Rebellion*, ALCOHOL AND TOBACCO TAX AND TRADE BUREAU, http://www.ttb.gov/public_info/whisky_rebellion.shtml (last updated Aug. 21, 2014).

[78] FRITZ, *supra* note 74, at 153, 174.

[79] *Whiskey Rebellion*, ENCYCLOPEDIA.COM (2005), http://www.encyclopedia.com/topic/Whiskey_Rebellion.aspx.

[80] HISTORIC U.S. COURT CASES: AN ENCYCLOPEDIA 38 (John W. Johnson ed., 2d. ed., 2005). President Washington subsequently pardoned both shortly after their convictions. *See id.* at 40.

nation.[81] Justice Paterson's conclusion is based not on a factual occurrence but on a logical inference, known as a "constructive treason." The concept of constructive treason originated in England when "tyrannical princes [] had abundant opportunities to create . . . forced and arbitrary constructions, to raise offences into the guilt and punishment of treason, which were not suspected to be such."[82] Constructive treason broadened the reach of the Treason Clause to those acts that *would have* resulted in the levying war or adherence to enemies without an *actual* act occurring. Americans voiced their disdain for this concept, with commentators such as Francis Scott Key arguing "[i]f 100 men conspire, and only 50 actually levy war, the latter only are guilty as principals."[83]

Several years after the convictions of Vigol and Mitchell, a second related rebellion led to another set of famous treason trials. In 1798 the U.S. Congress imposed a direct tax to fund military efforts during the "Quasi War" with France.[84] In response, a Pennsylvanian named John Fries led an unsuccessful rebellion against the U.S. government.[85] As a result of this uprising, over forty Americans faced trial for their participation, eleven of whom faced treason charges.[86] Fries, the leader of the rebellion, faced two treason trials due to an issue Justice James Iredell had with one juror during the first trial.[87] During the second trial, Justice Samuel Chase instructed the jury that the overt act of levying war consists of an actual assemblage of persons with actual violence or force, regardless of whether it is sufficient violence or force, and a universal or general intention among the participants to "resist or oppose the execution of any statute of the United States . . .."[88] For Justice Chase, the key factor of

---

[81] *See id.* at 40. After accepting this notion in Mitchell's case, Justice Paterson instructed the jury that Mitchell "must be pronounced guilty." *Id.*

[82] *See* Story, *supra* note 35, § 1791.

[83] R. Kent Newmyer, The Treason Trial of Aaron Burr: Law, Politics, and the Character Wars of the Nation 61 (2012).

[84] *See* Paul D. Newman, Fries's Rebellion: The Enduring Struggle for the American Revolution 60, 67–68 (2004).

[85] Thomas Carpenter, The Two Trials of John Fries 201–02 (1800).

[86] Newman, *supra* note 84, at 241.

[87] The Supreme Court: Controversies, Cases, and Characters from John Jay to John Roberts 96–97 (Paul Finkelman ed., 2014).

[88] Carpenter, *supra* note 85, at 197 (relating the judge's instructions to the jury).

levying war against the United States was *actual* force. As he explained to the jury, conspiracy or combination to levy war does not amount to treason.[89]

The Whiskey Rebellion and the rebellion of John Fries serve as the foundation of American treason jurisprudence. These seminal cases helped clarify the language in the Treason Clause, but in the instance of the Whiskey Rebellion, diverged from the intent of its drafters. With the incorporation of constructive treason, U.S. courts departed from the actual text of the Treason Clause and opened the door to constructing new forms of treason. However, this possibility became less problematic when former Vice President Aaron Burr stood trial after purportedly attempting to form his own nation in Spanish-controlled territories.

Described as "the greatest criminal trial in American history and one of the notable trials in the annals of the law,"[90] the trial of Aaron Burr was pivotal in shaping the Treason Clause. With much engagement by President Thomas Jefferson, the Aaron Burr trial was full of personal vendettas and scandal.[91] After serving as Vice President and relinquishing his role as a U.S. Senator, Burr set out on an expedition along the Mississippi, allegedly to evaluate which territories would become his new nation.[92] While filled with mystery, the plot likely included the seizure of New Orleans and parts of Mexico.[93] The plan never came to fruition, however, after members of the Ohio militia helped disperse a group of men dedicated to the enterprise assembled at Blennerhassett Island in December 1806.[94] Burr himself was not present on the island, located on the Ohio River.[95] After the events at Blennerhassett Island, Burr and several main collaborators were arrested and stood trial for treason.[96]

---

[89] *See id.*

[90] NEWMYER, *supra* note 83, at 1 (quoting constitutional historian Edward Corwin).

[91] *See* THE TREASON TRIALS OF AARON BURR viii (Peter C. Hoffer ed., 2008) (explaining President Jefferson claimed Burr was guilty before the trial began).

[92] *See id.* at 42. His initial plot allegedly began while he was still Vice President, when he spoke with English Minister to the United States Anthony Merry about the "independence" of parts of the western United States. *Id.* at 40.

[93] *See Ex parte* Bollman, 8 U.S. 75, 133 (1807).

[94] JAMES E. LEWIS, JR., THE BURR CONSPIRACY: UNCOVERING THE STORY OF AN EARLY AMERICAN CRISIS 148 (2017).

[95] *See id.* at 159.

[96] *See id.*; United States v. Burr, 25 F. Cas. 55, 168 (C.C.D. Va. 1807) (No. 14,693).

Prior to Burr's trial, Erick Bollman and Samuel Swartwout, two of Burr's associates, were tried for levying war against the United States at Blennerhassett Island.[97] The case eventually reached the Supreme Court, where Chief Justice John Marshall found them not guilty.[98] Although Bollman and Swartwout claimed to have seized New Orleans and robbed banks to fund their operation, these statements alone did not amount to proof of an overt act of treason.[99] Chief Justice Marshall defined levying war as "an actual assemblage of men for the purpose of executing a treasonable design."[100] Chief Justice Marshall elaborated that merely traveling to the rendezvous point is not sufficient to commit treason.[101] Bollman and Swartwout failed to engage in rebellion and only "rendezvoused" on Blennerhassett Island.[102]

During Burr's trial, Chief Justice Marshall presided over the case at the U.S. Circuit Court for the District of Virginia.[103] The trial, described as "of infinite importance" for the United States, featured a myriad of complex legal issues.[104] The most important legal question of the trial was whether a treason suspect could levy war against the United States if he were not a part of a treasonous assemblage of men.[105] The prosecution argued Burr was legally present at the assemblage on Blennerhassett Island due to his role as leader and advisor beforehand.[106]

In his famous opinion, Chief Justice Marshall explained that a treason suspect who was not an actual member of an assemblage of men levying war must perform an overt act constituting "a 'part' in the fact of levying war" to

---

[97] *Ex parte Bollman*, 8 U.S. at 76.

[98] *Id.* at 135.

[99] *Id.*

[100] *Id.* at 127.

[101] *Id.* at 134.

[102] *Id.* at 135.

[103] Lewis, *supra* note 94, at 294.

[104] *See id.* (quoting Delaware Republican George Read and Maryland Federalist Luther Martin). *See generally id.* at 294–300 (issues included battles over the size of the grand jury, the first use of executive privilege by a U.S. president, and debates over whether the prosecution must produce two witnesses to the same overt treasonous act before reaching the question of treasonous intent).

[105] *See id.* at 299–300.

[106] *See* United States v. Burr, 25 F. Cas. 55, 169–70 (C.C.D. Va. 1807) (No. 14,693).

be found guilty.[107] A suspect merely serving in an advisory role to men who later assembled to levy war could not be found guilty under the U.S. Constitution.[108] Chief Justice Marshall stated "[t]hose only who perform a part, and who are leagued in the conspiracy, are declared to be traitors. . . . [T]hey must 'perform a part,' which will furnish the overt act; and they must be 'leagued in the conspiracy.' The person who comes within this description in the opinion of the court levies war."[109]

Conspiracy without an actual overt act is not enough to satisfy the Treason Clause. As outlined by Chief Justice Marshall, a purported traitor must be accused of executing a specific, overt act.[110] In the case of *Burr*, the prosecution accused Burr of levying war at Blennerhassett Island.[111] However, Burr was not on Blennerhassett Island in early December 1806. Due to this fact, the court could not legally find Burr to be guilty of committing treason.[112] The Chief Justice explained that a purported traitor could not be constructively present at a treasonous assemblage of men, for "if many conspire to levy war, and some actually levy it, they may not be indicted for levying war generally."[113]

In concluding his opinion, Chief Justice Marshall ruled the jury could not consider any of Burr's statements revealing his intent to betray the United States because Burr was not on Blennerhassett Island in December 1806.[114] The court said this testimony was at most corroborative, which may enter into evidence only after an overt act is proved.[115] Since the prosecution could not prove Burr was a part of the December 1806 assemblage on Blennerhassett

---

[107] *Id.* at 182.

[108] *See generally id.*

[109] *Id.* at 161 (citing *Ex parte Bollman*).

[110] *See id.* at 169–70.

[111] *See id.*

[112] *See id.* at 179.

[113] *Id.* at 173–75 (referencing Lord Hale).

[114] *Id.* at 180 (quoting "No testimony relative to the conduct or declarations of the prisoner elsewhere, and subsequent to the transaction on Blennerhassett's Island, can be admitted; because such testimony, being in its nature merely corroborative and incompetent to prove the overt act in itself, is irrelevant until there be proof of the overt act by two witnesses.").

[115] *See id.* at 170.

Island, the court barred it from entering Burr's statements and actions into evidence.[116]

Chief Justice Marshall's legal determinations in both *Bollman* and *Burr* overturned the precedent set by the Whiskey Rebellion cases and reinstated the original interpretation of the Treason Clause. In doing so, Chief Justice Marshall left a legacy of legal restraint for the Treason Clause, which limited the ability of courts to construct new forms of treason.

B. John Brown's Raid and the Civil War

Prior to the Civil War, several prominent treason charges, cases, and convictions caught the eye of the American public. Charges of attempting to form a monarchy along the Mississippi River[117] and a conviction for betraying an individual state[118] are representative of the wide array of acts that warranted judicial scrutiny. However, with the outbreak of the American Civil War, treason case law reached an entirely new level of challenge and complexity. The U.S. courts faced the difficult task of providing guidance for how to deal with an enemy consisting of half of the nation.

On October 16, 1859, prior to South Carolina's secession from the Union, outspoken abolitionist John Brown staged a raid on the federal armory in Harper's Ferry, Virginia (now West Virginia) with the goal of sparking a

---

[116] *Id.* at 180.

[117] *Warrant for Arrest of Joseph Smith on the Charge of Treason (June 25, 1844)*, UMKC Sch. of L., http://law2.umkc.edu/faculty/projects/ftrials/carthage/treasonwrit.html (last visited Oct. 4, 2018) (describing the indictment against the founder of the Church of Latter Day Saints for committing treason against Illinois); *see* Alex Beam, American Crucifixion: The Murder of Joseph Smith and the Fate of the Mormon Church xiv (2014) (stating that before Joseph Smith could stand trial, a mob broke into his prison cell and killed him).

[118] *See* Amasa M. Eaton, *Thomas Wilson Dorr, in* 5 Great American Lawyers The Lives and Influence of Judges and Lawyers Who Have Acquired Permanent National Reputation, and Have Developed the Jurisprudence of the United States 175, 228 (William Draper Lewis ed., 1908); *Ex parte* Dorr, 44 U.S. 103, 104–06 (1844) (denying a request to issue a writ of habeas corpus because the Court did not have jurisdiction over a person convicted of treason under a competent state court unless that person was being called as a witness in a federal case).

rebellion against the south and its institution of slavery.[119] After seizing the armory, a bloody battle ensued between Brown's men and townspeople. The ordeal quickly ended after President James Buchanan sent U.S. troops led by Colonel Robert E. Lee to Harper's Ferry.[120] After President Buchanan declined to prosecute a federal case against the captured Brown and several of his raiders, the Commonwealth of Virginia prepared for trial.[121]

In an already divided nation, the Brown trial garnered nationwide interest.[122] Held in Charlestown, Virginia, the trial resulted in Brown's conviction for levying war against Virginia.[123] The guilty verdict posed several problems not adequately addressed by the state court. The most pressing issue was whether Brown, a nonresident of Virginia, could be found guilty of betraying the state. The court dismissed Brown's argument that he could not, stating "the Constitution did not give rights and immunities alone but also imposed responsibilities."[124] A federal prosecution would have better rebutted Brown's argument because a citizen of a state is also a citizen of the collective United States, thus owing allegiance to the entire nation. English common law supports the notion that a citizen has the responsibility to maintain his allegiance to his entire country, not only to his local government.[125] Comparable to English precedent, the connection between the United States and its citizens or residents forms duties inherent in the concept

---

[119] BRIAN MCGINTY, JOHN BROWN'S TRIAL 42, 127 (2009).

[120] *See generally id.* at 49-62.

[121] *See id.* at 82 (noting that both the United States and Virginia had jurisdictional claims over the armory).

[122] *Id.* at 120.

[123] *Id.* at 216–217.

[124] *See* Carlton F.W. Larson, *The Forgotten Constitutional Law of Treason and the Enemy Combatant Problem*, 154 U. PA. L. REV. 863, 888 (2006) (offering a detailed outline of Brown's arguments and issues regarding the verdict).

[125] *See* John Adams et al., *supra* note 611, at 430; Sir Michael Foster, *Discourse on High Treason* (1762) 183–90, 193–98, 200–01, 205–11, 213, 216–19, 221–24, 220–46, 249–50, *in* 4 THE FOUNDERS' CONSTITUTION 410 (Philip B. Kurland & Ralph Lerner eds., 1987) ("High Treason being an Offence committed against the Duty of Allegiance . . .. The Duty of Allegiance, whether Natural or Local, is founded in the Relation the Person standeth in to the Crown, and in the Privileges He deriveth from that Relation. Local Allegiance is founded in the Protection a Foreigner enjoyeth for his Person, his Family or Effects during his Residence here[.]").

of allegiance.[126] In the case of Brown, one could argue that because Brown held American citizenship, and because he was in Virginia at the time of the insurrection, he owed allegiance to that state. Though the state court failed to adequately answer this question, treason jurisprudence would progress further still during the largest insurrection the United States ever faced.

In the early hours of April 12, 1861, General P.G.T. Beauregard bombarded Fort Sumter, initiating the bloodiest conflict in U.S. history.[127] The ensuing American Civil War posed several distinct issues related to the Treason Clause. First, almost half of U.S. citizens betrayed their allegiance to the Union by openly waging war against the United States.[128] When the citizens of the southern states seceded, they defied all duties and obligations inherent in citizenship. These states also entered into open rebellion with the intent to overthrow the U.S. government operating in the South.[129] By supporting these secessionist efforts and participating in open conflict against the United States, Americans who supported the Confederate States committed treason.

Second, unlike previous American insurrections such as the Whiskey and Fries rebellions, the Civil War was more akin to a traditional war warranting a congressional declaration. However, during the course of the conflict, Congress never formally exercised its Article I power to declare war against the Confederacy.[130] Without a formal declaration of war, potential issues arose

---

[126] *See* Carlisle v. United States, 83 U.S. 147, 154 (1873) (stating that "'allegiance' is . . . the obligation of fidelity and obedience which the individual owes to the government under which he lives, or his sovereign in return for the protection he receives.").

[127] *See* SABRINA CREWE & MICHAEL V. USCHAN, FORT SUMTER: THE CIVIL WAR BEGINS 16 (2004).

[128] Thirteen states seceded from the Union during the Civil War. *See Secession Acts of the Thirteen Confederate States*, CIVIL WAR TRUST, https://www.battlefields.org/learn/primary-sources/secession-acts-thirteen-confederate-states (last visited Apr. 2, 2016) (listing all acts and ordinances issued by the seceding states supporting secession).

[129] *See Carlisle*, 83 U.S. at 156 (citing President Johnson's December 25, 1868 pardon of all people participating directly or indirectly in insurrection during the Civil War).

[130] *See* U.S. CONST. art. I, § 8, cl. 11. *See also Official Declarations of War by Congress*, U.S. SENATE,

concerning the legality of U.S. military operations against the secessionist states[131] and the use of treason against ordinary citizens living within them.[132]

President Andrew Johnson shed some light on which citizens committed treason against the United States when he issued Proclamation 179, which fully pardoned all rebels who participated in the Civil War and granted them amnesty.[133]   This proclamation, issued on Christmas Day 1868, offered "amnesty and pardon to persons who had been or were concerned in the late rebellion against the lawful authority of the Government of the United States," which included "every person who, directly or indirectly, participated in the late insurrection or rebellion."[134]   The all-encompassing nature of this identified group of Americans appeared to indicate that most, if not all, of those who contributed in any way to the war effort against the Union were guilty of treason. Judging by the scope of Proclamation 179, contributions to the war effort included conducting business with the Confederacy[135] and merely residing within one of the thirteen seceding states as a citizen of the Confederacy.[136]   However, the Civil War treason cases did not address

---

http://www.senate.gov/pagelayout/history/h_multi_sections_and_teasers/WarDeclar ationsbyCongress.htm (last visited Feb. 28, 2019).

[131] *See* The Prize Cases, 67 U.S. 635, 636 (1863) (challenging President Lincoln's ability to blockade Confederate ports and capture ships within those ports without a congressional declaration of war).

[132] *See, Carlisle*, 83 U.S. at 155 (holding British citizens domiciled in the United States have committed treason by manufacturing saltpeter and selling it to the Confederacy).

[133] Gerhard Peters & John T. Woolley, *Proclamation 179—Granting Full Pardon and Amnesty for the Offense of Treason Against the United States During the Late Civil War*, THE AMERICAN PRESIDENCY PROJECT, https://www.presidency.ucsb.edu/documents/ proclamation-179-granting-full-pardon-and-amnesty-for-the-offense-treason-against-the (last visited Oct. 4, 2018).

[134] *Id.*

[135] *See Carlisle*, 83 U.S. at 155–56.

[136] James Hurst argues that during the Constitutional Convention, the Framers chose to not limit the Treason Clause's ability to reach those participating in a civil war against the United States. *See* HURST, *supra* note 29, at 134 (stating "[t]he only respects in which the Convention may be said to have rejected opportunities to confine the scope of the offense were in rejecting the suggestions that the states be denied any authority to define treason against themselves, and that participation in a civil war, between a state and the nation, be excepted.").

whether remaining a citizen of the Confederacy constituted an overt act of treason.[137]

In *The Prize Cases*, the Supreme Court remained focused on what constituted an act of levying war. *The Prize Cases* presented the question of whether President Abraham Lincoln could legally blockade Confederate ports and take violators' cargo as a "prize" without a congressional declaration of war.[138] To determine the legality of President Lincoln's actions, the Court examined whether a state of war existed at the time of the blockade, and to what extent the President may act to thwart hostile actors absent congressional action.[139] The Court concluded that a state of war did exist at the time of the blockade and the President, through his constitutional powers as Commander-in-Chief, had the duty to "resist force by force" when it was thrust upon the nation.[140] The Court clarified that while the President may not initiate or declare war, he must counter insurrection or hostilities "without waiting for any special legislative authority."[141] For the Treason Clause, the holding in *The Prize Cases* applies the reasoning in the case of the Whiskey and Fries rebellions that levying war occurs when Americans engage in rebellion even without a congressional declaration of war. When rebellion or insurrection occurs within the United States, all direct and indirect participants are subject to the Treason Clause.

The Civil War featured several prominent treason cases, some of which posed major issues for criminal procedure and the constitutional right to a fair criminal trial.[142] Throughout the conflict, Union forces made examples of Southerners who committed acts disrespectful to the United States. In one particular instance, Union forces executed a gambler named William

---

[137] Note that one should construe the term "overt act" broadly to justify the inclusion of people remaining in a State in open rebellion but who choose not to participate further in hostilities against the U.S. government.

[138] The Prize Cases, 67 U.S. 635, 636 (1863).

[139] *Id.* at 659, 666.

[140] *Id.* at 668–69.

[141] *Id.*

[142] *See* U.S. CONST. amends. V, VI (codifying rights in criminal cases and the right to a fair trial).

Mumford after he tore down and desecrated a U.S. flag in New Orleans.[143] Mumford's trial took place within the Union-occupied city and featured a jury comprised of officers handpicked by the de-facto military governor, General Benjamin Butler.[144] During his trial, Mumford faced various treason charges, including "maliciously and willfully tear[ing] down said flag from said building and trail[ing] it ignominiously through the public streets, and . . . destroy[ing] [it]."[145] Upon conclusion of the trial, the jury found Mumford guilty and sentenced him to death.[146] On June 7, 1862, Mumford was hanged by Union troops next to the same building from which he removed the American flag several weeks earlier.[147] This trial appeared inherently unjust to the citizens of New Orleans and was arguably unconstitutional because it lacked an impartial judge and jury.[148]

The Civil War also presented one of the first treason cases dealing with the "Aid and Comfort" provision of the Treason Clause. In *United States v. Greathouse*, several seamen were indicted for levying war against the United States and giving aid and comfort to the Confederacy for attempting to intercept and seize mail ships traveling between California and the port of Panama and capture the U.S. fort at Alcatraz in March 1863.[149] The men had previously received a letter of marque from Confederate President Jefferson Davis to engage in hostilities but were apprehended by authorities before achieving their objective.[150] Before the sailors could leave the port of San

---

[143] BENJAMIN F. BUTLER, AUTOBIOGRAPHY AND PERSONAL REMINISCENCES OF MAJOR-GENERAL BENJ. F. BUTLER 438–42 (1892).

[144] *See id.*

[145] *Id.*

[146] *Id.*

[147] *Id.*

[148] *See id.* Treason trials must protect the defendant's right to due process and a fair trial. *See* U.S. CONST. art. III, § 3; U.S. CONST. amends. V, VI.

[149] *See* United States v. Greathouse, 26 F. Cas. 18, 18–21 (C.C.N.D. Cal. 1863) (No. 15,254) (involving defendants indicted under An Act to Suppress Insurrection, to Punish Treason and Rebellion, and Confiscate the Property of Rebels, and for Other Purposes, 12 Stat. 589 (1862)).

[150] *See id.*

Francisco, however, U.S. revenue officers seized their schooner and arrested them.[151]

The court in *Greathouse* made two significant contributions to treason jurisprudence when it outlined to the jury what acts constituted treason. First, the court explained that to aid and comfort the enemy, one must provide assistance to subjects of a foreign nation and *not* rebels or insurrectionists.[152] Because the defendants in *Greathouse* supported the Confederacy, the court instructed the jury to omit any consideration of aiding and comforting the enemy.[153] Second, the court stated that a crew's postponement of actual hostilities did not preclude a guilty verdict.[154] The court's instructions required the jury to find the defendants guilty of treason if it determined the purpose of the attempted voyage was to fulfill the letter of marque, disrupt U.S. commerce, and commit hostilities against the United States.[155] The court explained that if a hostile voyage is postponed for a lengthy amount of time and the ship resumes legal and innocent voyages, the original treasonous intent could not lead to a guilty verdict.[156] However, the most important question for the jury was whether "the vessel sail[ed] under the letter and in the service of the rebel government[.]"[157] *Greathouse* offered needed clarification for the scope of an "Aid and Comfort" charge by demonstrating how to assess instances where hostilities were thwarted properly.

---

[151] *See id.* at 18.

[152] *See id.* at 22 (instructing to the jury that "[t]he term 'enemy' . . . applies only to the subjects of a foreign power in a state of open hostility with us. It does not embrace rebels in insurrection against their own government. An enemy is always the subject of a foreign power who owes no allegiance to our government or country.").

[153] *Id.* (explaining that all parties assisting rebels effectively levy war themselves against the United States because they are "equally involved in guilt."); *id.* at 23.

[154] *See id.* at 28 (instructing the jury that "it can hardly be contended that the mere postponement of actual hostilities can deprive the voyage of character stamped upon it by its main purpose and design.").

[155] *Id.*

[156] *Id.* at 28. *See also* Medway v. United States, 6 Ct. Cl. 421, 432 (1870) (holding that writing letters to the president of the Confederacy offering support and aid during the Civil War did not amount to treason because they were not sent or uttered).

[157] *Greathouse*, 26 F. Cas. at 29.

The Civil War cases presented many issues regarding how to properly conduct treason trials during obstreperous times. These cases also helped clarify ambiguous terms within the Treason Clause. Specifically, *The Prize Cases* better defined when war is levied against the United States.[158] President Johnson's Proclamation 179 offered insight into who commits treason during a major rebellion.[159] *Greathouse* clarified the scope of the Aid and Comfort provision and outlined the importance of a treasonous intent after U.S. officials thwarted traitorous acts[160] In many ways, the Civil War cases helped future courts deal with traitors during World War II.

C. World War II and the Rise of Aid and Comfort Convictions

When the Japanese bombarded Pearl Harbor on December 7, 1941, the United States quickly entered into the already raging global conflict, aptly named World War II.[161] Soon after the attack, Congress officially declared war on the major Axis powers of Japan, Germany, and Italy.[162] With these declarations came open and total warfare. The global conflict ushered in new treason cases and legal issues of first impression. Instances of a German-American saboteur scheming on U.S. soil,[163] American propagandists operating on behalf of the Axis powers,[164] and Nazi sympathizers helping German soldiers escape from prison camps[165] became almost commonplace during the war. With the dawn

---

[158] *See* The Prize Cases, 67 U.S. 635, 668–69 (1863).

[159] *See* Peters & Woolley, *supra* note 133.

[160] *Greathouse*, 26 F. Cas. at 18–20, 28.

[161] *See* STEVEN M. GILLON, PEARL HARBOR: FDR LEADS THE NATION INTO WAR ix (2011).

[162] *See id.* (discussing Congress's declaration of war against the major Axis Allies as well as Bulgaria, Hungary, and Rumania the following year); *see also Official Declarations of War by Congress, supra* note 130.

[163] *See, e.g., Ex parte* Quirin, 317 U.S. 1, 2 (1942).

[164] *See, e.g.,* Best v. United States, 184 F.2d 131, 137 (1st Cir. 1950) (convicting an American of treason for serving as a commentator for the Nazi Third Reich); Chandler v. United States, 171 F.2d 921, 925–26 (1st Cir. 1948) (stating that the defendant was the highest paid Nazi commentator in the U.S.A. Zone Short Wave Station of the German Radio Broadcasting Company).

[165] *See, e.g.,* Stephan v. United States, 133 F.2d 87, 90 (6th Cir. 1943) (finding an American guilty of treason for assisting a Nazi soldier in attempting to escape a prison camp in Ontario, Canada).

of modern warfare emerged a new norm for treason law: prosecuting Americans for aiding and comforting the enemy.[166]

In the first major treason case of World War II, *Cramer v. United States*, the Supreme Court overturned a treason conviction against Anthony Cramer, an American who met with German saboteurs in New York and agreed to hold their money belt for safekeeping.[167] In reversing the lower court's judgment, the Supreme Court explained that without proof Cramer provided *actual* aid and comfort with *intent* to betray his nation, the prosecution's case must fail.[168] The Court further explained that "[t]he very minimum function that an overt act must perform . . . is that it show sufficient action by the accused, in its setting, to sustain a finding that the accused actually gave aid and comfort to the enemy."[169] Thus, an overt act and an intent to betray one's nation are so intertwined that intent must be inferred from the overt act itself.[170] In citing Lord Reading, the Court explained the significance of an overt act and its portrayal of the traitor's criminal intent.[171] In *Cramer*, the Court was not convinced that Cramer intended to betray the United States by meeting with German citizens and agreeing to hold a money belt for safekeeping.[172]

In a similar case, the Supreme Court affirmed a treason conviction because the accused provided aid and comfort to a saboteur in order to help him complete his mission.[173] This case, *Haupt v. United States*, was intimately related to *Ex parte Quirin*, one of the most prominent cases of World War II. In *Ex parte Quirin*, a German-American named Herbert Hans Haupt and several

---

[166] *See* HURST, *supra* note 29, at 25 (explaining that of ten reported World War II cases dealing directly with treason, nine resulted in convictions for adhering to an enemy of the United States by offering some form of aid and comfort).

[167] Cramer v. United States, 325 U.S. 1, 4, 48 (1945).

[168] *Id.* at 30–31.

[169] *Id.* at 34–35. The Court also held that two witnesses must validate and prove the "sufficient" overt act occurred. *See id.* at 33.

[170] *Id.* at 31.

[171] *Id.* at 45 (quoting Lord Reading's statement that "[o]vert acts are such acts as manifest a criminal intention and tend towards the accomplishment of the criminal object. They are acts by which the purpose is manifested and the means by which it is intended to be fulfilled.").

[172] *Id.* at 48.

[173] *See* Haupt v. United States, 330 U.S. 631, 635 (1947).

other members of the Nazi Third Reich arrived in the United States via submarine to plant explosives in New York City.[174] Before the saboteurs could execute their plan, American officials intervened.[175] The saboteurs were subsequently placed before a military commission and tried as enemy combatants, where they all received guilty verdicts.[176] Several days later, Haupt was executed for participating in the plot.[177]

In *Haupt*, Herbert Hans' father Hans Max faced prosecution for treason after he gave his son shelter, helped him purchase a car, and assisted him in attaining employment in a lens factory.[178] Unlike in *Cramer*, the Court in *Haupt* was convinced Hans Max's actions revealed an intent to betray the United States and assist in Herbert Hans' mission.[179] The Court believed that providing his son shelter for six days and helping him purchase a car and find work were central enough to Haupt's plot to warrant a treason conviction for Hans Max.[180]

The outcomes in *Cramer* and *Haupt* illustrate the importance of how subtle factual differences lead a court to identify treasonous intent. For the Supreme Court, only a few details in *Haupt* led to the affirmation of a treason conviction.[181] Though the facts in *Cramer* and *Haupt* may seem too similar to easily distinguish, each case provides distinct guidance for courts overseeing treason prosecutions. The *Cramer* opinion offers a restricted view of the Treason Clause by limiting the potential for new constructive treasons. The ruling in *Cramer* also remains true to both the text of the Treason Clause and Founding Fathers' intent to limit the scope of the crime, much like Chief Justice Marshall's rulings in *Ex parte Bollman* and *Burr*.[182] In contrast, *Haupt* represents

---

[174] *See Ex parte* Quirin, 317 U.S. 1, 21 (1942).

[175] *Id.*

[176] *Id.* at 25.

[177] *See Nazi Saboteurs and George Dasch*, FED. BUREAU OF INVESTIGATION, https://www.fbi.gov/history/famous-cases/nazi-saboteurs-and-george-dasch (last visited March 25, 2019).

[178] *Haupt*, 330 U.S. at 635.

[179] *Id.* at 635–36 (describing such actions as "essential" to furthering Hans Herbert's mission of sabotage).

[180] *Id.*

[181] *See Haupt*, 330 U.S. at 635–36.

[182] *See* HURST, *supra* note 29, at 187–89.

the notion that although an act may appear innocent on its face, it may rise to the level of treason if the evidence reveals the actor *intended* to aid and comfort the enemy.[183] In conjunction, these cases demonstrate the hardships courts face when determining the scope of the Treason Clause, in particular, the crime of aiding and comforting the enemy.

A more straightforward case of aid and comfort for the Supreme Court was *Kawakita v. United States*. In *Kawakita*, a dual-citizen of Japan and the United States was convicted of treason for providing aid and comfort to the Japanese when he abused American prisoners-of-war.[184] When the United States formally declared war on Japan, Tomoya Kawakita acted as an interpreter for the Japanese in a prison camp housing captured U.S. soldiers.[185] The Court held Kawakita adhered to the enemy by offering aid and comfort in abusing American soldiers and inflicting punishment on them.[186] The Court explained that Kawakita's acts were treasonous because "they were acts which tended to strengthen the enemy and advance its interests," which amounted to "more than sympathy with the enemy, more than a lack of zeal in the American cause, [and] more than a breaking of allegiance to the United States."[187] If the Supreme Court found Hans Max's actions of helping his Nazi son obtain shelter, a job, and a car to be treasonous, the Court had no issue determining Kawakita's acts of violence against U.S. prisoners-of-war in Japan amounted to treason.[188]

Kawakita presented the unique issue of dual-citizenship. In his defense, Kawakita argued a dual-citizen could only commit treason against the country in which he currently resides.[189] The Court quickly dismissed this argument by explaining the Treason Clause contains no territorial limitation, extending

---

[183] *See id.* at 247–49 (arguing the Court convoluted the intent and overt act elements of the Treason Clause in *Cramer*, and that the *Haupt* opinion provided much needed clarification).

[184] Kawakita v. United States, 343 U.S. 717, 737–41 (1952).

[185] *Id.* at 737.

[186] *Id.* at 740–41.

[187] *Id.* at 741.

[188] *See id.* at 737.

[189] *See id.* at 732.

to Americans living abroad.[190] The Court continued by declaring, "American citizenship, until lost, carries obligations of allegiance as well as privileges and benefits."[191]   After *Kawakita*, the duties of loyalty inherent in citizenship expressly applied to not only U.S. citizens and resident aliens residing within the United States,[192] but also all American dual-citizens regardless of whether they lived inside or outside American territory.[193] If any person within these categories levies war against the United States or adheres to enemies by offering aid and comfort, he commits treason.

World War II also introduced a new breed of propagandist traitors whose sole overt act of betrayal was speaking on behalf of U.S. enemies in Europe and Asia.[194] Two of the most infamous propagandists, "Axis Sally" and "Tokyo Rose," became household names.[195] These two women received jail sentences after working for German and Japanese radio broadcast services and targeting both U.S. soldiers and citizens with propaganda.[196] Both women, named Mildred Gillars and Iva Ikuko Toguri D'Aquino, were found guilty of treason because their speech helped further the enemy's propaganda efforts.[197] Like *Kawakita*, both Gillars and D'Aquino committed treason while living in

---

[190] *See id.* at 732–33.

[191] *Id.* at 734.

[192] *See* Carlisle v. United States, 83 U.S. 147, 154 (1872) ("[t]he citizen or subject owes an absolute and permanent allegiance to his government or sovereign, or at least until, by some open and distinct act, he renounces it and becomes a citizen or subject of another government or another sovereign."); Adams, et al., *supra* note 61.

[193] *See Kawakita*, 343 U.S. at 732–33.

[194] *See* D'Aquino v. United States, 192 F.2d 338, 348 (9th Cir. 1951); Gillars v. United States, 182 F.2d 962, 968–69 (D.C. Cir. 1950); Best v. United States, 184 F.2d 131, 137 (1st Cir. 1950); Chandler v. United States, 171 F.2d 921, 925–26 (1st Cir. 1948).

[195] *See* RICHARD LUCAS, AXIS SALLY: THE AMERICAN VOICE OF NAZI GERMANY vii (2010); YASUHIDE KAWASHIMA, THE TOKYO ROSE CASE: TREASON ON TRIAL xi, 39–41 (2013).

[196] *See Gillars*, 182 F.2d at 968–69; *D'Aquino*, 192 F.2d at 348.

[197] *See Gillars*, 182 F.2d, at 971 (holding that Gillars' words were "spoken as part of a program of propaganda warfare (*sic*), in the course of employment by the enemy in its conduct of war against the United States, to which the accused owes allegiance, may be an integral part of the crime."); *D'Aquino*, 192 F.2d, at 353 (stating it is "psychologically possible" for a person to intentionally commit treason while still feeling compassion for individual prisoners).

enemy territory.[198] Their overt acts consisted of recording propaganda for the Axis powers from abroad, which was enough to uphold guilty verdicts. While these cases sparked intense First Amendment debates,[199] they also expanded the scope of the Treason Clause to include propagandists who supported a wartime enemy of the United States.

With the conclusion of World War II came the end of treason case law.[200] As global governance began to evolve through the creation of institutions such as the United Nations, several legal scholars began to argue that the Treason Clause should be left by the wayside.[201] Although the decades following World War II featured prominent U.S. conflicts where Americans joined the ranks of oppositional forces or helped issue enemy propaganda, the Treason Clause remained dormant.[202] Instead of charging defectors with treason, the U.S. government began using other statutes, such as the Espionage Act.[203] After the September 11 terrorist attacks, the U.S. government continued to ignore the Treason Clause, instead seeking convictions under terrorism statutes.[204]

---

[198] See LUCAS, *supra* note 195, at viii; KAWASHIMA, *supra* note 195, at xi.

[199] See, e.g., KAWASHIMA, *supra* note 1955, at 166–67 (arguing the verdict in *D'Aquino* was a political ploy which distorted the constitutional right to make critical speech against the U.S. government).

[200] *Kawakita* was the last treason conviction in the United States. *See* Dan Eggen & Karen DeYoung, *U.S. Supporter of Al Qaeda is Indicted on Treason Charge*, WASH. POST (Oct. 12, 2006), http://www.washingtonpost.com/wp-dyn/content/article/2006/10/11/AR2006101101121.html.

[201] See Eichensehr, *supra* note 34, at 1445 ("[c]ommentators argued that the crime was antiliberal, too difficult to prove, unnecessary in times of stability and security, and based on a sense of loyalty to the state that has become extinct in the modern era.").

[202] See Henry M. Holzer, *Why Not Call it Treason? From Korea to Afghanistan*, 29 S.U. L. REV. 181, 194 (2002) (arguing that traitors from the Korean War, Vietnam War, and the War on Terror in Afghanistan should have been tried for treason).

[203] See *id.* at 182 (citing the famous Cold War case against the Rosenbergs for committing espionage). *See also* Espionage and Censorship, 18 U.S.C. pt. 1, ch. 37.

[204] See *Attorney General Transcript: News Conference – Indictment of John Walker Lindh*, DEP'T OF JUSTICE (Feb. 5, 2002), https://www.justice.gov/archive/ag/speeches/2002/020502transcriptindictmentofjohnwalkerlindh.htm (stating that John Walker Lindh was indicted on 10 separate counts by a grand jury in the Eastern District of Virginia for conspiring with the Taliban, training with al Qaeda, carrying firearms and destructive devices, and conspiring to kill Americans).

Although the U.S. government chose to not charge American members of al Qaeda under the Treason Clause, the constitutional crime remains a viable option in the future. The executive branch's decision to refrain from pursuing treason convictions during any conflict after World War II should not be interpreted as rendering the Treason Clause moot. For example, the limited use of the Treason Clause is not comparable to when the Supreme Court significantly restrained the 14th Amendment's Privileges or Immunities Clause in the *Slaughter-House Cases*.[205] Unlike this pivotal instance in constitutional precedent, the Court has placed zero restraints on the Treason Clause. The Court understands and acknowledges the Treason Clause is as much a tactical weapon as it is a legal one and must be used as such.[206]

The Treason Clause should be viewed as a potential option for prosecutors to use against Americans who join and fight for ISIS. ISIS is currently levying war against the United States as a new and unconventional enemy, notwithstanding the recent collapse of the Islamic State. This does not mean all ISIS sympathizers are automatically subject to treason liability. The analysis must focus on distinct types of ISIS fighters and sympathizers, including: (1) Americans who travel to the Middle East intending to join ISIS; (2) Americans who commit terrorist attacks against U.S. citizens on behalf of ISIS in the United States and abroad; (3) Americans who are featured in ISIS propaganda videos; and (4) Alien residents who commit terrorism on American soil. This analysis guarantees the appropriate and effective use of the Treason Clause in accordance with the Founding Fathers' original intent to limit the use of treason for the "preservation of liberty."[207]

---

[205] *See* Slaughter-House Cases, 83 U.S. 36, 78 (1872) (holding the Privileges or Immunities Clause has no application to a state's own citizens).

[206] *See* Cramer v. United States, 325 U.S. 1, 45 (1945) ("the treason offense is not the only nor can it well serve as the principal legal weapon to vindicate our national cohesion and security.").

[207] *See* RECORDS FROM THE FEDERAL CONVENTION, *supra* note 532, at 435 (quoting Gouverneur Morris).

III.　THE TREASON CLAUSE AS
##　　　APPLIED TO ISIS

According to the Program on Extremism at The George Washington University, about 250 Americans either attempted to or successfully traveled to Syria and Iraq to join ISIS since Fall 2015.[208] American affiliates of ISIS have killed Americans on U.S. soil[209] and have fought on the battlefield in Iraq.[210] Based on the willingness of some Americans to join the ranks of ISIS, the Executive Branch should consider using the Treason Clause against those who violate their allegiance to the United States. To determine whether applying a charge of treason against ISIS is indeed legal, the following must be established: (1) American members of ISIS levy war against the United States; or (2) ISIS is an "enemy" of the United States.[211] If neither is true, then any American who joins ISIS cannot be tried under the Treason Clause. However, if either is true, an assessment of the four aforementioned categories of ISIS members is warranted.

A.　Has ISIS Levied War Against the United States?

Is ISIS currently levying war against the United States? The answer to this question is not easily ascertainable. The terror group's heinous acts against Americans in U.S. territory and abroad support the claim that it is levying war against the United States.[212] For the Treason Clause to apply to American ISIS

---

[208] LORENZO VIDINO & SEAMUS HUGHES, ISIS IN AMERICA: FROM RETWEETS TO RAQQA ix (2015).

[209] *See* Karimi, et al., *supra* note 6 (San Bernardino terrorist attacks).

[210] *See* Barbara Starr & Ryan Browne, *Two Americans Accused of Fighting for ISIS Were Captured in Syria, Militia Says*, CNN (Jan. 6, 2019), https://www.cnn.com/2019/01/06/middleeast/american-isis-fighter-suspects/index.html; Kamil Kakol & Nicholas Fandos, *Amid ISIS Battles, American Surrender in Iraq*, N.Y. TIMES (Mar. 14, 2016), http://www.nytimes.com/2016/03/15/world/middleeast/american-isis-fighter.html?_r=1.

[211] *See* U.S. CONST. art. 3, § 3, cl. 1.

[212] *See, e.g., US Missed Chattanooga Attack but Foiled 'Over 60' Isis-Linked Plots: Security Chair*, THE GUARDIAN (July 19, 2015), http://www.theguardian.com/us-news/2015/jul/19/chattanooga-isis-terror-plots-homeland-security (writing that naturalized U.S. citizen Mohammad Youssef Abdulazeez killed four marines and one sailor at the Navy Operational Support Center and Marine Corps Reserve

members, these Americans must actually "assemble[] for the purpose of effecting by force a treasonable purpose."[213] As explained by Chief Justice Marshall in *United States v. Burr*, "where a body of men are assembled for the purpose of making war against the [U.S.] government and are in a condition to make that war, the assemblage is an act of levying war."[214]

Certain assemblages are more easily discernable as an actual levying of war. As stated by Lord Coke, levying war "must be such an assembly as carries with it *speciem belli*, the appearance of war."[215] In the United States, Congress's eleven formal declarations of war are the most straightforward examples of when war was levied against the United States.[216] When Congress declares war, it expressly acknowledges an already-existing state of warfare or consents with the President's utilization of the U.S. military to counter hostilities.[217] As observed in *The Prize Cases*, however, the United States may engage in war absent a congressional declaration.[218] A formal acknowledgment of hostilities by Congress was not necessary during the Civil War because of the force used against the United States.[219] The degree of fighting and the assemblage of troops managed by the self-declared Confederate States of America constituted a total war.

Center in Chattanooga, Tennessee. Authorities believe the attack was inspired by ISIS); *see also* Chelsea J. Carter, *supra* note 10; Amir Abdallah, *URGENT Video: ISIS Beheads American Journalist Steven Sotloff*, IRAQI NEWS (Sept. 3, 2014), http://www.iraqinews.com/features/urgent-video-isis-beheads-american-journalist-steven-sotloff/ (reporting ISIS's beheading of American journalist Steven Sotloff); Amir Abdallah, *URGENT Video: Peter Kassig Beheaded by ISIS with 16 Syrians*, IRAQI NEWS (Nov. 16, 2014), http://www.iraqinews.com/features/urgent-video-peter-kassig-beheaded-isis-16-syrians/ (reporting ISIS's beheading of American journalist Peter Kassig).

[213] *See* Ex parte Bollman, 8 U.S. (4 Cranch) 75, 126 (1807).

[214] United States v. Burr, 25 F. Cas. 55, 162 (C.C.D. Va. 1807) (No. 14,693).

[215] *See id.* at 163 (quoting Lord Coke). In *Burr*, "the judges proceeded entirely on the idea that a warlike posture was indispensable to the fact of levying war." *Id.* at 164.

[216] *See Official Declarations of War by Congress*, *supra* note 13030.

[217] *See* Youngstown Sheet & Tube Co. v. Sawyer, 343 U.S. 579, 642 (Jackson, J., concurring) ("a state of war may in fact exist without a formal declaration [of war].").

[218] The Prize Cases, 67 U.S. 635, 668–69 (1863).

[219] *See id.*

The Supreme Court has also recognized the existence of "limited, partial, war."[220] When the United States engaged in the "Quasi-War" with France, Congress did not declare war but authorized certain types of forces to engage in hostilities under certain circumstances.[221] In analyzing this situation, the Supreme Court found a state of "public war" existed.[222] The key factor of "public warfare" is the public nature of hostilities, meaning the relevant governments hold authority over those participating in the conflict.[223] Limited and partial war may best describe the Whiskey and Fries rebellions. In both examples, the insurrectionists committed treason by using open but limited rebellion to inhibit the U.S. government's ability to collect taxes.[224] Although these hostilities did not rise to the level witnessed during the Civil War, the rebels legally levied war against the United States.[225]

Warfare is difficult to analyze in the context of terrorism because wars, excluding internal conflicts, are traditionally fought between *nations*.[226] ISIS is not a nation, but is a designated Foreign Terrorist Organization[227] employing "soldiers" waging unconventional and asymmetric warfare against civilians

---

[220] *See* Bas v. Tingy, 4 U.S. (4 Dall.) 37, 43 (1800) (determining that an partial and limited war existed with France).

[221] *See id.*

[222] *See id. See also Imperfect War*, BLACK'S LAW DICTIONARY (10th ed. 2014) ("[a]n intercountry war limited in terms of places, persons, and things."); *Mixed War*, BLACK'S LAW DICTIONARY (10th ed. 2014) ("[a] war between a country and private individuals.").

[223] *See Public War*, BLACK'S LAW DICTIONARY (10th ed. 2014) ("[a] war between two countries under authority of their respective governments.").

[224] *See* FRITZ, *supra* note 74, at 153; NEWMAN, *supra* note 84, at 60, 67–68, 241.

[225] The governmental response was significant, however. For example, President Washington led 13,000 militiamen in battle during the Whiskey Rebellion. *See* IDEAS AND MOVEMENTS THAT SHAPED AMERICA: FROM THE BILL OF RIGHTS TO "OCCUPY WALL STREET" 984 (Michael S. Green & Scott L. Stabler eds., 2015).

[226]*See* NORMAN ABRAMS, ANTI-TERRORISM AND CRIMINAL ENFORCEMENT 210 (2008) ("[c]lassical wars traditionally involve a battle against sovereign states"); John L. Gaddis, *And Now This: Lessons from the Old Era for the New One, in* THE AGE OF TERROR: AMERICA AND THE WORLD AFTER SEPTEMBER 11 (Strobe Talbott & Nayan Chanda eds., 2001). *But see* Eichensehr, *supra* note 34, at 1495 (arguing that treason applies to "an armed conflict equivalent to a war").

[227] *See* Foreign Terrorist Organizations, *supra* note 7.

and military personnel alike.[228] Thus, the term "war" in the traditional sense may not appear to apply to the United States' conflict with ISIS.

Yet the definition of "war" has evolved since September 11, 2001.[229] Though terrorist groups are not sovereign states, the U.S. government treats them as enemies of the United States due to their aggressiveness, objectives to defeat or topple governments, merciless attacks, and combative behavior.[230] Throughout the War on Terror, the United States has fought terrorist groups such as al Qaeda and governments such as the Taliban on traditional battlefields.[231] As President Bush explained after al Qaeda executed the September 11 attacks, "[t]he terrorists and their supporters declared war on the United States, and war is what they got."[232]

In the early stages of U.S. engagement with ISIS, the Obama administration relied on congressional authorizations implemented during the Bush administration. To justify air strikes against ISIS operatives, President Barack Obama cited both the 2001 and 2002 Authorizations for Use of United States Armed Forces ("AUMFs") against al Qaeda and Iraq as providing sufficient legal authority.[233] The President also argued the War

---

[228] See ANTHONY H. CORDESMAN, TERRORISM, ASYMMETRIC WARFARE, AND WEAPONS OF MASS DESTRUCTION: DEFENDING THE U.S. HOMELAND 1 (2002).

[229] See Authorization for the Use of United States Armed Forces, Pub. L. 107-40 (2001) (authorizes the President to "use all necessary and appropriate forces against those nations, organizations, or persons" determined to be a part of the September 11 terrorist attacks). This congressional authority was used as the legal basis to invade Afghanistan shortly after the September 11 terrorist attacks.

[230] See ABRAMS, supra note 2266, at 195 (distinguishing the War on Terror with similar "wars" against organized crime, white collar crime, and drugs).

[231] See id.

[232] See id. at 210.

[233] See Charlie Savage, Obama Sees Iraq Resolution as a Legal Basis for Airstrikes, Official   Says,   N.Y.   TIMES   (Sept.   14,   2014), http://www.nytimes.com/2014/09/13/world/americas/obama-sees-iraq-resolution-as-a-legal-basis-for-airstrikes-official-says.html (including a written statement by an administration official citing the 2002 AUMF). See also Authorization for Use of Military Force, Pub. L. 107-40 (2001) (authorizing the President to "use all necessary and appropriate forces against those nations, organizations, or persons" determined to have planned, authorized, committed, or aided the September 11 terrorist attacks, or harbored those responsible); Authorization for Use of Military Force against Iraq, Pub. L. 107-243 (2002) (authorizing the President to "use [] all

Powers Resolution's 60-day limitation barring military operations absent congressional authorization did not apply because "the operations are authorized by a statute."[234] According to President Obama, because ISIS existed as an al Qaeda faction in 2004, both AUMFs grant the executive branch the power to conduct air strikes and deploy U.S. troops to the region.[235] Because the 2001 AUMF applies to ISIS, President Obama argued the executive branch could continue operations past the 60-day limitation created by the War Powers Resolution.[236] Similarly, the Trump administration has cited both AUMFs to support the continued deployment of U.S. troops to the region.[237]

This legal theory is not without criticism, however. Commentators have argued that applying the 2001 and 2002 AUMFs against ISIS is not valid because ISIS is a major enemy of al Qaeda.[238] Some speculators believe the Obama administration's use of the 2001 and 2002 AUMFs was an attempt to

---

necessary means to enforce United Nations Security Council Resolution 660 (1990) and subsequent relevant resolutions and to compel Iraq to cease certain activities that threaten international peace and security . . .).

[234] *See* The White House, Letter from the President – War Powers Resolution Regarding Iraq (Sept. 23, 2014), https://obamawhitehouse.archives.gov/the-press-office/2014/09/23/letter-president-war-powers-resolution-regarding-iraq; Press Release, The White House, Background Conference Call on the Presidents' Address to the Nation (Sept. 10, 2014), https://www.whitehouse.gov/the-press-office/2014/09/10/background-conference-call-presidents-address-nation.

[235] *See* Spencer Ackerman, *Obama's Legal Rationale for Isis Strikes: Shoot First, Ask Congress Later*, THE GUARDIAN (Sept. 10, 2014), http://www.theguardian.com/world/2014/sep/11/obama-isis-syria-air-strikes-legal-argument (citing an Obama administration official).

[236] *See* Press Release, *supra* note 234. *See also* Congressional Action, 50 U.S.C. § 1544(b) (1973).

[237] *See* Letter from Deputy Under Secretary of Defense for Policy, David J. Trachtenberg to Senator Tim Kaine (Jan. 29, 2018), https://www.documentcloud.org/documents/4383185-Kaine-Trump-ISIS-war-power-letters.html [hereinafter Letter to Senator Kaine].

[238] *See, e.g.*, Ankit Panda, *A Bad Idea: Using the 2001 AUMF as Legal Rationale for Striking ISIS*, THE DIPLOMAT (Sept. 11, 2014), http://thediplomat.com/2014/09/a-bad-idea-using-the-2001-aumf-as-legal-rationale-for-striking-isis/.

avoid the legislative process of declaring war.[239] Commentators also argue that since President Obama submitted a request to Congress to pass a new AUMF to counter ISIS, the 2001 and 2002 AUMFs do not properly extend to the ISIS conflict.[240] Opponents of the legal theory also believe President Obama's call for repealing the 2001 and 2002 AUMFs conflicts with his argument that both laws support military action against ISIS.[241] It is important to note the U.S. Supreme Court has yet to make a legal determination on the merits of this argument.[242]

The absence of a specific ISIS AUMF does not indicate Congress does not acknowledge that war exists between the United States and ISIS. At the very least, Congress's failure to pass a new AUMF acts as a form of congressional acquiescence, described by Justice Jackson as a "zone of twilight."[243] In his

---

[239] *See, e.g., id.* ("[t]he 2001 AUMF is a delightfully expansive law if you're a member of the U.S. Executive Branch looking to swiftly implement strategy in a far-flung land. Whereas under normal circumstances, Congress has to declare war or authorize the use of force, the executive is free under the AUMF to carry out this action provided that it is actively targeting an al Qaeda affiliate.").

[240] *See* Letter from President Obama to Congress, Authorization for the Use of United States Armed Forces in Connection with the Islamic State of Iraq and the Levant (Feb. 11, 2015), https://www.whitehouse.gov/the-press-office/2015/02/11/letter-president-authorization-use-united-states-armed-forces-connection [hereinafter Letter from President Obama to Congress]; Kristina Wong, *White House Legal Strategy for ISIS Fight Gets Blurry*, THE HILL (Aug. 8, 2015), http://thehill.com/policy/defense/250619-white-house-legal-strategy-for-isis-fight-gets-blurry.

[241] *See, e.g.*, Derek Tsang, *To Justify ISIS Airstrikes, Obama Using Legislation He Wants Repealed*, PUNDITFACT (Sept. 18, 2014), https://www.politifact.com/punditfact/statements/2014/sep/18/julie-pace/justify-airstrikes-against-islamic-state-obama-usi/.

[242] *See* MICHAEL J. GARCIA & JENNIFER K. ELSEA, CONG. RESEARCH SERV., R43720, U.S. MILITARY ACTION AGAINST THE ISLAMIC STATE: ANSWERS TO FREQUENTLY ASKED LEGAL QUESTIONS 18 (2014). The D.C. Court of Appeals recently dismissed as moot a former U.S. Army Captain's claim seeking declaratory judgment that Operation Inherent Resolve violated the War Powers Resolution and was unconstitutional. *See* Smith v. Trump (D.C. Ct. App. No. 1:16-cv-00843) (July 10, 2018). The U.S. Army Captain argued the 2001 and 2002 AUMFs did not provide proper legal authority to fight ISIS. *See id.*

[243] *See* Youngstown Sheet & Tube Co. v. Sawyer, 343 U.S. 579, 637 (1952) (Jackson, J. concurring) ("[w]hen the President acts in absence of either a congressional grant or denial of authority, he can only rely upon his own independent powers, but there is a zone of twilight in which he and Congress may have concurrent authority, or in

famous concurring opinion in *Youngstown Sheet & Tube Co. v. Sawyer*, Justice Jackson explained the President and Congress held "concurrent authority" during this "zone of twilight," which "enables" or "invites" the President to act within his constitutional powers to combat an emerging threat.[244]

However, the "zone of twilight" rationale is not the strongest indicator that Congress believes the United States is at war with ISIS and supports the executive branch's wartime efforts. The strongest indicator is the annual appropriations Congress continuously passes to counter ISIS, valued in the billions of dollars.[245] The power of the purse is the most important mechanism Congress can use to support military efforts, especially during imperfect or mixed wars.[246] Based on its continuous passage of appropriations to fund U.S. military activities countering ISIS, Congress implicitly acknowledges the United States is at war with the terror organization, or at the very least acquiesces to executive action.[247]

The United States is also at war with ISIS due to its obligations under the North Atlantic Treaty Organization ("NATO"). As a member of NATO, the United States adheres to Article 5 of the Washington Treaty, which provides that any armed attack against a NATO ally is an attack against all of NATO.[248] This concept is known as "collective self-defense."[249] Under the Washington Treaty an "armed attack" includes any attack:

---

which its distribution is uncertain. Therefore, congressional inertia . . . may sometimes . . . enable, if not invite, measure on independent presidential responsibility.").

[244] *See id.*

[245] *See* GARCIA & ELSEA, *supra* note 242, at 12; Jennifer Bendery, *Congress Just Voted to Fund the War Against ISIS. Did They Authorize it, Too?*, HUFFINGTON POST (Dec. 18, 2015), http://www.huffingtonpost.com/entry/congress-war-authorization-isis_us_56743423e4b0b958f656590a (arguing that U.S. appropriations funding efforts against ISIS constitutes a de facto authorization of hostilities).

[246] *See* JENNIFER K. ELSEA ET AL., CONG. RESEARCH SERV., R41989, CONGRESSIONAL AUTHORITY TO LIMIT MILITARY OPERATIONS 4, 19 n.104 (2013); *cf.* Louis Fisher, Congressional Abdication on war and Spending xiii-xiv (2000) (arguing that because Congress has delegated much of its war and spending authorities to the executive, congressional funding should not be seen as an expression of its intent).

[247] *See* GARCIA & ELSEA, *supra* note 242, at 12.

[248] The North Atlantic Treaty, art. 5, Apr. 4, 1949, 63 Stat. 2241, 34 U.N.T.S. 243.

[249] *See Collective Self-Defence – Article 5*, NORTH ATLANTIC TREATY ORGANIZATION, https://www.nato.int/cps/en/natohq/topics_110496.htm# (last updated June 12, 2018).

> on the territory of any of the Parties in Europe or North America, on the Algerian Departments of France, on the territory of Turkey or on the Islands under the jurisdiction of any of the Parties in the North Atlantic area north of the Tropic of Cancer; [or]
>
> on the forces, vessels, or aircraft of any of the Parties, when in or over these territories or any other area in Europe in which occupation forces of any of the Parties were stationed on the date when the Treaty entered into force or the Mediterranean Sea or the North Atlantic area north of the Tropic of Cancer.[250]

Article 6's definition of "armed attack" further authorizes NATO operations south of the Tropic of Cancer.[251]

In the event of an armed attack against any NATO ally, every NATO member, to include the United States, must exercise the right of individual or collective self-defense recognized in Article 51 of the United Nations Charter.[252]   Thus, per the Washington Treaty, ISIS's attacks in Paris on November 13, 2015 and Brussels on March 22, 2016 constitute an armed attack against all of NATO.[253] Furthermore, the phrase "shall be considered an attack against them all" in NATO Article 5 *requires* all NATO allies to use collective self-defense when a NATO ally encounters an armed attack.[254] Based on these NATO obligations, the United States must recognize any ISIS attack against a NATO ally as triggering NATO Article 5's collective self-defense provisions. For the purposes of the Treason Clause, ISIS attacks in Paris and Brussels easily fit the definition of "levying war," especially when compared with the small Whiskey and Fries rebellions.

---

[250] The North Atlantic Treaty, art. 6, Apr. 4, 1949, 63 Stat. 2241, 34 U.N.T.S. 243.

[251] *See Collective Self-Defence – Article 5*, NORTH ATLANTIC TREATY ORGANIZATION, https://www.nato.int/cps/en/natohq/topics_110496.htm# (last updated June 12, 2018).

[252] *Id.; see also* U.N. Charter art. 51.

[253] *See* The North Atlantic Treaty art. 5, Apr. 4, 1949, 63 Stat. 2241, 34 U.N.T.S. 243; Collective Self-Defence – Article 5, North Atlantic Treaty Organization, https://www.nato.int/cps/en/natohq/topics_110496.htm# (last updated June 12, 2018).

[254] The North Atlantic Treaty art. 5, Apr. 4, 1949, 63 Stat. 2241, 34 U.N.T.S. 243.

The fact that ISIS targets and kills Americans,[255] attacks NATO members,[256] aspired to be and functioned as a *de facto* nation-state,[257] and openly engages in hostilities against the United States with tens of thousands of fighters[258] logically supports the conclusion that the terror group is not only capable of levying war against the United States but has already done so. Though Congress has not yet passed an AUMF specific to ISIS,[259] both President Donald Trump and President Obama have cited the 2001 and 2002 AUMFs as statutory support for legally conducting air strikes against ISIS fighters.[260] Congressional appropriations which fund U.S. military efforts against ISIS provide additional support for interpreting Congress's intent.[261] Based on these executive and legislative actions, both governmental branches arguably believe ISIS is levying war against the United States. Furthermore, Congress's actions reveal its implicit support of the President's use of military action against ISIS, thus supporting the executive's claim of statutory and constitutional authority to do so.

B. Are ISIS Members "Enemies" of the United States?

Although congressional and executive actions tend to reveal a belief that ISIS is levying war against the United States, it is necessary to determine whether ISIS members are considered "enemies." If Congress expressly prohibits

---

[255] *See, e.g.*, Carter, *supra* note 10.

[256] *See* Higgins & Freytas-Tamura, *supra* note 14.

[257] *See* BRIGITTE L. NACOS, TERRORISM AND COUNTERTERRORISM (5th ed. 2016) (describing ISIS as "a pseudo-state led by a conventional army.") (quoting terrorism expert Audrey Kurth Cronin).

[258] *See* Ryan Pickrell, *As Many as 30,000 ISIS Fighters Still in Iraq and Syria*, BUS. INSIDER (Aug. 14, 2018), https://www.businessinsider.com/as-many-as-30000-isis-fighters-still-in-iraq-and-syria-2018-8.

[259] President Obama proposed a new AUMF specifically against ISIS but unsuccessfully convinced Congress to pass it. *See* The Obama White House, Authorization for Use of Military Force against the Islamic State of Iraq and the Levant (proposed Feb. 11, 2015), https://obamawhitehouse.archives.gov/sites/default/files/docs/aumf_02112015.pdf.

[260] *See* Letter to Senator Kaine, *supra* note 237; Letter from President Obama to Congress, *supra* note 240.

[261] *See* JENNIFER K. ELSEA ET AL., CONG. RESEARCH SERV., R41989, CONGRESSIONAL AUTHORITY TO LIMIT MILITARY OPERATIONS 4, 19 n.104 (2013); Bendery, *supra* note 245.

military operations against ISIS or declares that the terror group is not at war with the United States, the Treason Clause may still apply to ISIS members. To commit treason under the Constitution, a person who owes loyalty to the United States must either levy war against the nation or adhere to its enemies by offering them aid and comfort.[262] If ISIS is an enemy of the United States, anyone owing allegiance to the United States who offers aid or comfort to the terror organization is guilty of treason.

The term "enemy" historically applied to a person when: (1) He is a subject of a foreign power; (2) The foreign power was in open hostilities with the United States; and (3) The subject had no allegiance to the United States.[263] In describing the Treason Act of 1351, William Blackstone explained that "enemies are here understood the subjects of foreign powers with whom we are at war", and the "[Treason Act of 1351] is taken strictly, and a rebel is not an *enemy*; an enemy being always the subject of some foreign prince, and one who owes no allegiance to the crown of England."[264] As explained by Circuit Judge Field in his jury instruction for *United States v. Greathouse*, an enemy of the United States cannot be an American rebel or insurrectionist.[265] Black's Law Dictionary follows this traditional view by defining "enemy" as "[a] person possessing the nationality of a state with which one is at war."[266]

This understanding of "enemy" contains two major factors which seem to exclude members of a non-state actor such as ISIS: an enemy must be a subject

---

[262] U.S. CONST. art. 3, § 3, cl. 1.

[263] United States v. Greathouse, 26 F. Cas. 18, 22 (C.C.N.D. Cal. 1863) (No. 15,254) (instructing the jury that "[t]he term 'enemy' . . . applies only to the subjects of a foreign power in a state of open hostility with us. . . . An enemy is always the subject of a foreign power who owes no allegiance to our government or country.").

[264] *See* 4 WILLIAM BLACKSTONE, COMMENTARIES 74-91, 350-51 (1769) (located in 4 THE FOUNDERS' CONSTITUTION 426 (Philip B. Kurland & Ralph Lerner eds., 1987) (explaining that imposing war against one's king is treason.).

[265] *Greathouse*, 26 F. Cas. at 22 (stating anyone performing or aiding in a treasonous act are to be considered traitors).

[266] *See Enemy*, BLACK'S LAW DICTIONARY (10th ed. 2014) (defining '*enemy*' as: "1. An opposing military force; 2. A state with which another state is at war; and 3. A foreign state that is openly hostile to another whose position is being considered"). *See also Alien enemy*, BLACK'S LAW DICTIONARY (10th ed. 2014) ("[a] citizen or subject of a country at war with the country in which the citizen or subject is living or traveling.").

of a foreign power engaged in hostilities with the United States, and the subject must not owe allegiance to the United States. Because ISIS is not a "foreign power," it cannot be recognized as a nation. However, Blackstone anticipated this conundrum and explained further that "[a]s to foreign pirates or robbers, who may happen to invade our coasts, without any open hostilities between their nation and our own, and without any commission from any prince or state at enmity with the crown of Great Britain, the giving them any assistance is also clearly treason."[267]

If Blackstone's reasoning is applied in the modern era, it is apparent the term "enemy" in the Treason Clause applies to ISIS. Similar to the pirates and robbers described by Blackstone, ISIS members are non-state actors from various nations not at war with the United States, led by a private Iraqi citizen named Abu Bakr al-Baghdadi.[268] ISIS cannot be described as an American uprising and (excluding American members) none of its foreign fighters owe allegiance to the United States when located physically outside of American territory. ISIS members also arguably qualify for the designation of "enemy combatants." An enemy combatant is a person who "belongs to or actively supports forces (such as al Qaeda) hostile to or in conflict with the United States or its allies."[269] Congress renamed the term to "unprivileged enemy belligerent" in the Military Commissions Act of 2009, but the basic premise remains the same: irregular fighters affiliated with non-state actors are enemies of the United States.[270]

---

[267] BLACKSTONE, *supra* note 264, at 426 (explaining that providing support to enemies is treason).

[268] *See* Massimo Calabresi, *Person of the Year: The Short List No. 2: Abu Bakr al-Baghdadi*, TIME, http://time.com/time-person-of-the-year-2015-runner-up-abu-bakr-al-baghdadi/ (last visited Apr. 21, 2016); *see, e.g.*, Paul D. Shinkman, *ISIS by the Numbers in 2017*, U.S. NEWS (Dec. 27, 2017), https://www.usnews.com/news/world/articles/2017-12-27/isis-by-the-numbers-in-2017 (listing countries and regions in which ISIS and its affiliates operated in 2017).

[269] *Enemy Combatant*, BLACK'S LAW DICTIONARY (10th ed. 2014).

[270] *See* 10 U.S.C. § 948a(7) (2018) ("[t]he term 'unprivileged enemy belligerent' means and individual (other than a privileged belligerent) who — (A) has engaged in hostilities against the United States or its coalition partners; (B) has purposefully and materially supported hostilities against the United States or its coalition partners; or (C) was a part of al Qaeda at the time of the alleged offense under this chapter.").

This term reflects Congress's intent to differentiate between traditional forces loyal to a sovereign nation and the modern-day terrorist, who holds allegiance to a non-state entity.[271] The U.S. Supreme Court has recognized Congress's authority to designate terrorists as enemy combatants, although these individuals must receive some form of due process to satisfy the 1949 Geneva Conventions.[272] This recognition is useful when applying the Treason Clause's definition of "enemy" to ISIS members.[273] The Supreme Court previously acknowledged the legitimacy of the "enemy combatant" – or "unprivileged enemy belligerent" – status in the context of irregular forces.[274] When applied to modern terrorism, the "enemy combatant" status provides support sufficient to legally deem terrorists as enemies of the United States. As argued by Blackstone, the original understanding of "enemy" in the context of treason embraced the idea that enemies may act on behalf of non-

---

[271] *See* Michael T. McCaul & Ronald J. Sievert, *Congress's Consistent Intent to Utilize Military Commissions in the War against al Qaeda and its Adoption of Commission Rules that Fully Comply with Due Process*, 42 St. MARY'S L. J. 595, 609 (2011) (explaining that by creating the term "unprivileged enemy belligerent", Congress sought to, *inter alia*, differentiate between al Qaeda and its affiliates and prisoners of war).

[272] *See* Hamdan v. Rumsfeld, 548 U.S. 557, 631–32 (2006) (holding that Common Article 3 of the Geneva Conventions applies to procedures used by military commissions); *see also* Geneva Convention Relative to the Treatment of Prisoners of War art. 3(1)(d), Aug. 12, 1949, 6 U.S.T. 3316, 75 U.N.T.S. 135 (guaranteeing the following to *hors de combat* currently in detention: "the passing of sentences and the carrying out of executions without previous judgment pronounced by a regularly constituted court, affording all the judicial guarantees which are recognized as indispensable by civilized peoples.").

[273] Some commentators argue the unprivileged belligerent enemy status provided a means to prosecute Americans with using procedural rules less stringent than those provided by the Treason Clause. *See* Larson, *supra* note 123, at 868 (explaining *Hamdi v. Rumsfeld* affirmed *Ex parte Quirin*); Benjamin A. Lewis, Note, *An Old Means to a Different End: The War on Terror, American Citizens, and the Treason Clause*, 34 HOFSTRA L. REV. 1215, 1230 (2005–2006) (citing *Ex parte Quirin* as precedent).

[274] *See Ex parte* Quirin, 317 U.S. 1, 37–38 (1942) ("[b]y passing our boundaries for such purposes without uniform or other emblem signifying their belligerent status, or by discarding that means of identification after entry, such enemies become unlawful belligerents subject to trial and punishment.").

state actors like pirates and robbers.[275] Based on a modern understanding of an "enemy combatant" and Blackstone's explanations related to non-state actors, ISIS members are justifiably enemies of the United States.

The term "enemy" is conditioned on the existence of actual hostilities. As explained by the District Court for the Southern District of New York, "[o]n the breaking out of [World War I] between the United States and [Germany], the subjects of the [German] Emperor . . . were enemies . . . and remained such enemies during the continuance of the war."[276] According to the court, a sovereign nation is not considered an enemy until it thrusts war upon the United States.[277] For ISIS to be an "enemy", it must engage in actual warfare against the United States. When analyzing application of the Treason Clause to ISIS, it is imperative to not limit the discussion to hostilities between sovereign nations. Non-state actors such as ISIS may also engage in hostilities with the United States when they coordinate attacks against American and NATO troops.[278] For example, ISIS in the Greater Sahara conducted a coordinated attack against U.S. and Nigerien troops, resulting in the deaths of four Americans.[279] ISIS is, in fact, levying war against the United States when it targets and kills Americans at home and abroad.

Since ISIS meets the criteria for an enemy levying war against the United States, an inquiry into whether the Treason Clause applies to Americans supporting ISIS is appropriate. However, a treason analysis must be individualized and assess American ISIS members in smaller, distinct categories. This procedure offers credence to the Founding Fathers, who

---

[275] *See* BLACKSTONE, *supra* note 264, at 426 (explaining that providing assistance to "foreign pirates or robbers who may happen to invade Our coasts without any open hostilities between their nation and the United States, and without any commission . . . would be treason . . . because such unauthorized invaders are to be considered as enemies . . . .").

[276] United States v. Fricke, 259 F. 673, 675 (S.D.N.Y. 1919).

[277] *See id.*

[278] *See* Thomas Gibbons-Neff & Helene Cooper, *U.S. Identifies 3 ISIS Militants Who Led Deadly Ambush in Niger*, N.Y. TIMES (May 29, 2018), https://www.nytimes.com/2018/05/29/us/politics/isis-militants-ambush-niger.html.

[279] *See id.*

intentionally limited the scope of the Treason Clause to avoid the formation of "new-fangled and artificial treasons."[280]

IV. APPLYING THE TREASON CLAUSE TO AMERICAN MEMBERS AND SUPPORTERS OF ISIS

ISIS is the poster child for terrorist recruitment. The organization's utilization of social media to recruit fighters is so successful that Congress has debated whether it should regulate social media corporations such as Facebook and Twitter.[281] ISIS's efforts have also convinced significant numbers of Americans to join their ranks in the Middle East.[282] According to the Center for National Security at Fordham Law, U.S. federal government prosecutions have led to 173 terrorism cases, 115 of which resulted in criminal convictions.[283] In 2015 alone, officials conducted 900 investigations against suspected ISIS members and sympathizers in every state in America.[284] Although European nationals account for a larger proportion of ISIS recruits,[285] Americans actively seek to join the terror group and execute terrorist attacks on U.S. soil.[286]

In determining that ISIS is an enemy actively levying war against the United States, any American who joins, wages war on behalf of, or offers aid

---

[280] See generally THE FEDERALIST NO. 43 (James Madison).

[281] See Charlie Hebdo and the Jihadi Online Network: Assessing the Role of American Commercial Social Media Platforms Before the Subcomm. on Terrorism, Nonproliferation, and Trade of the H. Comm. on Foreign Affairs, 114th Cong. 67 (2015) (testimony of Evan F. Kohlmann); Paulina Wu, Impossible to Regulate: Social Media, Terrorists, and the Role for the U.N., 16 CHI. J. OF INT'L L. 281, 292 (2015) (explaining how social media and the internet have become increasingly used in recruitment efforts and its regulation has become a hot topic among the UN).

[282] See VIDINO & HUGHES, supra note 208, at ix (estimating 250 Americans traveled to or attempted to join ISIS in Syria and Iraq).

[283] Research, CENTER ON NATIONAL SECURITY AT FORDHAM LAW (last visited Jan. 9, 2019), https://www.centeronnationalsecurity.org/research/.

[284] See VIDINO & HUGHES, supra note 208, at ix.

[285] See PETER BERGEN ET AL., ISIS IN THE WEST: THE NEW FACES OF EXTREMISM 10, 16, 45 (2015) (including data on the number of European nationals who joined ISIS.

[286] Id. at 4–6, 11.

and comfort to ISIS can be convicted of committing treason. However, courts should ensure criminal defendants are convicted of treason using a series of categories of traitors. The following categories will be analyzed to define which types of ISIS members and sympathizers qualify for a treason conviction: (1) Americans who were arrested while en route to the former "Islamic State"; (2) Americans who execute terror attacks in the United States or abroad on behalf of ISIS; (3) Americans who propagandize for ISIS; and (4) Aliens who commit terror attacks in the name of ISIS on American soil.

A. Americans Traveling to the Former Islamic State

On June 29, 2014, ISIS declared a caliphate traversing the borders of Iraq and Syria.[287] In doing so, it formed the "Islamic State," a self-proclaimed nation for ISIS members and sympathizers.[288] The Islamic State officially fell on March 23, 2019, when American-backed forces took the village of Baghuz, Syria.[289] The Federal Bureau of Investigation ("FBI") estimated over 200 Americans traveled or attempted to reach Syria to enter ISIS-controlled territory since 2014.[290] In one particular instance, Jaelyn Delshaun Young and her proclaimed husband Muhammad Oda Dakhlalla, both U.S. citizens, attempted to travel to Syria to join ISIS.[291] Before the couple could reach Syria, the FBI arrested and charged both with attempting to provide material support to ISIS.[292] Young

---

[287] See Matt Bradley, *ISIS Declares a New Islamist Caliphate*, WALL ST. J. (June 29, 2014), http://www.wsj.com/articles/isis-declares-new-islamist-caliphate-1404065263 (describing ISIS's declaration of statehood).

[288] *Id.*

[289] See Rukmini Callimachi, *ISIS Caliphate Crumbles as Last Village in Syria Falls*, N.Y. TIMES (Mar. 23, 2019), https://www.nytimes.com/2019/03/23/world/middleeast/isis-syria-caliphate.html.

[290] See *Counterterrorism, Counterintelligence, and the Challenges of "Going Dark" Before the S. Select Comm. on Intelligence*, 114th Cong. 5057 (2015) (statement of FBI Director James B. Comey), https://www.intelligence.senate.gov/sites/default/files/hearings/S.%20Hrg.%20114-739.pdf#page=54 (discussing the efforts underway in identifying fighters traveling to join and support ISIS).

[291] See Complaint at 2, United States v. Young, 3:15MJ32-SAA (D.C.N.D. Miss. May 21, 2015) [hereinafter Young Complaint] (stating the steps taken by Young and Dakhlalla in attempting to travel to Syria to join ISIS).

[292] See *id.* at 1; see also Providing Material Support or Resources to Designated Foreign Terrorist Organizations, 18 U.S.C. § 2339B (2015) (defining *'material support'* as

and Dakhlalla received prison sentences of twelve and eight years, respectively.[293]

Although Young and Dakhlalla never reached the Islamic State, their attempt to join ISIS does raise the question of whether they committed treason. In planning their trip to Syria, did Young and Dakhlalla perform an overt act sufficient to reveal a treasonous intent? Is an attempt to join ISIS an act of treason, or is the fact that they never reached Syria enough to disqualify them from treason scrutiny? These questions are important and must be answered, especially in light of the number of Americans currently facing terror charges for attempting to offer material support to ISIS. These legal questions must also be answered before the executive branch can begin forming policies necessary to leverage the Treason Clause against ISIS. Without clear legal insight, any treason policy will be tenuous and justifiably challenged by legal scholars.

For the Treason Clause to apply to Americans like Young and Dakhlalla, they must owe allegiance to the United States and execute an overt act in furtherance of a treasonous plot.[294] Since Young and Dakhlalla are U.S. citizens, they automatically owe allegiance to the United States through duties inherent in American citizenship.[295] The question then becomes whether their attempt to reach the former Islamic State is an intentional, overt act of treason.[296]

---

providing any property, tangible or intangible, or service, including currency or monetary instruments or financial securities, financial services, lodging, training, expert advice or assistance, safehouses, false documentation or identification, communications equipment, facilities, weapons, lethal substances, explosives, personnel (one or more individuals who may be or include oneself), and transportation, except medicine or religious materials to foreign terrorist organization).

[293] Press Release, DEP'T OF JUSTICE, Mississippi Woman Sentenced to 12 Years for Conspiring to Provide Material Support to ISIL (Aug. 11, 2016), https://www.justice.gov/opa/pr/mississippi-woman-sentenced-12-years-prison-conspiring-provide-material-support-isil; Press Release, DEP'T OF JUSTICE, Mississippi Man Sentenced to 8 Years in Prison for Conspiring to Provide Material Support to ISIS (Aug. 24, 2016), https://www.justice.gov/opa/pr/mississippi-man-sentenced-eight-years-prison-conspiring-provide-material-support-isil.

[294] See Cramer v. United States, 325 U.S. 1, 34–35 (1945).

[295] See Kawakita v. United States, 343 U.S. 717, 734 (1952).

[296] See HURST, supra note 29, at 205–06.

As the Supreme Court explained in *Cramer*, treasonous intent can be inferred by the overt act itself.[297] The Court in *Cramer* emphasized, however, that "mental attitudes or expressions should not be treason[.]"[298] It is not enough to conclude that Young and Dakhlalla are guilty of treason because they sought to aid and comfort ISIS or levy war against the United States by joining ISIS.[299] This would be a blatant example of constructive treason the Supreme Court quashed in *Cramer* and *Burr*.[300] The act of boarding a plan in an *attempt* to join ISIS must be determined to be an overt treasonous act to result in a treason conviction.

For the Young and Dakhlalla situation, the key word is *attempt*. When Americans like Young and Dakhlalla never leave the United States, a prosecutor cannot reasonably argue they assembled with ISIS fighters or sympathizers. Since an actual assemblage is required to levy war against the United States,[301] it appears Young and Dakhlalla did not commit treason by levying war. The Supreme Court explained in *Ex parte Bollman* that the act of traveling to a rendezvous point does not equate to an actual assemblage.[302] Americans who fail to leave the United States may intend to join the actual warlike assemblage in Syria and Iraq. However, these Americans fail to implement their traitorous intentions when apprehended by U.S. officials. Similar to the case of Aaron Burr,[303] the fact the alleged perpetrators never physically joined the ISIS ranks is enough to exonerate them from the crime of treason by levying war.

It is noteworthy to revisit the case of *United States v. Greathouse* before concluding that Americans attempting to travel to Syria and Iraq cannot legally commit treason.[304] In *Greathouse*, the court explained that when war is

---

[297] *See Cramer*, 325 U.S. at 31.

[298] *Id.* at 28.

[299] *Id.*

[300] *See id.* at 39–40; United States v. Burr, 25 F. Cas. 55, 143, 171–72 (C.C.D. Va. 1807) (No. 14,693).

[301] *Ex parte* Bollman, 8 U.S. (4 Cranch) 75, 127 (1807).

[302] *See id.* at 75, 134.

[303] *Burr*, 25 F. Cas. at 113 (explaining Aaron Burr was not guilty of treason because he was not present at the assemblage of men on Blennerhassett's Island).

[304] *See* United States v. Greathouse, 26 F. Cas 18, 22 (C.C.N.D. Cal. 1863) (No. 15,254).

thrust upon the United States, "all who engage in the rebellion [or war effort] at any stage of its existence, or . . . give to it any species of aid and comfort, in whatever part of the country they may be, stand on the same platform; they are all principals in the commission of the crime; they are all levying war against the United States."[305] If boarding a plane to join ISIS is a part of the war effort against the United States, these Americans commit treason. However, this is simply not the case. In most instances, Americans seeking to join ISIS are never in actual contact with ISIS leaders and are not following military orders. Instead, they tend to be "lone wolves" inspired by online ISIS news and propaganda.[306] Neither Young nor Dakhlalla received orders from ISIS leaders to travel to Syria or execute a mission on behalf of ISIS.[307] Young and Dakhlalla informed undercover FBI agents of their *desire to join* ISIS in Syria on their own volition.[308] ISIS lone wolves are fundamentally different from the *Greathouse* defendants, who received a letter of marque from Confederate President Davis to carry out specific acts of armed aggression against U.S. ships.[309] If Americans in the United States specifically receive orders from ISIS leaders or reach ISIS fighters in Syria and Iraq, they are more likely to be found guilty of treason.[310] However, an attempt to board a plane in the United States, without more, cannot qualify as an overt act of treason.

The act of boarding a plane in an attempt to travel to the Islamic State may still be a treasonous overt act if it is "essential to [the] design for treason."[311] The factor of essentiality pertains to the "Aid and Comfort" provision of the Treason Clause, as explained in *Haupt*.[312] Americans attempting to travel to

---

[305] *Id.*

[306] *See, e.g.*, Christal Hayes, *ISIS in our own Backyard: Group's U.S. Followers are Diverse, in Places Large and Small*, USA TODAY (updated Jan. 5, 2018), https://www.usatoday.com/story/news/2018/01/04/fight-against-isis-teenager-playing-basketball-fbi-agent-and-couple-their-honeymoon-heres-how-isis-s/953954001/.

[307] *See* Young Complaint, *supra* note 291, at 2.

[308] *See id.*

[309] *See Greathouse*, 26 F. Cas. at 18, 24.

[310] *Id.*

[311] Haupt v. United States, 330 U.S. 631, 635 (1947).

[312] *Id.*

Syria and Iraq may commit treason if the act of boarding a plane or planning a trip to the former Islamic State constitutes an overt act essential to offering aid and comfort to ISIS and its members.

Americans arrested while attempting to travel to Syria and Iraq may offer some form of existential support to ISIS. When the public media reports the arrest of these Americans, each specific instance of betrayal may act as an ISIS advertisement, which may add fuel to the ISIS fire. Though any press is good press, this is not sufficient aid to qualify as an overt act essential to ISIS's mission. While news coverage may provide some marginal benefits to ISIS, the fact Young and Dakhlalla never met or worked with ISIS members or reached ISIS territories to fight NATO and the United States is significant. In relation to the Treason Clause, Americans cannot commit the crime of offering aid and comfort ISIS if they fail to leave the United States. This is not to say Americans must be in Syria and Iraq in order to aid and comfort ISIS. To the contrary, if ISIS were to commit a terrorist attack on U.S. soil and Americans offered ISIS sleeper cells a place to live or helped prepare weaponry for the attack, they assuredly commit treason. Yet, for those Americans who intend to betray the United States by leaving for Syria and Iraq but are first arrested, they never committed treason because they never provided aid or comfort to ISIS. The Supreme Court previously advised against applying the Treason Clause to "doubtful cases."[313] When Americans do not reach the enemy, a court could only find treason constructively, which renders the case as inherently doubtful.

In *Haupt*, the Supreme Court upheld Hans Max's treason conviction because he provided his son shelter, a car, and employment while knowing his son's intended on executing a mission for the Nazis.[314] The key difference between the situation in *Haupt* and that of Americans like Young and Dakhlalla is the actual rendering of assistance to an enemy. Young and Dakhlalla wanted to assist ISIS but could not while Hans Max provided assistance to his Nazi son in multiple ways.[315] Young and Dakhlalla's inability

---

[313] *See Ex parte* Bollman, 8 U.S. (4 Cranch) 75, 127 (1807) (advising against the use of constructive treasons).

[314] *See Haupt*, 330 U.S. at 635.

[315] *Id.*

to execute the treasonous act saves them from treason scrutiny but should not save them from criminal terror charges. An entire section of the U.S. Code is devoted to dealing with attempts to join terrorist groups or commit terrorism.[316] The executive branch should continue to use these terrorism statutes to prosecute Americans who attempt to join ISIS abroad instead of pursuing treason convictions. Treason is inapplicable to this class of ISIS supporters and would justifiably be dismissed by any court.

B. Americans Who Commit Armed Attacks on U.S. Soil or the Battlefield

Perhaps the classification of ISIS traitors arousing the greatest emotional response from Americans is U.S. citizens who commit armed attacks within the United States or on the battlefield. Since 2014, ISIS members and sympathizers have conducted several attacks against American civilians, military personnel, and police.[317] One of the most notable and alarming attacks occurred in San Bernardino, California by U.S. citizen Syed Rizwan Farook and his wife Tashfeen Malik, a permanent U.S. resident,[318] with the assistance of U.S. citizen Enrique Marquez, Jr.[319] Just as alarming was a report in early January 2019 of Syrian Democratic forces capturing two Americans in Syria for allegedly fighting on behalf of ISIS.[320] The capture of these Americans, named Warren Christopher Clark and Zaid Abed al-Hamid, supports the claim that Americans are on the front lines in Syria and Iraq.[321] The San Bernardino killers and the two alleged ISIS fighters share in common

---

[316] *See generally* Terrorism, 18 U.S.C. ch. 113B (2015).

[317] *See, e.g.*, Ray Sanchez et al., *ISIS Goes Global: 143 Attacks in 29 Countries have Killed 2,043*, CNN (Oct. 10, 2018, 6:20 PM), http://www.cnn.com/2015/12/17/world/mapping-isis-attacks-around-the-world/ (last updated Apr. 13. 2016).

[318] *See* Saeed Ahmed, *Who were Syed Rizwan Farook and Tashfeen Malik*, CNN (Dec. 4, 2015), https://www.cnn.com/2015/12/03/us/syed-farook-tashfeen-malik-mass-shooting-profile/index.html.

[319] *See* Indictment at 1–7, United States v. Marquez, No. 15-93 JGB (C.D. Cal. 2015), https://www.scribd.com/doc/294325546/Federal-Indictment-of-Enrique-Marquez [hereinafter Marquez Indictment] (indicted on five counts of conspiring to provide material support to terrorists, providing firearms to terrorists, and committing visa fraud).

[320] *See* Starr & Browne, *supra* note 210.

[321] *See id.*

a desire to fight and kill on behalf of ISIS.[322] The San Bernardino killers and American ISIS fighters also share the common bond of betrayal. Not only do both levy war against the United States, but they also adhere to U.S. enemies by offering them aid and comfort.

When Syed Rizwan Farook gunned down fourteen Americans and attempted to detonate a pipe bomb inside the Inland Regional Center,[323] he conducted an armed attack against the United States in the name of ISIS. For his actions to be considered treasonous, Farook must have either levied war against the United States or provided aid and comfort to an enemy.[324] In all likelihood, both Farook (and Marquez) were self-radicalized and never contacted ISIS members in the former Islamic State.[325] Farook made the decision to use firearms and construct a pipe bomb to kill Americans in the name of ISIS, an enemy of the United States. Unlike the official directions provided by the Confederate States of America to the *Greathouse* defendants,[326] ISIS did not plan the attack but did unofficially sanction it afterward and encouraged future attacks.[327] The United States recognizes terrorism as a new form of asymmetric warfare akin to an imperfect or mixed war, as evidenced by the wars in Afghanistan and Iraq.[328] Additionally, ISIS declared war on the

---

[322] *See* Marquez Indictment, *supra* note 319, at 1–7; Ahmed, *supra* note 318.

[323] *See* Richard Winton & James Queally, *FBI is Now Convinced that Couple Tried to Detonate Bomb in San Bernardino Terror Attack*, L.A. TIMES (Jan. 15, 2016), http://www.latimes.com/local/lanow/la-me-ln-fbi-san-bernardino-bombs-20160115-story.html.

[324] *See* United States v. Greathouse, 26 F. Cas. 18, 22 (C.C.N.D. Cal. 1863) (No. 15,254); *Ex parte* Bollman, 8 U.S. (4 Cranch) 75, 127 (1807).

[325] *See* Bill Chappell, *ISIS Praises San Bernardino Attackers; 'We Will Not be Terrorized,' Obama Says*, NPR (Dec. 5, 2015), http://www.npr.org/sections/thetwo-way/2015/12/05/458578960/isis-praises-san-bernardino-attackers-we-will-not-be-terrorized-obama-says.

[326] *See Greathouse*, 26 F. Cas. 18, 24 (C.C.N.D. Cal. 1863) (No. 15,254).

[327] *See* Chappell, *supra* note 325.

[328] *See* Authorization for Use of Military Force against Iraq, Pub. L. No. 107-243 (2002); Authorization for Use of Military Force, Pub. L. No. 107-40 (2001). *See also Imperfect War*, BLACK'S LAW DICTIONARY (10th ed. 2014); *Mixed War*, BLACK'S LAW DICTIONARY (10th ed. 2014).

United States as early as 2012.[329] Based on these facts, any armed attack against Americans by ISIS lone wolves or sleeper cells, especially on U.S. soil, must be deemed an act of warfare executed by ISIS.

Farook cannot stand trial for treason because police killed him in a shootout shortly after the attacks, leaving Marquez as the only living member of the San Bernardino trio.[330] Since Marquez helped purchase firearms for Farook and Malik, it is warranted to examine whether his actions constitute an overt act of treason. As the Supreme Court stated in *Ex parte Bollman*, "all those who perform any part [of the treasonous act], however minute, or however remote from the scene of action, and who are actually leagued in the general conspiracy, are to be considered as traitors."[331] To be guilty of levying war against the United States, Marquez must have been a member of an ISIS assemblage formed to wage war against his nation.[332] To be guilty of aiding and comforting a U.S. enemy, Marquez must have provided *actual* aid and comfort with *intent* to betray his nation.[333]

Marquez's actions played an important part in the San Bernardino attack because the shooters used the firearms Marquez to kill Americans.[334] Though Farook and Malik used Marquez's firearms to kill Americans in the name of ISIS, the timeline of the purchase matters in identifying any treasonous intent. Marquez purchased the firearms for Farook and Malik several years prior to the actual attacks.[335] Marquez previously conspired with the shooters to

---

[329] *See* John Sexton, *ISIS Declared War on US Homeland in 2012, Promising an Attack Worse than 9/11*, BREITBART.COM (Oct. 1, 2014), http://www.breitbart.com/blog/2014/10/01/isis-declared-war-on-us-homeland-in-2012-promising-an-attack-worse-than-9-11/ (purportedly quoting a speech given by Abu Bakr al-Baghdadi, the leader of ISIS).

[330] *See* Winton & Queally, *supra* note 323.

[331] *Ex parte* Bollman, 8 U.S. (4 Cranch) 75, 126 (1807).

[332] *See* United States v. Burr, 25 F. Cas. 55, 162 (C.C.D. Va. 1807) (No. 14,693).

[333] Cramer v. United States, 325 U.S. 1, 29–31 (1945).

[334] *See 25 Years Urged for Buyer of Rifles Used in Terror Attack*, ASSOCIATED PRESS (Apr. 10, 2018), https://www.apnews.com/cea2b7c35cda4a9b8e45dd5d6764dd4c.

[335] *See* Richard Rojas & Ian Lovett, *Enrique Marquez, Buyer of Guns Used in San Bernardino Attack, is Studied*, N.Y. TIMES (Dec. 8, 2015), https://www.nytimes.com/2015/12/09/us/enrique-marquez-buyer-of-guns-used-in-san-bernardino-attack-is-studied.html.

conduct terror attacks, but not the San Bernardino attack specifically.[336] Marquez also did not provide additional support or aid during the San Bernardino attack.[337] Marquez's situation is comparable to that of Aaron Burr's, who likely conspired in a treasonous plot but did not conduct an actual overt act.[338] Based on this context, Marquez would not be liable for levying war against the United States. Marquez would also likely not be guilty of providing aid and comfort because he did not specifically aid Farook and Malik in executing the San Bernardino attack.[339]

Americans fighting for ISIS on the battlefield present the most straightforward instance of treason. When Americans fight against the United States on behalf of or alongside enemy fighters, they are the epitome of a traitor.[340] These individuals blatantly breach their allegiance by taking up arms against their country without remorse. Not only do they assemble with enemy fighters, but they also intend to kill American and NATO troops. These overt acts are enough to reveal a treasonous intent.[341] Assuredly, the intent to kill Americans on the battlefield is the type addressed in the Treason Clause.[342] Attempting to kill U.S. soldiers on the battlefield is more extreme than the torture and abuse outlined in *Kawakita*, where Kawakita abused Americans in a Japanese prison camp.[343]

The holding in *Ex parte Quirin* poses a problem for prosecuting American ISIS fighters for treason, however. In *Quirin*, the Supreme Court distinguished between the crimes of treason and unlawful belligerency.[344] The Court

---

[336] *See 25 Years Urged for Buyer of Rifles Used in Terror Attack, supra* note 334.

[337] *See id.*

[338] *See* United States v. Burr, 25 F. Cas. 55, 180 (C.C.D. Va. 1807) (No. 14,693).

[339] Regardless, prosecutors successfully reached a guilty plea with Marquez for providing material support to terrorists. *See 25 Years Urged for Buyer of Rifles Used in Terror Attack, supra* note 334.

[340] *See* Sir Michael Foster, *Discourse On High Treason* Ch. 2 § 12, *in* 4 THE FOUNDERS' CONSTITUTION 416 (Philip B. Kurland & Ralph Lerner eds., 2000).

[341] *See* Cramer v. United States, 325 U.S. 1, 8 (1945) (quoting Lord Reading's statement that "'[o]vert acts are such as manifest a criminal intention and tend towards the accomplishment of the criminal object.'").

[342] *See* Hamdi v. Rumsfeld, 542 U.S. 507, 554 (2004) (Scalia, J. dissenting).

[343] Kawakita v. United States, 343 U.S. 717, 733–38 (1952).

[344] *Ex parte* Quirin, 317 U.S. 1, 38 (1942).

outlined the essential elements of unlawful belligerency to include an American citizen who attempts or commits a hostile act against the United States while not wearing a proper uniform or holding military identification.[345] The Court then explained that these essential elements were distinct from those of the crime of treason.[346] Yet, an American ISIS fighter may levy war against the United States without wearing proper uniforms or holding military identification.[347] It is important to understand that the crime of treason should not be removed from a prosecutor's legal arsenal merely because a suspect also committed other crimes. The crimes of treason and unlawful belligerency are not mutually exclusive.[348] What is essential to the crime of treason is an intent to betray the United States when conducting an overt act.[349] When an American ISIS member fires upon a member of the U.S. military on the battlefield, he affirmatively acts in furtherance of his treasonous intent. As long as the U.S. government can produce two witnesses to prove this overt act occurred, the American ISIS fighter may be found guilty of treason.[350]

Americans who fight and kill for ISIS, like Farook or allegedly Clark and al-Hamid, are more easily found to be traitors because their actions unquestionably reveal an intent to betray the United States. Motivations behind an American's decision to join a group like ISIS are always complex.[351] This complexity should not shield this category of ISIS supporters from treason scrutiny though, because the simple fact remains: whatever their motivations are, they still intend on betraying the United States.[352] For these

---

[345] *Id.*

[346] *See id.*

[347] *See* Larson, *supra* note 124, at 914 (arguing treason applies to certain terrorist activities).

[348] *See* Cramer v. United States, 325 U.S. 1, 45 (1945).

[349] *See id.* at 53-54.

[350] *See* U.S. CONST. art. III, § 3, cl. 1.

[351] *See* VIDINO & HUGHES, *supra* note 208, at 15 (explaining how some Americans joined ISIS for religious and ideological reasons while others sought to help in the formation of a "utopian Islamic society.").

[352] *See* 18 U.S.C. § 2381 (2018).

reasons, as long as two witnesses can testify to the same overt act, these American ISIS members are justifiably considered traitors.

C. American ISIS Propagandists

One of the most unique and disturbing characteristics of ISIS is its use of propaganda films and social media. The group is notorious for its beheading videos and Twitter feeds.[353] Much like the constitutional issues raised in the World War II propaganda cases of Axis Sally and Tokyo Rose,[354] the legal problems surrounding treason's application to American ISIS propagandists are numerous. For example, application of the Treason Clause is difficult and potentially harmful to an American's constitutional right to free speech.[355] These are valid concerns for any presidential administration seeking to counter ISIS and deter Americans from joining the terror group. For the purposes of this inquiry, the question must focus not on the particular policy choices of whether an administration should prosecute American ISIS propagandists, but rather on whether a prosecution is viable.

Since speech cannot be construed as an assemblage of men holding a treasonous intent, any prosecutions of ISIS propagandists for committing treason will assessed only under the "Aid and Comfort" provision of the Treason Clause.[356] During World War II, U.S. courts found Americans adhered to the Axis Powers by making propaganda films and radio broadcasts.[357] These courts determined that when an American's speech equates to an act "in furtherance of a program of an enemy[,]" the speaker "gives aid with intent to betray his own country," thereby committing

---

[353] *See, e.g.*, Carter, *supra* note 10; VIDINO & HUGHES, *supra* note 208, at ix.

[354] *See, e.g.*, KAWASHIMA, *supra* note 195, at 166–67 (arguing the *D'Aquino* decision infringed on the constitutional right to criticize the U.S. government).

[355] For an excellent assessment of technology and the implications of applying the Treason Clause to the War on Terror, *see generally* Tom W. Bell, *Treason, Technology, and Freedom of Expression*, 37 ARIZ. ST. L. J. 999 (2005).

[356] *See* D'Aquino v. United States, 192 F.2d 338, 348 (9th Cir. 1951); Gillars v. United States, 182 F.2d 962, 968–69 (D.C. Cir. 1950); Best v. United States, 184 F.2d 131, 137 (1st Cir. 1950); Chandler v. United States, 171 F.2d 921, 925–26 (1st Cir. 1948).

[357] *See, e.g.*, *Gillars*, 182 F.2d at 968–69.

treason.[358] For an American ISIS propagandist to "aid and comfort" a U.S. enemy, his speech must be a part of an ISIS propaganda program established to counter U.S. efforts and he must intend to betray the United States.[359] The category of American ISIS propagandists may be the most difficult to assess in regard to the Treason Clause due to the First Amendment's free speech protections.[360] Specifically, the First Amendment protects an American's speech on his views, opinions, and criticisms of the United States.[361]

The World War II propaganda cases offer much insight into this conundrum. In *Gillars v. United States*, the U.S. Court of Appeals for the District of Columbia Circuit found that "Axis Sally" committed treason when she made broadcasts on behalf of the German Radio Broadcast Company to dishearten American soldiers before the Allied invasion of Europe.[362] The court reasoned that speech may constitute treason if the speaker seeks to adhere to the enemy by providing aid and comfort to the enemy and intends to betray the United States.

Similarly in *D'Aquino*, the Ninth Circuit found that "Tokyo Rose" committed treason when she recorded statements directed toward U.S. troops in the Pacific Theater on behalf of the Imperial Japanese Government and Broadcasting Corporation of Japan.[363] The Ninth Circuit agreed with the lower court that these statements were intended to "destroy the confidence" of U.S. troops and sought to "undermine" the war effort by lowering morale.[364]

After assessing the World War II propaganda cases, one can conclude that Americans who independently use Twitter to express their support for ISIS without the terror group's knowledge or sanction do not commit treason. Though these Americans make vile statements in support of an evil organization, the actors are legally expressing their views. Absent proof that these Americans tweet as official ISIS propagandists, these instances arguably

---

[358] *See id.* at 971.

[359] *See id.*

[360] *See* R.A.V. v. St. Paul, 505 U.S. 377, 382 (1992).

[361] *See Gillars*, 182 F.2d at 971 ("In addition, the First Amendment bars enlarging treason to include the mere expression of views, opinion or criticism.").

[362] *Id.* at 968.

[363] D'Aquino v. United States, 192 F.2d 338, 348 (9th Cir. 1951).

[364] *See id.*

fall within the "doubtful cases" for which the Supreme Court advises against prosecuting under the Treason Clause.[365]

Conversely, any American who participates in a beheading video, an Internet video alongside ISIS members, or radio broadcast aimed at U.S. and allied troops commits treason against the United States. In these instances, there is sufficient proof the American is a propagandist adhering to ISIS by offering his aid and comfort to dishearten Americans and undermine the U.S. war effort.[366] Establishing the existence of treasonous intent is possible because an American assuredly knows he is aiding the enemy when he is among ISIS's ranks and propagandizes on its behalf.[367] Assessing an American ISIS sympathizer's online footprint and network is important to determine when online speech transforms into an essential facet of ISIS operations.[368] Americans use social media to voice their support of ISIS attacks against Americans and swear allegiance to the terror group.[369] Oftentimes ISIS does not officially sanction these statements but avidly encourages Americans to conduct armed attacks in the United States and abroad.[370] Further complicating the issue is ISIS's global and semi-autonomous online network.[371]

---

[365] See Ex parte Bollman, 8 U.S. (4 Cranch) 75, 127 (1807) (holding the principles of the constitution defined treason narrowly and should be held as such, allowing lesser crimes to be charged on their own).

[366] See D'Aquino v. United States, 192 F.2d 338, 348; Gillars v. United States, 182 F.2d 962, 968–69 (D.C. Cir. 1950).

[367] See Cramer v. United States, 325 U.S. 1, 31 (1945).

[368] See Haupt v. United States, 330 U.S. 631, 635 (1947) (holding that testimony by two eyewitnesses of a meeting between the defendant and an enemy agent not sufficient to view words as treasonous).

[369] See, e.g., Scott Shane et al., Americans Attracted to ISIS Find an 'Echo Chamber' on Social Media, N.Y. TIMES (Dec. 8, 2015), https://www.nytimes.com/2015/12/09/us/americans-attracted-to-isis-find-an-echo-chamber-on-social-media.html.

[370] See, e.g., The Islamic State's (ISIS, ISIL) Magazine, THE CLARION PROJECT (Sept. 10, 2014), https://clarionproject.org/islamic-state-isis-isil-propaganda-magazine-dabiq-50/ (last viewed Apr. 24, 2016) (containing issues of ISIS' English language propaganda magazine entitled Daqib).

[371] See Alessandria Masi, ISIS Recruiting Westerners: The 'Islamic State' Goes After Non-Muslims and Recent Converts in the West, INT'L BUS. TIMES (Sept. 8, 2014), http://www.ibtimes.com/isis-recruiting-westerners-how-islamic-state-goes-after-non-

In the case of an American swearing allegiance to ISIS, treason is applicable if the American's social media presence tends to strengthen ISIS and advance its interests.[372] For example, an American's online oath of allegiance to ISIS is arguably an act strengthening ISIS and advancing its interests. The American's oath of allegiance conveys an intent to betray the United States and become an ISIS member. However, social networking sites are vulnerable to hackers, making the Treason Clause's two-witness requirement likely very difficult to meet. The fact still remains that an American swearing allegiance to ISIS on social media may never encounter actual ISIS operatives or execute official ISIS instructions. In U.S. case law, propagandists were found guilty of treason when they propagandized on behalf of an enemy in an official capacity, not on their own volition.[373] An American who independently declares allegiance to ISIS shows his initial support for ISIS and can begin to pursue avenues to meet ISIS members. The speech indirectly supports ISIS in the form of a positive externality. A swearing of allegiance to ISIS cannot be treasonous, though, because the individual is not speaking as an official agent of the terror group.

An American swearing allegiance to ISIS on social media is also not an actual member of an ISIS plot or program; further evidence would be necessary to show official ties with ISIS.[374] Swearing allegiance on social media may reveal the American's desire to collaborate with ISIS in the future. However, this act is not treasonous until the American actually joins ISIS and officially coordinates with the group in person or online.[375]

The same can be said for an American using social media to celebrate or condone an ISIS attack in the United States. While sickening, this speech is

---

muslims-recent-converts-west-1680076 ("[ISIS recruiters] act autonomously, but they feed into the same product, which is bringing guys over, guys that they know are trustworthy and that ISIS can use as fodder.") (quoting former Taliban recruiter and current Canadian national security operative Mubin Shaikh).

[372] Kawakita v. United States, 343 U.S. 717, 737 (1952).

[373] *See* D'Aquino v. United States, 192 F.2d 338, 348 (9th Cir. 1951); Gillars v. United States, 182 F.2d 962, 971 (D.C. Cir. 1950).

[374] *See* Best v. United States, 184 F.2d 131, 133–36 (1st Cir. 1950) (outlining Best's official ties to German radio propaganda).

[375] *See* Cramer v. United States, 325 U.S. 1, 31 (1945).

closer to the non-treasonous opinions, views, and criticisms the Supreme Court outlined in *Gillars*.[376] This is not to say that swearing allegiance to ISIS or praising a terrorist attack on social media is always protected speech. For example, the United States Code includes an anti-riot statute criminalizing the promotion or encouragement of carrying on a riot.[377] The right to free speech is not unlimited and cannot be used to commit crimes.[378] In relation to the Treason Clause, an American's postings on social media pledging allegiance to ISIS or praising an ISIS terror attack, without more, are not overt acts of treason.

D. Resident Aliens Acting on Behalf of ISIS

The final category to be assessed is resident aliens of the United States who become radicalized by ISIS and act on its behalf. After the Civil War, the Supreme Court determined that resident aliens are capable of committing treason against the United States.[379] The concept that aliens owe allegiance to their host country is not new and was discussed during the drafting of the Constitution.[380] It was commonly understood that any alien residing in a nation or passing through it owes some level of allegiance to that nation because he benefits from its laws.[381] This doctrine applies to resident aliens in the United States today as much as it did in 1789.

The question, therefore, becomes whether treason applies to U.S. resident aliens like Tashfeen Malik, one of the San Bernardino shooters and co-conspirators, when they are radicalized by ISIS and act on its behalf. In the case of *Carlisle v. United States*, the Supreme Court found that British citizens who were legal residents of the United States had committed treason when

---

[376] *See Gillars*, 182 F.2d at 971 (D.C. Cir. 1950) (stating that without intent to betray one's nation, words or actions alone do not usually constitute treason).

[377] *See* Riots, 18 U.S.C. § 2101 (1996).

[378] *See* United States v. Rahman, 189 F.3d 88, 116–17 (2d Cir. 1999) (acknowledging the First Amendment does not protect all speech, referencing several U.S. crimes committed by speech alone).

[379] Carlisle v. United States, 83 U.S. (16 Wall.) 147, 148 (1872).

[380] *See* Adams et al., *supra* note 61.

[381] *See id.*

they sold gunpowder to the Confederacy during the Civil War.[382] The Court explained that when they sold gunpowder to the Confederacy, the British citizens were "participators in the treason of the Confederates equally as if they had been original conspirators with them".[383]

If the sale of gunpowder to the Confederacy was an act of treason, then collaborating and executing an armed attack in the name of ISIS against Americans on U.S. soil must be treason. If Malik survived a shootout with police after the attacks, she would have been a prime candidate for a treason conviction. As an alien resident of the United States, Malik was a U.S. citizen for the purposes of the Treason Clause.[384] Malik intended to levy war against the United States and violate her owed allegiance when she killed Americans in California in the name of ISIS. The obviousness of her intent to betray the United States, her host nation, is comparable to Tomoya Kawakita's blatant intent to betray the United States when he abused American soldiers in Japanese internment camps during World War II.[385]

A more difficult scenario to discern is if an illegal alien decides to act on behalf of ISIS. To be sure, there is no indication that ISIS has previously sent aliens through illicit channels to settle in America or radicalized illegal aliens already residing in the United States.[386] There is also no evidence that any illegal immigrants currently support ISIS or plan to do so in the near future. However, the question is still important when examining the boundaries of the Treason Clause. The Founding Fathers were silent on this issue and did not discuss the allegiance owed by aliens residing in the United States illegally.[387] The inquiry must therefore assess legal norms related to those rights afforded to illegal immigrants.

---

[382] *Carlisle*, 83 U.S. (16 Wall.) at 150–51.

[383] *Id.*

[384] *See* Adams et al., *supra* note 61.

[385] *See* Kawakita v. United States, 343 U.S. 717, 737–38, 744 (1952).

[386] *See, e.g., Anti-Immigrant Movement Links Immigration to Terrorism*, ANTI-DEFAMATION LEAGUE (Oct. 21, 2014), http://www.adl.org/civil-rights/immigration/anti-immigrant-movement-links.html (arguing that "anti- immigration" organizations try to use fears of terrorism to pursue anti-immigration agendas).

[387] *See* Adams, et al., *supra* note 61 (discussing "all persons abiding within any of the United Colonies" and not differentiating between legal and illegal status).

The Fourteenth Amendment provides that no state shall "deny to any person within its jurisdiction the equal protection of the laws."[388] When the Supreme Court interpreted this language, it declared that no state "shall deny to any person the benefit of jurisdiction in the equal protection of the laws[,]" including illegal immigrants seeking to attend public school.[389] Illegal immigrants also enjoy the full protection of the Due Process Clause of the Fourteenth Amendment.[390] Since aliens who illegally enter the United States are afforded significant and important rights under the U.S. Constitution, they owe allegiance to the United States.[391] As explained by the Supreme Court, a person who receives benefits from the laws of the United States assuredly owes it allegiance.[392] By benefitting from some of the most fundamental laws of the United States, illegal aliens owe a certain level of allegiance.

If an illegal immigrant becomes radicalized by ISIS, he must face similar treason scrutiny. The level of scrutiny should equate to the type of rights afforded to the alien. That is, if illegal immigrants benefit from fundamental rights such as equal protection and due process, they must also owe an equivalent level of allegiance to the United States. Illegal aliens who join ISIS should receive the same procedural protections included in the Treason Clause irrespective of their legal status. At the same time, they should not receive a preference higher than that of American citizens. If an illegal immigrant executes a terror attack in America on behalf of ISIS, he should be tried in a civilian court in conformity with the standards and requirements outlined in prior treason cases.

V.   CONCLUSION

The crime of treason remains one of the most polarizing crimes in the U.S. criminal code and continues to garner much debate over its application to

---

[388] U.S. CONST. amend. XIV, § 2.

[389] *See* Plyler v. Doe, 457 U.S. 202, 202, 210 (1982).

[390] *See* Zadvydas v. Davis, 533 U.S. 678 (2001) ("once an alien enters the country, the legal circumstance changes, for the Due Process Clause applies to all 'persons' within the United States, including aliens, whether their presence here is lawful, unlawful, temporary, or permanent.").

[391] *See id.*

[392] *See* Carlisle v. United States, 83 U.S. (16 Wall.) 147, 154 (1872).

modern terrorism.[393] From Aaron Burr's plot to form a new nation in Spanish territories, to the secession of the Confederate States of America, to World War II propagandists, American treason cases are some of the most famous in U.S. history.   Treason remained an important crime for state and federal governments to use against traitors up until World War II.[394]   Upon the conclusion of that conflict, treason convictions all but disappeared.[395] In its place, Congress passed several statutes criminalizing terrorism, espionage, and seditious conspiracy.[396]   While these laws are appropriate for certain instances of wrongdoing, they did not repeal the Treason Clause. Despite arguments claiming treason is immoral and prone to illiberal application,[397] the Treason Clause offers important procedural safeguards.[398] The crime will also likely continue to be used sparingly by the U.S. government. Allegiance remains one of the most important aspects of the nation-state, and betrayal of this civic duty should be punished.[399]   The U.S. government should demonstrate restraint in punishing Americans for violating their allegiance to the nation. The Founding Fathers valued the idea of restricting constructive treason by including the limited Treason Clause in the U.S. Constitution.[400] They sought to ensure treason applied only to those who either actually levied war against the United States or adhered to its enemies through offering aid and comfort.[401]

---

[393] *See, e.g.*, Sam Finegold & Gina Kim, *Treason in the War on Terror*, HARV. POL. REV. (Dec. 7, 2011), http://harvardpolitics.com/covers/constitution/treason-in-the-war-on-terror/.

[394] *See generally supra* PART III. (discussing charges of treason through America's history).

[395] *See supra* PART II.C.

[396] *See generally* 18 U.S.C. ch. 113B (2018); 18 U.S.C. pt. 1, ch. 37. (2018) (criminalizing terroristic actions).

[397] *See, e.g.*, Eichensehr, *supra* note 34, at 1443, 1445, 1462–64.

[398] *See* U.S. CONST. art. III, § 3.

[399] *See generally* KATHERINE L. HERBIG, ALLEGIANCE IN A TIME OF GLOBALIZATION, U.S. DEP'T OF DEF. TECH. REP. 08-10 (2008), http://www.dtic.mil/dtic/tr/fulltext/u2/a549258.pdf (discussing challenges of allegiance in an age of globalism and its impact on traditional nation state paradigm).

[400] *See Records From The Federal Convention, supra* note 52.

[401] *See id.*

As established earlier, ISIS qualifies as both a *de facto* and a *de jure* enemy of the United States in the age of terrorism.[402] Although the Islamic State has all but disappeared, ISIS continues to kill American soldiers on the battlefields in Iraq[403] and Syria, as well as American civilians globally.[404] Any actual levying of war by an American in the name of ISIS should be interpreted as an indication of intent to commit treason against the United States. Americans who adhere to ISIS by offering aid and comfort should be found guilty of committing treason.[405] The constitutional crime must also apply to those aliens within the United States who either levy war against the United States or provide aid and comfort to its enemies.[406]

At the same time, treason should not be used in "doubtful cases" described by the Supreme Court in *Ex parte Bollman*.[407] Doubtful cases include instances where Americans are arrested while en route to the former Islamic State, independently use social media to support terrorist attacks, sympathize with ISIS but have yet to meet or join the ranks of ISIS, or offer ISIS monetary assistance.[408] By excluding these doubtful cases, the Treason Clause will function as a crime used against those who are traitors in fact while avoiding the creation of constructive treasons.[409]

---

[402] *See supra* PART III.A–B.

[403] *See, e.g.*, Barbara Starr, et al., *Navy SEAL Charles Keating IV Gave Life Rescuing Others from ISIS*, CNN (May 5, 2016, 7:35 AM), http://www.cnn.com/2016/05/03/politics/us-service-member-killed-iraq-mosul/.

[404] *See* Dragana Jovanovic, *2 American Cyclists Among 4 Dead in Tajikistan Attack Claimed by ISIS*, ABC NEWS (July 31, 2018), https://abcnews.go.com/International/american-cyclists-dead-terror-attack-tajikistan/story?id=56911753.

[405] *See generally* Richard Engel, et al., *The Americans: 15 Who Left the United States to Join ISIS*, NBC NEWS (May 16, 2016, 7:13 AM) https://www.nbcnews.com/storyline/isis-uncovered/americans-15-who-left-united-states-join-isis-n573611 (reporting on Americans and aliens that traveled abroad to join ISIS).

[406] *See* U.S. CONST. art. III, § 3, cl. 1.

[407] *Ex parte* Bollman, 8 U.S. (4 Cranch) 75, 127 (1807).

[408] *See generally* Jack Healy & Matt Furber, *3 Somali-Americans Found Guilty of Trying to Join Islamic State*, N.Y. TIMES (June 3, 2016) https://www.nytimes.com/2016/06/04/us/somali-americans-verdict-minneapolis-isis.html (discussing guilty verdict for men stopped while traveling to join ISIS).

[409] *See generally supra* PART I.B. (discussing the measures the drafters of the Treason Clause took to make it more restrictive).

It is important to note the responsibilities of Congress in clarifying the ambiguity surrounding the charge of treason. To avoid erroneous use of the Treason Clause, Congress must be proactive in drafting new treason legislation. Treason laws should unambiguously designate ISIS as an enemy of the United States through Congress's constitutional power to declare war.[410] For example, Congress may pass a new ISIS AUMF, upon which the U.S. government could rely during treason trials. A new ISIS AUMF should specifically explain that any person owing allegiance to the United States becomes a traitor when he levies war on behalf of ISIS or provides it aid and comfort. With this clarification, American citizens and aliens residing in the United States would be on notice that joining or supporting ISIS is an act of treason. These clarifications are vital because a treason conviction carries the potential of the death penalty.[411] Congress recently attempted to define "an organization that the Secretary of State has designated as a foreign terrorist organization" as an enemy of the United States.[412] Although this bill failed to become law, the draft language could be used as a baseline for a new ISIS AUMF. Regardless, Congress must act to clear any ambiguities surrounding treason's application to ISIS. Congressional action is necessary for the constitutional crime of treason to be utilized effectively against ISIS. With these policy and legal concerns in mind, the U.S. government needs to reconsider the Treason Clause as a viable weapon for the war against ISIS.

---

[410] U.S. CONST. art. I. § 8, cl. 11.

[411] *See* 18 U.S.C. § 2381 (1994).

[412] *See* Treason and Passport Revocation Act of 2015, H.R. 2020, 114th Cong. (2015).

Congress-in-Chief: Congressional Options to Compel Presidential War-Making

Clark H. Campbell*

Abstract

The last time Congress declared war was in 1942 against Rumania. Since then American troops have been sent into action with, and in some cases without, authorizations to use force instead of a formal declaration of war. Americans are accustomed to hearing about the President using more force than he is technically allowed by the Constitution, over the objections of Congress. But what if the roles were switched? If Congress declares war over the objections of the President, can the President be forced to make war in accordance with Congress' demands? When Congress makes a formal declaration of war in accordance with Article I Section 8 of the Constitution, is the President obligated to direct US troops into battle against the enemy state or group? If Congress asks the President to use force, is the President required to comply?

* **Clark Campbell** is a 2016 graduate (Juris Doctor) of the J. Reuben Clark School of Law at Brigham Young University. He is a Captain in the United States Air Force Judge Advocate General's Corps and currently serves as Chief, Adverse Actions at Scott Air Force Base in Illinois.

TABLE OF CONTENTS

INTRODUCTION

The last time Congress declared war was in 1942 against Rumania.[1] Since then American troops have been sent into action with, and without, authorizations to use force rather than with a formal declaration of war.[2] Americans are accustomed to hearing claims that the current President has used more force than he is explicitly allowed by the Constitution, over the objections of Congress.[3] But what if the roles were reversed? If Congress declares war[4] over the objections of the President, can Congress force the President to make war[5] in accordance with its demands? When Congress makes a formal declaration of war in accordance with Article I Section 8 of the Constitution, is the President obligated to direct US troops into battle against the enemy state or group? If Congress asks the President to use force, is the President required to comply? The Supreme Court in *Youngstown Sheet & Tube Co. v. Sawyer* told us that "[w]hen the President takes measures incompatible with the expressed

---

[1] U.S. Senate: Official Declarations of War by Congress https://www.senate.gov/pagelayout/history/h_multi_sections_and_teasers/WarDeclarationsbyCongress.htm (last visited Aug. 26, 2018).

[2] *See, e.g.*, Off. Legal Counsel, 2011 WL 1459998, Authority to Use Military Force in Libya (2011); *see also* Kevin Lamarque, *Should Obama consult Congress before conducting airstrikes in Syria?*, CBS NEWS (Aug. 28, 2014), http://www.cbsnews.com/news/should-obama-consult-congress-before-conducting-airstrikes-in-syria/.

[3] *See* Charles Babington & Juliet Eilperin, *House Votes to Require Assent for Ground Troops*, WASH. POST (Apr. 29, 1999), http://www.washingtonpost.com/wp-srv/politics/daily/april99/house042999.htm (evidencing allegations of Presidents using unauthorized force were made against President Clinton); *see also* Scott Wilson, *Obama administration: Libya action does not require congressional approval*, WASH. POST (Jun. 15, 2011), http://www.washingtonpost.com/politics/obama-administration-libya-action-does-not-require-congressional-approval/2011/06/15/AGLttOWH_story.html; Jacqueline Klimas, *Obama launches 2,800 strikes on Iraq, Syria without congressional approval*, WASH. POST (Apr. 27, 2015) http://www.washingtontimes.com/news/2015/apr/27/congress-still-not-specifically-authorizing-islami/?page=all.

[4] U.S. CONST. art. I, § 8, cl. 11 (Congress' power to declare war includes nuances and limitations that this article will not discuss).

[5] U.S. CONST. art. II, § 2, cl. 1. The President's constitutionally granted role of Commander in Chief includes the power to make war. *See id.* This article will not discuss the nuances and limitations of the President's power to make war. The power to make war will be treated as a simple power to command U.S. forces in both peace- and war-time.

or implied will of Congress, his power is at its lowest ebb, for then he can rely only upon his own constitutional powers minus any constitutional powers of Congress over the matter."[6] The idea of the President resisting military action may seem absurd, but has been borne out by history:

> Today, of course, we are so accustomed to thinking of Presidents as more hawkish than Congress that the hypothetical of a dovish President would strike many as preposterous. Yet, history provides a number of commonly ignored examples: John Adams resisted calls for a declaration of war against France in 1798 and instead sought authority for the limited and undeclared Quasi-War; James Madison was ambivalent about declaring war on Britain in 1812; Grover Cleveland in 1896 rebuffed the proposal by various members of Congress to declare war on Spain; William McKinley in 1898 reluctantly conceded to the same war fervor; and Woodrow Wilson successfully campaigned for reelection in 1916 on the slogan, "He kept us out of war."[7]

In fact, there are recent examples of Congress acting hawkish[8] over the objections of the President. In 2015, Senator Tom Cotton of Arkansas sent a letter to the leaders of Iran warning against making a nuclear deal with President Obama.[9] While Senator Cotton's actions did not amount to an outright threat of war, his actions represented a more hardline approach toward Iran than that of President Obama.

It may give helpful context to the reader to imagine possible scenarios based on political sentiment in the not-so-distant past when Congress could have taken a more hawkish approach than the President. First, Congress

---

[6] Youngstown Sheet & Tube Co. v. Sawyer, 343 U.S. 579, 637 (1952) (Jackson, J., concurring).

[7] J. Gregory Sidak, *To Declare War*, 41 DUKE L. J. 27, 85–86 (1991).

[8] *See Hawk*, Merriam-Webster, http://www.merriam-webster.com/dictionary/hawk (2018) (defining "hawk" as "one who takes a militant attitude and advocates immediate vigorous action; especially: a supporter of a war or warlike policy"); *see also Dove*, Merriam-Webster, http://www.merriam-webster.com/dictionary/dove (last visited Mar. 11, 2019) (defining "dove" as "one who takes a conciliatory attitude and advocates negotiations and compromise; especially: an opponent of war").

[9] Jennifer Steinhauer, *Senator Behind Iran Letter Is Latest Freshman Republican to Stir Things Up*, N.Y. TIMES (Mar. 11, 2015), http://www.nytimes.com/2015/03/12/us/politics/senator-behind-iran-letter-is-latest-freshman-republican-to-stir-things-up.html?_r=1.

could have sought a preemptive strike against Iran. As Senator Cotton's letter shows, popular sentiment to some degree opposed any course of action that could result in Iran gaining nuclear capabilities.[10] Senator Cotton seemed to be threatening a re-imposition of sanctions,[11] but if Congress wanted to disable Iran's nuclear program permanently, the President could have been pressured to attack locations vital to Iranian nuclear development. Second, Congress could seek a greater American military presence in Syria. If the terror group The Islamic State of Iraq and Syria (ISIS) becomes resurgent in and around Syria, Congress may push for military action to control the situation and end the conflict. Third, greater Russian involvement in Ukraine could encourage Congress to request military counteraction to control Russian aggression and protect Eastern Europe. Finally, Congress could ask the President to respond more forcefully against Boko Haram in Nigeria, as the Nigerian Ambassador requested early in 2015.[12] These scenarios, while not the most current examples of Legislative-Executive tension, will be helpful to illustrate the application of the principles discussed in this article. Modern warfare can include myriad methods including cyber-attacks, economic attacks, biological attacks, espionage, or political subversion.[13] However, this article will focus on how Congress could force the President to make war in a traditional, physical attack. Congressional power and approaches will differ if Congress seeks to pursue other methods of warfare.

I will proceed based on a hypothetical situation in which Congress declares war or passes an act calling for military action, and the President responds by expressing his unwillingness to make war or by exercising his

---

[10] Letter from U.S. Senators to Leaders of the Islamic Republic of Iran (Mar. 9, 2015), https://www.cotton.senate.gov/?p=press_release&id=120 [hereinafter Letter from U.S. Senators].

[11] *Id.* (reminding Iranian leaders that Congress must approve any agreement made with Iran).

[12] Amb. Adebowale Ibidapo Adefuye, *Nigeria and US must work together to fight Boko Haram*, THE HILL (Mar. 2, 2015), http://thehill.com/blogs/congress-blog/foreign-policy/234146-nigeria-and-us-must-work-together-to-fight-boko-haram.

[13] See Eric Talbot Jensen, *Future War, Future Law*, 22 MINN. J. INT'L L. 282, 282 (2013) (discussing the evolution of warfare and its impact on developments in the law).

veto.[14] After the President exercises his veto, Congress overrides that veto,[15] and expresses an intent to pursue military action over the President's objections. Congress then must decide under what theory of law the President must follow their orders or how Congress can force presidential action.

Congress would not lightly decide to override presidential objections and declare a war that the President refuses to support. But, the idea that Congress may seek war over the President's objections is not beyond imagination. This article will analyze that situation and the constitutional and practical issues attached to it. For this purpose, Congress will be treated as a single unit acting in concert against the President. In addition to prescribing avenues of action to a Congress seeking to compel the President, I hope to inspire thought and research into this and other areas of Legislative-Executive relations.[16]

Congress has many possible courses of action to attempt to compel the President to make war. The options, in decreasing order of severity, include impeachment, a lawsuit to compel the President to act, a lawsuit against another executive officer, use of the power of the purse to constrain the President, a loan of US troops to a state or organization willing to make war, or an act directing specific presidential action. If Congress successfully forces presidential action, a new question becomes important: to what degree must the President make war? This question will be discussed after presenting each possible approach for Congress.   Although there are some actions that Congress could take to compel the President to make war,[17] the most likely to succeed are the application of the power of the purse or passage of a specific law directing presidential action.

This article will examine the options available to Congress, following the order listed above. Sections II through VII will present the mechanisms Congress can use to compel the President to make war and discuss problems with each approach. Section VIII will address the question of the degree of war-making required of a President.

---

[14] *See* U.S. CONST. art. I, § 7, cl. 22.2.

[15] *See id.*

[16] *See* Letter from U.S. Senators, *supra* note 10.

[17] *See, e.g.,* Campbell v. Clinton, 203 F.3d 19, 23–24 (D.C. Cir. 2000) (exploring congressional and Executive war powers).

I.   IMPEACHMENT

A. *Constitutional Power to Impeach*[18]

Impeachment—or the threat of impeachment—of the President, is one option for Congress to respond to a President that is unwilling to make war. If a President can be galvanized to action by the threat or initiation of impeachment proceedings, Congress may be able to "force" war-making. Alternatively, if a President does not respond to the threat of impeachment, Congress could remove that President from office.[19] Once the President is removed, Congress could expect a more willing Executive to cooperate in plans for war. However, there are significant challenges to the use of impeachment as a tool to compel presidential action, the first being the ability of Congress to impeach.[20]

The Constitution of the United States grants power to Congress to remove the President from office if he is impeached by the House of Representatives and convicted by the Senate.[21] In the history of the U.S., no President has ever

---

[18] U.S. CONST. art. I, § 2, cl. 5 ("The House of Representatives shall choose their Speaker and other Officers; and shall have the sole Power of Impeachment."); U.S. CONST. art. I, § 3, cl. 6 ("The Senate shall have the sole Power to try all Impeachments. When sitting for that Purpose, they shall be on Oath or Affirmation. When the President of the United States is tried, the Chief Justice shall preside: And no Person shall be convicted without the Concurrence of two thirds of the Members present.").

[19] U.S. CONST. art. I, § 3. ("The Senate shall have the sole Power to try all Impeachments. When sitting for that Purpose, they shall be on Oath or Affirmation. When the President of the United States is tried, the Chief Justice shall preside: And no Person shall be convicted without the Concurrence of two thirds of the Members present. Judgment in Cases of Impeachment shall not extend further than to removal from Office, and disqualification to hold and enjoy any Office of honor, Trust or Profit under the United States: but the Party convicted shall nevertheless be liable and subject to Indictment, Trial, Judgment and Punishment, according to Law.")

[20] Cass R. Sunstein, *Impeaching the President*, 147 U. PA. L. REV. 279, 286 (1998). ("The third position, which ultimately carried the day, was that the President should be impeachable, but only for a narrow category of abuses of the public trust-for example, by procuring office by unlawful means, or using distinctly presidential authority for ends that are treasonous.")

[21] U.S. CONST. art. I, § 3, cl. 6.

been removed from office through the process of impeachment.[22] The Constitution grants Congress the power to impeach the President in cases of "high crimes and misdemeanors."[23] Scholars disagree over the meaning of high crimes and misdemeanors.[24] Some argue that "impeachment is an appropriate remedy only where a public officer has committed a criminal act while in office."[25] This would shut the door on the ability of Congress to impeach a President for any political action or inaction unless those acts can be prosecuted as a criminal offense. Others posit that "an impeachment offense is whatever a majority of the House [considers it] to be at a given moment in history."[26] This view gives much greater power to Congress, essentially turning impeachment into a political weapon to be used at the discretion of whichever elected representatives can command a majority of the House and a two-thirds majority of the Senate.

A possible hook for Congress' impeachment comes from the word "*high*" in the Constitution's description of impeachable offenses as high crimes and misdemeanors. This modifier, scholars suggest, does not apply to the magnitude of the offense, but rather to the nature of the crime or misdemeanor.[27] The word "high" suggests that an act for which Congress may

---

[22] Stephen B. Presser, *Standards for Impeachment*, *in* ESSAYS ON ARTICLE II, THE HERITAGE GUIDE TO THE CONSTITUTION: FULLY REVISED SECOND EDITION (David F. Forte & Matthew Spalding eds., 2014) http://www.heritage.org/constitution/#!/ articles/2/essays/100/standards-for-impeachment (last visited Aug. 29, 2018). Presidents Andrew Johnson and William Clinton were both impeached but were not convicted by the Senate. *See id.* President Richard Nixon resigned his office before the House was able to vote on articles of impeachment. *See id.*

[23] U.S. CONST. art. II, § 4, cl. 1.

[24] *See e.g.*, Raoul Berger, *Impeachment for "High Crimes and Misdemeanors"*, 44 S. CAL. L. REV. 394, 403 (1970–71); Laurence H. Tribe, *Defining High Crimes and Misdemeanors: Basic Principles*, 67 GEO. WASH. L. REV. 712, 717 (1998–99); Neil Kinkopf, *The Scope of High Crimes and Misdemeanors after the Impeachment of President Clinton*, 63 LAW & CONTEMP. PROBS. 201, 202 (2000).

[25] Harold Baer, Jr., *How Serious Is the Threat of Impeachment? And to Whom?*, 96 MICH. L. REV. 1598, 1599 (1998) (reviewing MICHAEL J. GERHARDT, THE FEDERAL IMPEACHMENT PROCESS — A CONSTITUTIONAL AND HISTORICAL ANALYSIS (1996)).

[26] *Id.* at 1602 (alteration in the original) (internal quotation marks omitted); *see also* Gary L. McDowell, *"High Crimes and Misdemeanors": Recovering the Intentions of the Founders*, 67 GEO. WASH. L. REV. 626, 634 (1999) (internal quotation marks omitted).

[27] Sunstein, *supra* note 20, at 283.

impeach is "a 'crime or misdemeanor' carried out against the commonwealth itself."[28]   In this case, certain political acts would fall within the range of Congress' ability to impeach. Congress could argue that a President who fails to follow Legislative directives, particularly a declaration of war, has put our nation at risk—committed a crime against the commonwealth.[29] Assuming Congress is unified enough to act together in declaring and seeking war, voting on articles of impeachment would not present a major challenge.[30]

B. *Impeachment of President Andrew Johnson*

The impeachment of President Andrew Johnson exemplifies the circumstances under which a president could be impeached for opposing the will of Congress. President Johnson was impeached for violating an act that sought to take a portion of his executive power.[31] The Tenure of Office Act, enacted in 1867, restricted the President's power to remove officers by requiring Senate approval for any removal.[32] The President vetoed the Act after it was passed.[33] Congress overruled the President's veto, and the Act became law.[34] The cabinet of President Johnson advised him that the Act was unconstitutional because it subjected the executive power of the President to

---

[28] McDowell, *supra* note 26, at 638. *See also* Joseph Isenbergh, Note, *The Scope of the Power to Impeach*, 84 YALE L. J. 1316, 1324 (1975).

[29] McDowell, *supra* note 26, at 641.

[30] *See, e.g.*, Isenbergh, *supra* note 28, at 1332 (ignoring the possibility of Congressional censure of the President). A President who vetoes an act of Congress and then ignores the subsequent overruling of his veto would not likely respond to a simple censure by Congress. Even if Congress formalized their censure and supported their actions with arguments based in the Constitution, an unwilling President would be unlikely to respond.

[31] *See generally* EDMUND G. ROSS, HISTORY OF THE IMPEACHMENT OF ANDREW JOHNSON (The Echo Library ed., 2007) (1868) (detailing an exhaustive history of the events leading up to and constituting the impeachment and trial of President Andrew Johnson).

[32] Tenure of Office Act, ch. 154, 14 Stat. 430 (1869); Post Office Department Act, ch. 335, 17 Stat. 284 (1872).

[33] *See* ROSS, *supra* note 31, at 66.

[34] *Id.* at 63; Myers v. United States, 272 U.S. 52, 176 (1926) (ruling the Act unconstitutional).

the review of Congress.[35] After being advised on the unconstitutionality of the Act, President Johnson suspended Secretary of War Edwin Stanton in direct violation of the Act and appointed Ulysses S. Grant to take Stanton's place.[36] As a result of President Johnson's violation of the Tenure of Office Act, he was impeached in February of 1868.[37] After the House approved the articles of impeachment, President Johnson was tried in the Senate.[38] He avoided conviction by just one vote.[39]

In the case of President Johnson's impeachment, Congress passed an act over the veto of the President. When President Johnson acted in violation of that act, Congress impeached the President for refusing to follow its directive.[40] Rather than refusing to act, as in the premise of this article, President Johnson acted in opposition to Congress, but the situations are closely related. The articles of impeachment adopted by Congress, although presented under the name of "high crimes and misdemeanors," evidence an attitude that an impeachable offense is "whatever a majority of the House [considers it] to be at a given moment in history."[41] The political nature of President Johnson's impeachment suggests that Congress was not above using its power of impeachment as a tool to force the President to take or refrain from taking certain actions. Considering the example of President Johnson, it is not difficult to imagine Congress taking a similar course of action to compel a President to make war. Impeachment is difficult, even when a President has clearly committed criminal acts, such as perjury.[42] The difficulty of conviction, especially based on non-criminal articles of impeachment, is a substantial roadblock to the use of impeachment to compel presidential action.

---

[35] *See* ROSS, *supra* note 31, at 63–64.

[36] *See* ROSS, *supra* note 31.

[37] *Id.*

[38] *Id.*

[39] *Id.*

[40] *See* ROSS, *supra* note 31, at 66–67.

[41] 116 Cong. Rec. H11913 (Apr. 15, 1970) (statement of Gerald Ford).

[42] Alison Mitchell, *The President's Acquittal: The Overview; Clinton Acquitted Decisively: No Majority for Either Charge,* N.Y. TIMES (Feb. 13, 1999), http://www.nytimes.com/1999/02/13/us/president-s-acquittal-overview-clinton-acquitted-decisively-no-majority-for.html.

C. Problems with Impeachment

Other problems with the impeachment approach are significant. First, the process of impeachment could take a significant amount of time. Declaration of war would be put on hold during the presentation of and voting on articles of impeachment and the trial and removal of the President from office. The longest impeachment trial in the U.S. lasted only three months,[43] but assuming Congress felt a pressing need for military action, even such a slight delay could prove disastrous. Second, once the President is successfully impeached and removed from office, Congress would have no guarantee of Executive action. The Vice President would assume the office of the President, and there is no guarantee that he would comply with Congress' intentions. The new President could appoint another Vice President, and the cycle would continue. If the Vice President were impeached concurrently with the President and the Speaker of the House assumed the Presidency, action would be more likely, because the Speaker would come from the body of Congress, which has declared and is seeking to make war. But that would only take place after having passed through the significant delay of two impeachments. Finally, articles of impeachment based on the President's failure to make war would be highly political. Congress' impeachment of President Johnson proves that such articles *can* result in impeachment, but that impeachment, and all other attempts at impeachment since, show that successful conviction is unlikely.

---

[43] *See* Douglas O. Linder, *Chronology, Famous American Trials: The Andrew Johnson Impeachment,* UKMC SCH. OF L., http://law2.umkc.edu/faculty/projects/ftrials/impeach/ Chronology.html (last visited Mar. 10, 2019) (providing a timeline of President Andrew Johnson's life from 1864 to the repealing of the Tenure of Office Act in 1887, including the dates for President Johnson's three-month impeachment trial); *see also* Douglas O. Linder, *The Impeachment Of President William Clinton: A Chronology,* UKMC SCH. OF L., http://law2.umkc.edu/faculty/projects/ftrials/clinton/clintonchrono.html (last visited Mar. 10, 2019) (discussing the timeline of the impeachment of President Bill Clinton).

II. LAWSUIT AGAINST THE PRESIDENT

A. Authority to Sue the President

Congress can seek to compel a President to take certain action by resorting to the third branch of the Government, the Judiciary.[44] Historical cases of individuals and groups suing the President of the United States have been numerous.[45] Courts have hesitated to assess judgments against the President, even when they had the authority to do so.[46] Two important cases in U.S. history have explored the option of compelling presidential action through lawsuit: *National Treasury Employees Union v. Nixon*,[47] and *Mississippi v. Johnson*.[48] Other pertinent cases, discussed at the end of this section, highlight problems with this approach.[49] A Supreme Court ruling against the President would be a major step for Congress toward compelling presidential action. The basis on which a lawsuit is brought affects the success and reach of that lawsuit and any resulting judgment. *Nixon* and *Johnson* provide valuable lessons for framing suits against the President.

---

[44] U.S. CONST. art. III, § 2, cl. 1; *see* Louis Jacobson, *Nancy Pelosi says U.S. House 'has never sued a sitting president in all of U.S. history'*, TAMPA BAY TIMES (Jul. 31, 2014), http://www.politifact.com/truth-o-meter/statements/2014/jul/31/nancy-pelosi/nancy-pelosi-says-us-house-has-never-sued-sitting-/.

[45] Sebastian Payne, *Republicans v. Obama – and other times the president has been sued*, WASH. POST (Jul. 11, 2014), http://www.washingtonpost.com/blogs/post-politics/wp/2014/07/11/republicans-v-obama-and-other-lawsuits-against-presidents/.

[46] *See, e.g.*, Nat'l Treasury Emp. Union v. Nixon, 492 F.2d 587, 616 (D.C. Cir. 1974) ("But because this Court possesses that jurisdiction and accordingly possesses the authority to mandamus the President to perform the ministerial duty involved herein does not mean that this Court must or should exercise that authority at this time. On the contrary, this Court may, if it believes it more appropriate, refrain at this time from issuing a writ of mandamus to the President and opt instead to act pursuant to the provisions of the Federal Declaratory Judgment Act, 28 U.S.C. § 2201 (1970)"); Franklin v. Massachusetts, 505 U.S. 788, 802 (1992) (". . . the District Court's grant of injunctive relief against the President himself is extraordinary, and should have raised judicial eyebrows.").

[47] 492 F.2d at 587.

[48] Miss. v. Johnson, 71 U.S. 475 (1867).

[49] *See, e.g.*, Baker v. Carr, 369 U.S. 186 (1962); Campbell v. Clinton, 203 F.3d 19 (2000).

i.   National Treasury Employees Union v. Nixon[50]

In *Nixon*, the National Treasury Employees Union (NTEU) sought to compel the President to perform his duties under an act of Congress, the Federal Pay Comparability Act (FPCA).[51] NTEU argued that the President was required to implement a comparability pay adjustment by a certain date or to inform Congress of an alternative pay adjustment plan.[52] The District Court for the District of Columbia dismissed the claim for lack of jurisdiction on separation of powers grounds.[53] The District Court also held that the statute directing the President to act was subject to various constructions and applications, and so was at the President's discretion in enactment.[54] But on appeal, the U.S. Court of Appeals for the D.C. Circuit found jurisdiction and decided that the FPCA created a ministerial duty that did not allow for presidential discretion.[55] The court found the duties required of the President to be "mandatory, involving no discretion."[56] Because the FPCA did not leave any discretion to the President in adjusting federal pay scales, the NTEU was entitled to have the President act according to the statute.[57] The court next considered the question of the remedy available to the NTEU.[58] Were the FPCA to require action of another federal official other than the President, a writ of mandamus would be the appropriate remedy, requiring little deliberation by the court.[59] After a lengthy discussion of constitutional principles and pertinent case law, the court decided that it also had the jurisdiction to issue a writ of mandamus compelling the President to fulfill his duty under the FPCA.[60] But the court declined to say that the power to issue a writ of mandamus necessarily implied

---

[50] 492 F.2d 587 (D.C. Cir. 1974).

[51] *Id.* at 591.

[52] *Id.* at 592.

[53] *Id.*

[54] *Id.* (holding that with no clear duty established by the statute, the President was free to act in a number of discretionary ways to meet the intent of the statute).

[55] *Id.* at 601.

[56] *Id.* at 616.

[57] *Id.*

[58] *Id.* at 602.

[59] *Id.*

[60] *Id.* at 616.

a duty to issue a writ.[61] The court instead issued a declaration of law, judging that to be sufficient to compel the President to act in this case.[62]

ii. *Nixon* Applied

The U.S. Court of Appeals for the D.C. Circuit decided in *Nixon* that it had the power to issue a writ of mandamus compelling the President to take action in certain cases.[63] The court specifically stated that it is the duty of the Judiciary to keep the Executive within Legislative limits.[64] In the case of President Nixon, the court failed to issue a writ of mandamus, instead issuing a declaratory ruling against the President for failure to faithfully execute the laws.[65] How does *Nixon* apply to the issue of compelling the President to make war?

As the court stated in *Nixon*, the fact that an actor is the President does not mean that all duties are discretionary.[66] Some areas could be so firmly within the Executive's realm that action in those areas cannot be compelled by the court.[67] The issue of areas committed to the Executive was addressed more fully in *Johnson*, but the primary focus here is that the *Nixon* court was clear that a statute giving only ministerial duties is one that does not raise a political question[68] and can thus be enforced by the court.[69] A problem arises when the clear ministerial duty is one that infringes on the President's Executive authority. Can Congress pass a law that removes the President's discretion from an Executive function?[70] But assuming that such a law could be passed in the area of war-making, it seems feasible that the court could find a power to compel the President to stay within the Legislative limits. Laws affecting

---

[61] *Id.*

[62] *Id.* at 616.

[63] *Id.* at 602, 616.

[64] *Id.* at 604.

[65] *Id.* at 616.

[66] *Id.* at 613.

[67] *Id.* at 615.

[68] *See* Baker v. Carr, 369 U.S. 186 (1962) (discussing political question doctrine).

[69] *Id.* at 603–04.

[70] *See* Discussion, *infra* Part VII.

the power to make war were more directly discussed by the Supreme Court over 100 years earlier, in *Johnson*.[71]

iii.   Mississippi v. Johnson[72]

The State of Mississippi filed a motion with the Supreme Court, asking for leave to file a bill restraining the President from enforcing the Reconstruction Acts.[73] Although Mississippi wanted to restrain the President from carrying out certain responsibilities, the Court found that the general principles that apply in restraining the President apply to compelling presidential action.[74] The Court decided that it did not have the power to compel the President to act in cases where Congress allowed the President any discretion in action.[75] Because the Reconstruction Acts allowed the President discretion, the Acts did not create a ministerial duty, and the Court could not compel or restrain presidential action.[76] The Court conspicuously distinguished their opinion from a discussion of ministerial duties.[77] In duties where the President has no discretion, the Court's decision in *Johnson* is less applicable.

iv.   *Johnson* Applied

The Court in *Johnson* recognized that there are certain presidential duties that cannot be compelled by the Court, even when a specific law directs those actions.[78] In areas "purely executive and political" the Court can have no power to force the President's hand.[79] Duties of the President that fall within his role as Commander in Chief are a prime example of "purely executive and

---

[71] *See* Miss. v. Johnson, 71 U.S. 475 (1867).

[72] *Id.*

[73] *Id.* at 497.

[74] *Id.* at 499 ("It is true that in the instance before us the interposition of the court is not sought to enforce action by the Executive under constitutional legislation, but to restrain such action under legislation alleged to be unconstitutional. But we are unable to perceive that this circumstance takes the case out of the general principles which forbid judicial interference with the exercise of Executive discretion.").

[75] *Id.* at 500.

[76] *Id.*

[77] *Id.* at 498.

[78] *Id.* at 500–01.

[79] *Id.* at 499.

political" duties.[80] Although in *Nixon* the Court ruled that they had the power to compel presidential action, the Court in *Johnson* declared that to compel the President as Commander in Chief would be "an absurd and excessive extravagance."[81] The power of the Judiciary to compel the President in war-making seems to be dubious at best. Therefore, Congress would have a problem using the Courts to compel the President to use force because the use of force is a purely Executive area of responsibility.

B. Problems with a Lawsuit Against the President

More problems await Congress in an attempt to compel presidential action through judicial process. The political question doctrine, ministerial law requirement, and requirements for standing make a lawsuit against the President an uphill battle. Even if Congress succeeds in a suit against the President, the judgment won could be unenforceable for the reasons discussed below.

i. Political question doctrine

First, the Judiciary may never accept a case based on the President declining to make war, in part because political questions are eschewed by the courts.[82] The courts will find that a political question exists when six factors are met.[83] The Court in *Baker* held that a political question involves (1) a commitment of the issue to another branch by the Constitution;[84] (2) an inability to apply judicial standards to the question;[85] (3) the need for an initial policy determination, not appropriate to be made by the Court;[86] (4) disrespect to another branch of government if a decision were made;[87] (5) a need to follow

---

[80] *Id.*

[81] *Id.*

[82] *See* Baker v. Carr, 369 U.S. 186, 217 (1962) (finding cases that involve a political question are nonjusticiable).

[83] *Id.*

[84] *Id.*

[85] *Id.*

[86] *Id.*

[87] *Id.*

political decisions that have already been made;[88] and (6) the potential for confusion and embarrassment if multiple branches of government gave differing guidance on an issue.[89] The Court distinguished political cases, which involve political rights or repercussions, from political questions.[90] Some areas of presidential action, such as foreign relations, were thought to always present political questions, thus outside the purview of the courts.[91] However, foreign affairs are not exclusively a political question, and the Supreme Court determined that those areas may sometimes involve questions subject to judicial determination.[92] On the other hand, compelling a President to make war is a situation so clearly fitting in the six factors for a political question[93] that the courts may choose to avoid it completely.[94]

ii.   Ministerial law requirement

The second problem for a lawsuit against the President is the need to pass a sufficiently ministerial law as to be enforceable by the courts.[95] A law that removes enough discretion from the President to be ministerial would likely be considered unconstitutional, for reasons discussed in Part VII of this article.[96] But the very creation of such a law would itself be difficult. The Supreme Court decided that even when the President made only the final act

---

[88] *Baker*, 369 U.S. at 217.

[89] *Id.*

[90] *Id.* at 211 (stating that cases involving the six elements that define a political question are nonjusticiable).

[91] *Id.*

[92] *See id.* at 209–24 (including specific examples of justiciable questions in traditionally political areas).

[93] *Id.* at 217 (listing the elements for identifying a question as a function of separation of powers, to include (1) Declaring and making war are clearly committed to the Legislative and Executive branches, respectively, excluding completely the Judiciary; (2) Judicial standards are ill-equipped to determine the providence of war-making; (3) whether or not to make war is soundly based on policy determinations by President and Congress; (4) a judicial determination would fly in the face of either Congress or the President; (5) second-guessing the state of war by the Court would cause confusion in Government and the Public; (6) embarrassment of either Congress or the President would be the sure result of a judicial determination of this issue.).

[94] *Id.*

[95] Nat'l Treasury Emp. Union v. Nixon, 492 F.2d 587, 609 (D.C. Cir. 1974).

[96] *See infra* Part VII.

in a long string of directed actions, that duty was not ministerial.[97] If a law were not sufficiently ministerial, leaving any discretion to the executive, the President would be immune from suit in performing that duty.[98] The difficulty involved in creating a ministerial duty to make war makes the prospect of suing the President unlikely.

iii. Requirement of standing

Courts only have the jurisdiction to decide cases brought by litigants who have suffered some actual injury and whose claims are meant to be addressed under the law.[99] In *Campbell v. Clinton*,[100] the U.S. Court of Appeals for the D.C. Circuit found that a group of congressmen did not have standing to sue the President[101] for committing U.S. forces to Yugoslavia without congressional authorization.[102] Congress sought a declaration from the court that the President had acted beyond the confines of the law.[103] Instead of reaching a decision on the merits of the case, the court held that the congressmen did not have standing to bring the suit.[104] Part of the court's reasoning was based on the myriad political tools available to Congress to restrain the President.[105] The congressmen brought the suit because they had been frustrated in their attempts to use those tools to restrain the President effectively.[106] The court held that unless a President acted in a way that nullified congressional votes, legislators should use the political means available to influence the President.[107] Although Congress in *Clinton* was seeking to restrain the

---

[97] Franklin v. Massachusetts, 505 U.S. 788, 800 (1992).

[98] *Nat'l Treasury Emp. Union.*, 492 F.2d 587 at 609.

[99] *Standing*, BLACK'S LAW DICTIONARY (10th ed. 2014)

[100] Campbell v. Clinton, 203 F.3d 19, 24 (D.C. Cir. 2000).

[101] *Id.; see also* Kucinich v. Obama, 821 F. Supp. 2d 110, 115 (D.D.C. 2011).

[102] *Campbell*, 203 F.3d at 20.

[103] *Id.*

[104] *Id.* at 23–25.

[105] *Id.* at 23.

[106] *Id.*

[107] While a presidential veto may be seen as a "nullification" of congressional votes, it is instead an override. The nullification spoken of is one that removes any effect from votes, essentially destroying the ability of congressional members to express their political opinions or desires. *Cf. id.*

President, similar arguments can be made when Congress seeks to compel presidential action. The availability of political means may result in a lack of standing for congressional efforts to compel the President by recourse to the Judiciary.

iv. Presidential indifference

Assuming there is recourse through the courts, the Judiciary may be unable to enforce any judgment against the President. A President who disagrees with a decision of the Judiciary could conceivably ignore any injunction issued by the court. The Supreme Court made this clear in *Johnson*: "[s]uppose the bill filed, and the injunction prayed for allowed. If the President refuses obedience, it is needless to observe that the court is without power to enforce its process."[108] The Court relies on the Executive to enforce its decisions, and this has resulted in a lack of obedience to Court decisions in the past.[109]

III.   LAWSUIT AGAINST ANOTHER OFFICER

A. Authority to Sue another Officer

Judicial action is not limited in application to the President. The Secretary of Defense could be sued,[110] resulting in an analysis similar to that of a suit against the President. Congress could also attempt to enforce their desires for war by bringing a lawsuit against another executive officer, such as a general in actual command of U.S. troops. The United States cannot be sued except as it allows itself to be sued, but exceptions to this rule may be made by Congress.[111] Courts have disallowed suits against military officers in the

---

[108] Miss. v. Johnson, 71 U.S. 475, 500–01 (1867).

[109] Examples include President Jackson's response to *Worcester v. Georgia*, 31 U.S. 515 (1832), and the slow response to *Brown v. Board of Education*, 347 U.S. 483 (1954).

[110]*See, e.g.,* Pauling v. McElroy, 278 F.2d 252, 253–55 (D.C. Cir. 1960) (per curiam); Lebron v. Rumsfeld, 670 F.3d 540, 543–61 (4th Cir. 2012); Mitchell v. McNamara, 352 F.2d 700, 701 (D.C. Cir. 1965) (per curiam).

[111] *See* U.S. v. Sherwood, 312 U.S. 584, 586–88 (1941) (stating that under the principle of sovereign immunity, the United States is generally immune from suit unless it gives its consents to being sued).

past,[112] but Congress has the authority to authorize lawsuits against executive officials.[113] The Supreme Court is especially willing to allow congressional suits in areas more subject to civilian control, such as the military.[114] Congress could conceivably allow a suit against not only the Secretary of Defense, but also against general officers of the military.[115]

B. Possible Outcomes of Suing Another Officer

This course of action, rather than compelling the President to act, seeks to circumvent the President and bring about the same result by effectively cutting the President out of the picture. At best, this approach would create an issue of conflicting directives to military commanders. Within the realm of reasonableness, there are three possible outcomes to a lawsuit seeking to compel an executive officer other than the President.

In the first possible outcome, a court would dismiss the suit as representing a political question. Since the power to make war is constitutionally committed to the Legislative and Executive branches, the doctrine of separation of powers suggests that those branches are the ones that should resolve the issue.[116] *Nixon* suggested that a statute allowing discretionary action would be a political question outside the realm of ministerial duties and, thus, outside the Court's right to decide.[117] The second possible outcome of a lawsuit against an executive officer would be a

---

[112] *See, e.g.,* Bork v. Carroll, 449 Fed. App'x 719, 720 (10th Cir. 2011) (rejecting a plaintiff-appellant's claims against U.S. military officers and the Secretary of Defense for lack of subject matter jurisdiction), aff'g 2010 WL 11519638, at *2 (W.D. Okla. Oct. 22, 2010).

[113] *See Sherwood,* 312 U.S. at 587–88.

[114] Gilligan v. Morgan, 413 U.S. 1, 10 (1973) ("[I]t is difficult to conceive of an area of governmental activity in which the courts have less competence. The complex, subtle, and professional decisions as to the composition, training, equipping, and control of a military force are essentially professional military judgments, subject always to civilian control of the Legislative and Executive Branches.").

[115] *Id.* at 11–12 ("[I]t should be clear that we neither hold nor imply that the conduct of the National Guard is always beyond judicial review or that there may not be accountability in a judicial forum for violations of law for specific unlawful conduct by military personnel whether by way of damages or injunctive relief.").

[116] *See* Baker v. Carr, 369 U.S. 186, 221 (1962).

[117] *See* Nat'l Treasury Emp. Union v. Nixon, 492 F.2d 587, 613 (D.C. Cir. 1974).

successful suit. In the case that a court decided that it had the power and right to decide the question, the court could issue a judgment ordering the official to follow the law.[118] The probability of such an outcome is extremely low, as it would require a law sufficiently specific to take all discretion from the officer in the making of war.[119] Such a law would almost certainly be unconstitutional.[120] But if a court did reach a decision compelling an executive officer to make war, the solution would be quite simple for the President: reassignment of the officer. The President could not remove the officer altogether without good cause,[121] but reassignment would be just as effective.[122]

The third outcome—and the ultimate outcome of the second course— would be the removal of the officer by the President as soon as the suit was filed, making the point moot. If an executive officer were to compromise the President's desire to remain aloof from war, the President would need only remove that officer from his place of duty by reassignment. Any attempt by Congress to restrict the ability of the President to remove an officer would surely be deemed unconstitutional, especially as applies to the removal of an official as closely connected with the Executive as a military commander.[123]

---

[118] *Id.* at 612–13.

[119] Another impediment in this scenario would be that the more liable to suit an officer is, the more likely she is to be far from the President, meaning she has more tactical decision-making ability but less ability to make strategic decisions.

[120] *See infra* Part VII; *Cf. Nat'l Treasury Emp. Union*, 492 F.2d at 612.

[121] *Cf.* McElrath v. United States, 102 U.S. 426, 437–38 (1880) ("[N]o officer of the military or the naval service should in time of peace be dismissed from service except upon and in pursuance of the sentence of a court-martial to that effect, or in commutation thereof.").

[122] Scott Wilson & Michael D. Shear, *Gen. McChrystal is Dismissed as Top U.S. Commander in Afghanistan*, WASH. POST (Jun. 24, 2010),
http://www.washingtonpost.com/wp-dyn/content/article/2010/06/23/AR2010062300689.html?sid=ST2010062504101.

[123] *See, e.g.*, Myers v. United States, 272 U.S. 52, 47 S. Ct. 21, 28 (1926); Free Enter. Fund v. Pub. Co. Accounting Oversight Bd., 561 U.S. 477, 484 (2010); Charles Tiefer, *Can Congress Make A President Step Up A War?*, 71 LA. L. REV. 391, 435 (2011) [hereinafter Tiefer, *Can Congress Make A President Step Up A War?*].

C. Problems with Suing Another Officer

The three outcomes discussed above clearly highlight the issues associated with a congressional attempt to compel war-making through a lawsuit against an executive officer. But other problems would further complicate a suit against another officer. The Supreme Court is reluctant to "extend the waiver of sovereign immunity more broadly than has been directed by the Congress."[124] And even an extension of the waiver may encounter difficulty in passing political question analysis.[125] Beyond what has been discussed, a lawsuit of this kind would entail great expense and large amounts of time. Congress could probably authorize suit against a military officer, file suit, and ultimately compel an officer to act or be removed, but the result would not be the fulfillment of congressional will.[126] The President could quickly replace the officer who was compelled to act or removed by Congress. If Congress were to attempt to pursue this route, it would almost surely be an exercise in futility.

IV.   THE POWER OF THE PURSE

A. Constitutional Authority for the Power of the Purse

The Legislative branch of the United States Government has one weapon that has been extremely effective in Legislative-Executive battles, the power of the purse. "This power over the purse may, in fact, be regarded as the most complete and effectual weapon with which any constitution can arm the immediate representatives of the people . . . ."[127] This power is especially pertinent as applies to the power to make war.[128] Congress' power to control the budget and spending of the President may be the best chance at controlling presidential action, especially in the realm of war-making.

---

[124] U.S. v. Shaw, 309 U.S. 495, 502 (1940).

[125] For a discussion of political question doctrine *see Baker v. Carr*, 369 U.S. 186, 209–52 (1962).

[126] *Myers*, 272 U.S. at 109–10.

[127] THE FEDERALIST NO. 58, (James Madison) (AVALON PROJECT DOCUMENTS IN L., HIST. & DIPL.), http://avalon.law.yale.edu/18th_century/fed58.asp.

[128] Peter Raven-Hansen & William C. Banks, *Article: Pulling the Purse Strings of the Commander in Chief*, 80 VA. L. REV. 833, 835 (1994).

This area of Congress' power has been extensively explored by scholars and repeatedly tested by the Judiciary.[129] The power of the purse has even been explored in its application to Congress' ability to compel war-making in an excellent article by Charles Tiefer.[130] Tiefer focused on the ability of Congress to use spending riders to force the President to increase the tempo and intensity of an ongoing war.[131] Drawing from the work of Tiefer and others allows greater insight into the ability and limitations of Congress not only to step up a war, but also to compel the President to enter a war.[132]

B. Appropriations Riders

The main route for Congress to exercise the power of the purse is through riders to appropriation bills.[133] Riders force a President to follow certain conditions or become subject to certain limitations to receive the funding appropriated.[134] While the President has discretion to reject the bill and the included rider, the funding would also be lost. Congress has much more solid ground on which to stand for limitation riders than riders compelling action, but both are available to Congress.[135] While many scholars and pundits argue against the power of Congress to compel presidential action, "even supporters of presidential power would concede that Congress could plainly and simply cut off funds" and end a war.[136] Past appropriation riders have sought to use limitations to prohibit the President from acting in various areas, for example continuing war in Afghanistan.[137]

---

[129] Notably, in 2007, the House Judiciary Committee held a special scholarly hearing on Congress's war powers. *See* Tiefer, *Can Congress Make A President Step Up A War?*, *supra* note 123, at 416.

[130] *See generally* Tiefer, *Can Congress Make A President Step Up A War?*, *supra* note 123, at 391–449.

[131] *Id.*

[132] *Id.*

[133] Neal Devins, *Appropriation Riders*, 1635 WM. & MARY FAC. PUBLICATIONS 67, 67–68 (1994), http://scholarship.law.wm.edu/facpubs/1635.

[134] *Id.* at 67.

[135] *See generally id.*

[136] Charles Tiefer, *Can Appropriation Riders Speed Our Exit from Iraq?*, 42 STAN. J. INT'L L. 291, 293 (2006) [hereinafter Tiefer, *Appropriations Riders Speed Exit*].

[137] *See* H.R. 780, 112th Cong. (2011–2012). This proposed bill restricted the use of military funds in Afghanistan "only for purposes of providing for the safe and orderly

Tiefer posits that the ability of Congress to attach enforceable conditions to appropriations bills falls into three categories, closely resembling the Jackson concurrence in *Youngstown Sheet & Tube Co. v. Sawyer*.[138] On one end of the spectrum, Congress is most likely to successfully attach riders when they deal with issues of shared responsibility between the Executive and Legislative branches.[139] In the middle, where Congress' ability to use riders is dubious, riders are attached to influence the President in areas where the President has Executive responsibility, but not central to those areas of Executive power.[140] The third category involves areas central to the President's responsibilities.[141] Tiefer states that due to *Youngstown*, in this last category, congressional attempts to legislate are presumptively unconstitutional because it infringes on one of the President's core powers – the power to make war.[142]

In the context of this article, Congress could attempt to add riders to appropriation bills forcing the President to make war. Riders would direct the President to take specific action against enemies of the United States. If the President wanted to keep the country funded and other projects operating, the bill would be approved, and the rider would come into effect. However, myriad problems erupt once the provisions of the appropriation rider become law. The main dilemma for Congress would be the invasion of the President's area of core Executive responsibility.[143] While the power to declare war rests firmly with the Congress,[144] the authority to make war belongs to the President

---

withdrawal from Afghanistan of all members of the Armed Forces and Department of Defense contractor personnel who are in Afghanistan." *Id.*

[138] 343 U.S. 579, 635–38 (1952).

[139] Tiefer, *Can Congress Make A President Step Up A War?*, *supra* note 123, at 417.

[140] *Id.* Tiefer gives the example of Congress increasing troop levels in a country neighboring a war zone. Allocation of troops outside of combat would not fall directly into the core responsibility of the President to make war but is an area where the President has executive responsibility and therefore falls into *Youngstown's* second category. *See id.*

[141] *Id.*

[142] *Id.*

[143] Youngstown Sheet & Tube Co. v. Sawyer, 343 U.S. 579, 637 (1952).

[144] U.S. CONST. art. I, § 8, cl. 11.

as Commander in Chief.[145]   Because the power to make war is a clearly Executive power, using Tiefer's analysis, this law would be presumptively unconstitutional as invading an area of core Executive responsibility.[146] Even assuming the law were constitutional, enforcement would still be an issue. Congress would have to resort to impeachment[147] or judicial action[148] to force the President to follow the law.   Therefore, while Congress would probably have some success compelling action through an appropriation rider, the passing of such a rider would only be the first step in compelling presidential action.

C. Government Shutdown

The second avenue open to Congress through the power of the purse is the equivalent of the nuclear option. Congress could refuse to allocate funding to *anything* unless the President responds to congressional directives to make war. Congress has threatened and carried out government shutdowns in the recent past, both purposefully and because of an inability to reach consensus.[149]   While this option seems to have great potential to force presidential action, it carries with it a host of issues. Constituents are likely to be unhappy with their representatives if a government shutdown occurs.[150] By precipitating a shutdown, Congress runs the risk of committing political suicide with the American people and permanently damaging relations with the Executive. Further, if a President is firm enough to ignore congressional requests, laws, and other congressional actions, there is a strong likelihood that the President would ignore the threat of a shutdown, even at great cost to

---

[145] U.S. CONST. art. II, § 2, cl. 1.

[146] *Id.*

[147] *See supra* Part II.

[148] *See supra* Part III.

[149] *US faces another partial government shutdown*, ALJAZEERA (Feb. 26, 2015), http://www.aljazeera.com/blogs/americas/2015/02/faces-partial-government-shutdown-150226040528670.html.

[150]Dareh Gregorian, *Angry furloughed federal workers protest shutdown at the White House, around the country* NBCNews.com (2019), https://www.nbcnews.com/politics/white-house/angry-furloughed-federal-workers-protest-shutdown-white-house-around-country-n957356 (last visited Feb 28, 2019).

the taxpayer.[151] Forcing a government shutdown would be unlikely to have the desired effects while causing harmful collateral damage.

D. Problems with the Power of the Purse

Congress faces many limitations in using the power of the purse to attempt control of the President. These limitations go beyond the political dangers described above and may limit the ability of Congress to use its power in the area of war-making altogether.[152] Such limitations on congressional power may be for the best.[153]

i. Practicality

Practicality limits Congress. Tiefer cautions, "[i]t is all but impossible to write . . . riders that carry out delicate and complex policies while satisfying the requirements for a limitation amendment."[154] Limitation riders—laws that restrict presidential action—are complex enough to cause serious issues for lawmakers. But crafting riders compelling the President to make war would be an almost impossible task. The complexities of logistics, strategy, joint operability, and tactical execution are only a few of the facets that Congress would have to address. Some scholars believe that riders that go beyond limitation may be unconstitutional.[155]

Tiefer's paradigm for analyzing appropriation riders is useful in this analysis.[156] The ability to make war is a function central to the Executive.[157] The actual operations of war-making, including target selection, strategy, and

---

[151] David E. Sanger, *Government Shutdown Cost Is Estimated at $700 Million*, N.Y. TIMES (Nov. 23, 1995), http://www.nytimes.com/1995/11/23/us/government-shutdown-cost-is-estimated-at-700-million.html.

[152] *See* Tiefer, *Appropriation Riders Speed Exit*, *supra* note 136.

[153] Nicolas L. Martinez, *Pinching the President's Prosecutorial Prerogative: Can Congress Use Its Purse Power to Block Khalid Sheikh Mohammed's Transfer to the United States?*, 64 STAN. L. REV. 1469, 1482 (2012) ("James Madison, for one, supported keeping the power of the purse at arm's length from the war power, and George Mason likewise counseled that the 'purse & the sword ought never to get into the same hands.'").

[154] Tiefer, *Appropriation Riders Speed Exit*, *supra* note 136, at 307.

[155] *See* Devins, *supra* note 133.

[156] *See* Tiefer, *Appropriation Riders Speed Exit* , *supra* note 136, at 307.

[157] U.S. Const. art. II, § 2, cl. 1

troop movements are core elements of the Executive's commander-in-chief power.[158] As the issue is so central to the Executive, a rider seeking to control the President in this area would be presumptively unconstitutional.[159] Some scholars suggest that Congress may not even be able to introduce riders in the area of foreign affairs generally.[160] For example,

> in the area of foreign affairs, Congress itself would violate the Constitution if it refused to appropriate funds for the President to receive foreign ambassadors or to make treaties. Congress . . . may not exercise this power in a manner inconsistent with the direct commands of the Constitution.[161]

Since the Constitution explicitly gives the President power to make war, and the drafting history of the Constitutional Convention suggests that the Framers specifically chose not to give this power to Congress, the specific acts of war-making seem to fall in the exclusive purview of the Executive.[162] One scholar suggests a two-step approach to determine if Congress has the authority to use riders to influence a specific area:

> In short, it seems to me that the starting point should be to first ask whether Congress, under an enumerated power, has the ability to legislate in the particular foreign affairs area that is under consideration, and if so, from where do they get the power. Further, it must be determined whether the power or ability of Congress to legislate derives from a specific grant or from some reasonable penumbra of a specific grant. The second question that must be

---

[158] Gilligan v. Morgan, 413 U.S. 1 (1973).

[159] *Id.; see also* Martinez, *supra* note 153, at 1491. These are what Tiefer calls "provisions that collide with one of the central issues for the Commander in Chief--command, disposition of forces, or campaigning." *See id.*

[160] *See* Kate Stith, *Congress' Power of the Purse*, 97 YALE L. J. 1343, 1350–51 (1988) (Asserting that Congress could run afoul of the Constitution by not funding constitutionally mandated Presidential activities). Although Congress is constitutionally barred from doing so, unconstitutional action by Congress would force the President to decide to sue Congress or let the rider stand. If the President were to sue Congress, a host of additional issues would result.

[161] *Id.; see also* John Norton Moore, *Do We Have an Imperial Congress?*, 43 U. MIAMI L. REV. 139, 153 n.25 (1988).

[162] John Yoo, *Declare War*, THE HERITAGE GUIDE TO THE CONSTITUTION, http://www.heritage.org/constitution/#!/articles/1/essays/49/declare-war (last visited Apr. 10, 2015).

> asked, even if the answer to the first question is yes, is whether Congress, in a particular case, has interfered with an area exclusively under presidential authority. An answer of no to the first question, or yes to the second, should prohibit congressional activism in the area.[163]

Whatever the approach, Congress is sure to walk a fine line of constitutionality when legislating in the area of war-making.

ii. Presidential counter-action

The President can also take some specific actions to counteract congressional efforts to introduce an appropriation rider. The President may take some action to directly attack the rider. The President does not have the option to veto just the appropriation rider while keeping the money appropriated. Presidents in the past have appealed to Congress to grant the Executive a line-item veto.[164] A line-item veto would give the President power to veto only a part of a bill, without affecting other parts of the bill. This power was granted for a short time, but the Supreme Court later found it unconstitutional.[165] As an alternative, Presidents have historically used signing statements to express their interpretation of a law or belief that a law is unconstitutional.[166] But signing statements do not have the force of law, and the President would therefore still be bound by the law.[167] A President can use the signing statement of a bill to express their belief that a law is unconstitutional, that the law does not apply in certain situations, or merely to express an unwillingness to follow the provisions of the rider. In fact, through a signing statement, a President can effectively ignore a rider. For example, President Clinton relied on the characterization of a law as unconstitutional when he "opined that the President could reject a condition on national security funding and yet still spend the funds."[168] A signing statement by President George W. Bush

---

[163] Moore, *supra* note 161, at 144–45.

[164] Clinton v. City of N.Y., 524 U.S. 417 (1998).

[165] *Id.*

[166] *Presidential Signing Statements*, LIBRARY OF CONGRESS, http://www.loc.gov/law/help/statements.php (last visited Apr. 10, 2015).

[167] *Id.*

[168] Tiefer, *Appropriations Riders Speed Exit*, *supra* note 136, at 312.

"asserted that the notice requirement of a funding bill concerning new military installations abroad might violate his constitutional grants of executive power as Commander in Chief."[169]   The President can also attempt to use public opinion against Congress.   President Theodore Roosevelt turned a limiting rider into a trap for Congress.[170] In such a situation, Congress is left with no real recourse but to pull the purse strings tighter and hope the President gives in to the pressure.

Although Congress' power of the purse is a mighty force in many other areas of legislation and governance, it seems that in compelling the President to make war this power may fall short.   If the President ignores efforts by Congress to use the power of the purse to compel war-making, Congress cannot do much in response.[171]   Even if the President does not ignore an appropriation rider, the will of Congress could still be frustrated.[172]

IV.   LOAN OF TROOPS

A. Possible Authority to Loan Troops

To circumvent the President and make war, Congress could try to loan U.S. troops to another actor. This option is not completely feasible and may be one that Congress would not even consider. However, the legal issues presented in this option are interesting and have been considered by advisors and scholars apart from this article.[173] A loan of troops to the United Nations or a U.S. ally would be a risky move, but a desperate Congress might make an

---

[169] *Id.* at 312–13 (internal quotations omitted).

[170] *Id.* at 332 ("[W]hen Congress halved the appropriation President Theodore Roosevelt had requested for a Navy fleet to sail around the world, he is said to have responded that he would have the fleet sail halfway around the world and leave it up to Congress if they wanted to bring it back.").

[171] Congress would likely have no ability to impeach or sue the President for allowing a shutdown, especially since the blame for a shutdown would be shared by Congress and the President.

[172] See Part VIII, *infra*

[173] *See, e.g., Placing of United States Armed Forces Under United Nations Operational or Tactical Control*, 20 U.S. Op. Off. Legal Counsel 182 (1996); *but see* Richard Hartzman, *Congressional Control of the Military in a Multilateral Context: A Constitutional Analysis of Congress's Power to Restrict the President's Authority to Place United States Armed Forces under Foreign Commanders in United Nations Peace Operations*, 162 MIL. L. REV. 50.

attempt. This course of action will almost surely fail because the Constitution directly grants the power of Commander in Chief to the President. [174] Supreme Court jurisprudence seems to concur.[175] In *Youngstown*, Justice Jackson, in his famous concurrence, states that the Commander in Chief clause "undoubtedly puts the Nation's armed forces under presidential command."[176]

B. Problems with Loaning Troops

Apart from the clear constitutional issues with loaning troops to another entity, Congress would encounter additional practical roadblocks. The President, as Commander in Chief, is possessed of established lines of communication to direct U.S. armed forces.[177] Because of easy communication and the historical arrangement of presidential command, U.S. armed forces would arguably be more likely to follow the directives of the Executive than those of Congress, were instructions from those parties to the conflict. American commanders and soldiers might also take issue with being asked to fight under the command of another entity, even if the alternative command were the United Nations.[178] If Congress left U.S. commanders enough control over troops to be effectively in charge, the President would likely be able to retain command. If Congress were to give over command of U.S. troops to

---

[174] U.S. Const. art. II, § 2, cl. 1

[175] Youngstown Sheet & Tube Co. v. Sawyer, 343 U.S. 579 (1952) ("Whatever the scope of this authority in other contexts, there can be no room to doubt that the Commander in Chief clause commits to the President alone the power to select the particular personnel who are to exercise tactical and operational control over U.S. forces.").

[176] *See id.; see also* Tiefer, *Can Congress Make A President Step Up A War?, supra* note 123, at 419.

[177] *See* U.S. Army, *U.S. Nat'l Military Chain-of-Command,* https://dde.carlisle.army.mil/ LLL/DSC/ppt/L19_2branches.pdf, (last visited Mar. 11, 2019) (delineating the formal lines of communication between the President and the armed forces; *see also* U.S. Dept. of Defense, *Meet the Team,* https://www.defense.gov/Our-Story/Meet-the-Team/ (last visited Mar. 11, 2019) (discussing the leadership and organizational structure of the Dept. of Defense.).

[178] U.S. forces do not typically operate under the operational control of other nations. *See* NATO, *Why SACEUR Has Always Been an American Officer,* https://shape.nato.int/ page214845858 (last visited Mar. 11, 2019) (discussing the rationale for U.S. command of NATO forces in Europe).

another entity, there could be repercussions more serious at home than any occurring abroad.

V.   SPECIFIC LAW DIRECTING PRESIDENTIAL ACTION

A. Constitutional Authority for Creating a Specific Law

Involved in many of the possible approaches discussed above is the matter of issuing a law specific enough to direct the President to act in accordance with congressional will without allowing him to undermine that will by exercising executive discretion. A ministerial law is necessary to allow the Supreme Court to issue a writ of mandamus directing the President to act.[179] A specific law would also be required in the suit of an executive official other than the President and in creating appropriations riders.[180] *Nixon* requires a law directing the President to perform a ministerial duty before that duty can be enforced by the Court.[181] *Johnson* also requires that Congress must act to remove presidential discretion before the Court can compel presidential action.[182]

In order to write a sufficiently narrow law, Congress would need to direct every aspect of war-making so as to deprive the President of any discretion. While Congress has shown itself to be expert in the crafting of complex legislation,[183] a law directing every aspect of war would be extremely difficult to create. However, assuming that Congress could create legislation meeting the requirements of a ministerial law, would the President be compelled to follow that law? Assume Congress could write a law to meet each of the proposed scenarios in Part I.[184] A law listing critical targets for disabling Iran's nuclear program, directing when strikes would take place, and which forces

---

[179] Nat. Treasury Emp. Union v. Nixon, 492 F.2d 587, 602 (D.C. Cir. 1974).

[180] *Id.*

[181] *Id.*

[182] *See* Miss. v. Johnson, 71 U.S. 475, 499 (1867) (stating that in the area of war-making even a specific law may not be allowed to compel the President).

[183] *See, e.g.,* U.S.C. Title 26 (demonstrating the thoroughness, complexity, and detail with which Congress can craft legislation).

[184] *See supra* Part I.

would carry out the strikes seems to be sufficiently specific to compel the President. The same would be true of laws directing specific detachments to make ground attacks on specific targets in Syria; designating cities in Ukraine as locations for stationing defensive military groups and equipment; or creating strategy to combat Boko Haram in Nigeria. Ministerial duties prescribed by law would require the President to take the action Congress ordered.[185] If a President chose to ignore those laws creating ministerial duties, Congress could then impeach the President with a firm legal basis.[186] Congress would encounter the same problems enumerated above [187] but would have a more certain argument for impeachment than they would in the absence of a specific law directing presidential action. A lawsuit against the President or another executive officer would also have a better chance of success after the passage of a specific law.[188] The Supreme Court would look more favorably on a request to issue a writ of mandamus if the President were refusing to follow specific directives set forth by congressional action.[189] Again, Congress would face many of the difficulties explained above but would stand on a more secure legal footing.

B. Immigration and Naturalization Service v. Chadha[190]

Does the Constitution even allow Congress to pass a law so specific as to take away the President's discretion in making war? The Supreme Court considered a similar question in the case *Immigration and Naturalization Service v. Chadha*.[191] Chadha, a foreign national, sued Congress challenging the constitutionality of a part of the Immigration and Nationality Act.[192] Congress had created a mechanism whereby a resolution from the House of Representatives could defeat immigration decisions of the Executive branch.[193]

---

[185] Nat'l Treasury Emp. Union v. Nixon, 492 F.2d 587, 602 (D.C. Cir. 1974).

[186] *Id.*

[187] *See supra* Part II.

[188] *Nat'l Treasury Emp. Union*, 492 F.2d at 604.

[189] *See supra* Part III; *Nat'l Treasury Emp. Union*, 492 F.2d at 604.

[190] I.N.S. v. Chadha, 462 U.S. 919 (1983).

[191] *Id.*

[192] 8 U.S.C. § 1254(c)(2).

[193] *Chadha*, 462 U.S. at 923.

This effectively created a legislative veto of executive action.[194] The Court found that the legislative veto was unconstitutional because it violated separation of powers principles.[195] Congress is required by the Constitution to involve both houses and the President in the creation of legislation.[196] Although the Court recognized that the legislative veto was a useful political invention,[197] Congress' violation of the President's constitutionally granted role made the law unconstitutional.[198]

C. Chadha *Applied*

The Court made clear that Congress cannot act in a way that violates the Constitution.[199]   As the Court decided in *Chadha*, Congress acts unconstitutionally by invading or removing constitutional powers of the President.[200] Separation of powers is one of the central principles of the Constitution of the United States and is inherent in the very structure of our Government.[201] Congress is limited to taking action in those areas delegated to it by the Constitution.[202] The position of Commander in Chief, holding the power to make war, is specifically delegated to the President by the Constitution.[203] Congress was given the power to *declare* war, arguably removing from Congress' purview the power to *make* war.[204] The President, while restricted from issuing a declaration of war, is the sole repository of the power to carry out war-making.[205] The Supreme Court described the duties of

---

[194] *Id.* at 944–45.

[195] *Id.* at 959.

[196] U.S. CONST. art. I, § 8, cl. 11.

[197] *Chadha*, 462 U.S. at 967–68.

[198] *Id.* at 960.

[199] *Id.*

[200] *Id.*

[201] *Id.* at 946.

[202] *Id.* at 957–58.

[203] U.S. CONST. art II, § 2, cl. 1; *see also* Madsen v. Kinsella, 93 F. Supp. 319, 323 (S.D.W. Va. 1950) *aff'd*, 188 F.2d 272 (4th Cir. 1951) *aff'd*, 343 U.S. 341 (1952) ("[T]he President, as commander-in-chief, is given the power to wage the war which Congress has declared.").

[204] U.S. CONST. art. I § 8, cl. 11; Yoo, *supra* note 162.

[205] Louis Fisher, *The "Sole Organ" Doctrine.*, LAW LIBRARY OF CONGRESS (2006), https://fas.org/sgp/eprint/fisher.pdf.

the Commander in Chief as "purely executive and political."[206] The specific areas of chain of command, disposition of forces, and military campaigning are central to the President's power to make war.[207] To allow Congress to control the President in those areas, or to allow the Court to do so, would be "an absurd and excessive extravagance."[208] The areas of core importance to the role of Commander in Chief are those which are necessary to making war.[209] Thus, if Congress were to seek to legislate in the area of war-making, any such law would almost certainly be found to offend to the Constitution.

D. Problems with a Specific Law

As discussed above, Congress faces significant hurdles when seeking to create a specific law directing the President to act. The practical issue of creating a law sufficiently specific to be ministerial is a major obstacle. If Congress left any discretion to the President, the law would not be enforceable as a ministerial duty.[210] Creating a law specific enough to be ministerial would be even more difficult because it would have to respect the separation of powers doctrine.[211] A law that gave Congress any of the powers specifically granted to the President would likely be found unconstitutional, leaving the President to act according to his discretion. As a result, although a specific law would give Congress powerful leverage to compel the President to act, significant obstacles militate against the use of this approach.[212]

VI. TO WHAT DEGREE?

Based on the discussion above, the ability of Congress to compel war may be quite limited. However, there have been various points in this article where analysis has shown that Congress might have a chance of compelling the President to make war. Assuming any of the points addressed in this paper are reached where the President or another officer is compelled to make war,

---

[206] Miss. v. Johnson, 71 US 475, 499 (1866).

[207] Tiefer, *Can Congress Make A President Step Up A War?*, *supra* note 123, at 400.

[208] *Miss.*, 71 U.S. at 499.

[209] Tiefer, *Can Congress Make A President Step Up A War?*, *supra* note 123, at 400.

[210] Franklin v. Mass., 505 U.S. at 788, 800 (1992).

[211] I.N.S. v. Chadha, 462 U.S. 919 (1983).

[212] *Id.*

to what degree can Congress commit the President to action? Consider one of the previously discussed scenarios: the military is poised to make a preemptive strike against Iran, move into Syria, take up defensive positions in Ukraine, or initiate a military campaign against Boko Haram. Is the President, reluctant up to this point to take any action, required to bring all the combined might of the U.S. military to bear to comply with a law compelling him to take military action? Could the President instead comply by launching one missile against the enemy? By dropping just one bomb? Could the President send one lone soldier into battle? While these actions would certainly not meet the vision of a Congress that sought war, would they satisfy the legal requirement to make war? Absent a law directing specific military action, which would likely be unconstitutional; Congress seems to have little power to directly control the military action taken by the President in making war.

The President has recently shown his willingness to water-down the actions directed by Congress.[213] Recently, Congress authorized sanctions, military coordination, and other actions in Ukraine and Syria.[214] The President has followed many of the directives in these bills but has, in some cases, taken actions of a lesser magnitude than Congress intended.[215] The power of Congress to compel action by the President is severely limited by the fact that the degree of action required is often unclear.[216] This is true especially when the constitution restricts Congress in the specificity of law allowed to be made due to constitutional restrictions.[217]

VII. CONCLUSION

For better or worse, a hawkish President seems to be the norm in modern U.S. politics. History books and the news are both full of examples of Presidents

---

[213] Josh Lederman, *Foreign Affairs chair says Trump is ignoring sanctions on Russia for former spy poisoning*, NBC NEWS (Jul. 26, 2018), https://www.nbcnews.com/politics/congress/foreign-affairs-chair-says-trump-ignoring-sanctions-russia-former-spy-n894961.

[214] S. Res. 2828, 11th Cong. (2014) (enacted).

[215] *See id.*

[216] Nat'l Treasury Emp. Union v. Nixon, 492 F.2d 587, 609 (D.C. Cir. 1974).

[217] *See supra* Part VII.

making war or using force without congressional approval.[218] The Office of Legal Counsel has argued that the President has the authority to make war, or take war-like actions, in many situations without the express approval of Congress.[219] While the ability of the President to take unilateral action has been examined and dissected, the opposite of the situation has not been analyzed. If the President takes a dovish approach and Congress acts hawkish, what is the result? Can Congress compel the President to make war?

In each of the scenarios presented in this article Congress would declare war or ask the President to use military force, the President would decline or veto Congress' request, and Congress would overrule the veto and continue to pursue the use of force. A declaration of war against Iran or Russia, a request of military action against ISIS or Boko Haram, or any other attempt to commit U.S. forces to action could create a situation where Congress is forced to seek an alternative method to compel presidential action. The scenarios presented may seem unlikely, but the legal issues surrounding them are both interesting and important. This article has analyzed various options for Congress in seeking to compel the President. This discussion has not been exhaustive, but the main points for each option have been presented and discussed.

Impeachment of the President requires that Congress frame the actions of the President as a high crime or misdemeanor.[220] Congress has shown itself willing to impeach for seemingly political offenses, as in the impeachment of President Johnson.[221] Yet, Congress would still face the problems of delay in the face of military threat while conducting the impeachment proceedings, as well as a potentially belligerent replacement for the impeached President.

---

[218] Every use of military force since World War II has been without a formal declaration of war. Many uses of military force have been conducted under authorizations for the use of force; but others have been carried out without any direct approval from Congress.

[219] *The President's Constitutional Authority to Conduct Military Operations Against Terrorists and Nations Supporting Them*, OFFICE OF LEGAL COUNSEL, http://fas.org/irp/agency/doj/olc092501.html (last visited Apr. 10, 2015).

[220] U.S. CONST. art. II, § 4, cl. 1.

[221] *See* Discussion, *supra* Part II.

Congress can sue the President to compel action, but only for his conduct in carrying out a ministerial duty[222] in an area not committed exclusively to the executive.[223] A suit by Congress would also face the issues of being dismissed by the court as presenting a political question or due to a lack of standing. Congress could sue an officer other than the President, but it would face issues similar to those posed by suing the President. Even in a successful case against another officer, the President could reassign that officer to another post and thwart Congress' efforts.

The power of the purse is available to Congress as a tool to compel presidential action. The use of appropriations riders or the threat of a government shutdown provides powerful leverage to force the President to act. Congress would face the issue of crafting riders specific enough to compel the President to take the action intended by Congress. Even if a specific rider where created, the President could discount the rider in a signing statement or even ignore it completely. But despite these problems, the power of the purse seems to be Congress' best bet at compelling the President to act.

Congress could attempt to loan U.S. forces to another nation for use in making war. However, as discussed above, loaning troops to another nation or entity would be completely ineffective both politically and practically. Congress would likely have the least amount of success in making war by this method.

Congress can write a law specific enough to be a ministerial duty, enforceable by the courts and by impeachment. However, congressional attempts to create a law including sufficient specificity would likely fall short and be ineffective or invade the constitutional powers of the President and be declared unconstitutional.

Congress is unlikely to compel the President to make war. Each of the above options is fraught with difficulty in both implementation and enforcement. Thus, although Congress has been given many constitutional tools to influence the balance of power between the branches of government, those tools seem better suited to restraining rather than compelling action. Justice Jackson famously wrote that "[w]hen the President takes measures

---

[222] Nat'l Treasury Emp. Union v. Nixon, 492 F.2d 587 (D.C. Cir. 1974).
[223] Miss. v. Johnson, 71 US 475, 499.

incompatible with the expressed or implied will of Congress, his power is at its lowest ebb . . . ."[224] But when, instead of *taking* measures, the President *refuses* to take action, it appears that Congress has little power to compel such action. Congressional power is often overtaxed when Congress seeks to restrain the President from the use of force, but it would be even more taxed to compel military action.

---

[224] Youngstown Sheet & Tube Co. v. Sawyer, 343 U.S. 579, 637 (1952) (Jackson, J., concurring).

www.ingramcontent.com/pod-product-compliance
Lightning Source LLC
Chambersburg PA
CBHW072132170526
45158CB00004BA/1338